GEOGRAPHY
History and Concepts
A Student's Guide

SECOND EDITION

ARILD HOLT-JENSEN
University of Bergen

English adaptation and translation by
BRIAN FULLERTON
Senior Lecturer in Geography
University of Newcastle-upon-Tyne

P·C·P

Paul Chapman
Publishing Ltd

British Library Cataloguing in Publication Data

Holt-Jensen, Arild
    Geography: history and concepts: a
    student's guide. — 2nd ed.
    1. Geography — History   2. Geography —
    Methodology
    I. Title   II. Fullerton, Brian
    III. Geografiens innhold og metoder.
    English
    910'.01   G80

ISBN 1-85396-011-X

Typeset by Burns and Smith, Derby.
Printed and bound by Butler & Tanner Ltd, Frome and London.

DQ
3
H
c.1

To my teacher in geography

Professor Fridtjov Isachsen
1906–79

Contents

Preface

Recent years have seen more active discussion of the philosophy and methodology of geography, and there has been a corresponding increase in the number of books and papers in this field. Much of this literature is written by specialists for specialists and assumes a knowledge of the history of geography and of the development of philosophical and methodological concepts a new student will not yet have. This book is intended to serve as an introduction to the way geographers have thought and now think, and to the methods they use. It also seeks to compare developments in geographical thought with contemporary developments in other disciplines.

The five main chapters of the book cover: the content and organizational structure of the discipline; the history of ideas in geography from antiquity to the present day; the 'quantitative revolution' in relation to the concept of 'paradigms' in science; the 'critical revolution', with its emphasis on the influence of values on research; the search for geographical synthesis as it has developed from simple description to systems analysis. The book restricts itself to basic explanations; it does not cover techniques (in cartography, fieldwork or statistical analysis) which may be needed at a specific stage of a research project for which there are already many good manuals.

It is always difficult to establish a satisfactory balance between an easily comprehensive account and a rigorous use of concepts in an introductory text. The problem is made worse in so far as authors who are cited have worked with slightly different definitions of several concepts that are central to geography. The reader may therefore still detect some inconsistencies. To help the student to monitor differences in the use of concepts among geographical thinkers and also for quick reference, there is a subject index (p. 183) that lists the pages on which concepts are defined. These concepts are italicized in the text, when they are introduced. An author and personality index provides brief biographical details of writers and scientists mentioned in the text.

An introductory work that is to be readable and also comprehensible to students must similarly simplify the story of the interactions between scholars. The sheer number of scientists in the modern world and the multiplicity of contacts beween them through books, conferences and academic visits makes it impossible to appreciate all the influences of one scholar upon another or to explain in detail why different trends in research emerged. I have been obliged to choose what I consider to be the major trends and influences, mentioning only a small number of the scientists who have taken part in the devolopment of geography and ignoring a number of personal contacts which may well have had a significant impact on the events described in the text. The reader should therefore be warned against the temptation to simplify the account even further in his or her own mind and so add to the many myths already in circulation about who or what influenced whom, which the persons concerned would like to modify or deny.

This book has developed through a number of stages. When I began to teach an elementary course on the history and philosophy of geography in Bergen in 1970, I could find no satisfactory text for students in either the English or Scandinavian languages. I therefore started to prepare a compendium on the basis of my lectures. Comments and corrections from colleagues and students, followed by more systematic reading on my own part, led to the publication of *Geografiens innhold og metoder* (Norwegian University Press, 1976). This book had a promising reception among Scandinavian students and also attracted a number of further comments and suggestions for improvements and alteration from fellow geographers. Starting from the Norwegian text, Brian Fullerton translated and supervised the first English edition (1981), which also included my additions and alterations. A number of encouraging (and some critical) reviews of the English edition induced me to continue my studies in order to improve subsequent editions in Norwegian, English and German. A Hebrew version, currently in preparation, has led to valuable discussions with Israeli geographers. An exchange visit to the University of Washington enabled me to spend the Spring Term of 1986 in Seattle and to achieve a better understanding of contemporary developments in North American geography.

The favourable reaction to the first English edition suggested that the structure and layout of the book was sound, so this edition retains the same framework. A large part of the text has, however, been completely rewritten in order to accommodate developments in geography during the 1980s, to include the expanded treatment of European geography found in the German edition and to refine the discussion of some arguments in the light of reviewers' comments on the first edition.

Chapter 1 has been rewritten in order to cover the role of the geographical societies in the development of geography from a cosmography to an institutionalized discipline and to explain the contemporary German debate on the nature of geography. Chapter 2 gives more space to the process of institutionalization and to the influences of Darwinism and anarchism on the development of geography. There is also a more extended coverage of physical geography and landscape geography. Chapter 3 includes a more precise discussion of Kuhn's 'paradigm' model and a review of his critics (Popper and Feyerabend) that was absent from the first edition. More comments have been added on recent developments within geography. Chapter 4 has been completely rewritten in order to give a more detailed presentation of different positivist and critical approaches and to include new sub-chapters on humanist and structuralist approaches within geography. Chapter 5 contains a more extended treatment of the role of explanation and description in geography, on practical uses of systems analysis and on organizational plans for the discipline. In order to keep the text reasonably short, a number of paragraphs from the first edition have been excluded from Chapter 5 and, to a lesser extent, from the other chapters. The present edition, like the first English edition, is a joint project between Brian Fullerton and myself, but responsibility for any defects or false conclusions rests wholly with the author.

I would also like to acknowledge the debts I owe, in particular to Ove Biilmann, Moshe Brawer, Olavi Granö, Jens-Christian Hansen, Torsten Hägerstrand, Jan Lunquist, Michael Morgan, Richard Morrill, Hans Skjervheim, Wolf Tietze, Aadel Brun Tschudi and Peter Weichart for good advice.

Undoubtedly, though, my biggest debt is to my wife, Elisabeth, and our two children, for their patience and forbearance with a husband and father absorbed in his geographical world of ideas both day and night.

Arild Holt-Jensen
Bergen
November 1987

Acknowledgements

The author and the publishers would like to thank the following for permission to reproduce copyright material:

Edward Arnold for Figures 3.2 and 5.7, from Harvey, D., *Explanation in Geography*, 1969, pp. 34 and 454; and Figure 3.5 and 3.6 from Haggett, P., Cliff, A.D. and Frey, A. *Locational Analysis in Human Geography*, 2nd ed. 1977.

Basil Blackwell for Figure 4.2, from Stoddart, D.R (ed.), *Geography, Ideology and Social Concern*, 1981, p. 24; and for Figure 4.3, Part C, from Johnston, R.J. *On Human Geography*, 1986, p. 60.

Verlag Franz Deuticke, for Figures 1.3, 5.12 and 5.13, from Weichhart, P.*Geographie im Umbruch*, 1975, pp. 11, 99 and 104.

Walter de Gruyter, Publishers, for Figure 1.2, from Schmithusen, J. *Allgmeine Synergetik*, 1976, and Figure 5.14, adapted from Hard, G. *Die Geographie, eine wissenschaftstheoretische Einführung*, 1973. Henk Meijer, for Figure 3.4, from *IDG: Zuyder Zee/Lake Issjel*, 1981.

The Geographical Association for Figure 5.3, from Kirk, W., *Geography*, Vol. 48, p. 364, 1973.

Harper & Row for fig 5.10 & 5.11 from Haggett, P., *Geography: A modern Synthesis*, 1984.

Methuen & Co. Ltd for Figure 5.9, from Chorley, R.J., *Directions in Geography*, 1973, p. 38; and Figure 5.2, from Haggett, P., *Models in Geography*, 1967, p. 533.

Pergamon Press for Figure 3.7, from Forer, P., *Progress in Human Geography*, Vol. 2, p. 247, 1978.

Anette Reenberg, for Figure 5.8, from *Det Katastroferamte SAHEL*, 2nd ed. 1984, Geografforlaget, Brenderup, p. 15.

1 What Is Geography?

Most people have only very vague notions about the content of scientific geography. School geography has left many with bad memories of learning the names of rivers and towns by rote. It is still common to meet people who think that geographers must have to learn a mass of facts, must know the population of towns all over the world and can name and locate all the new states in Africa. This idea of geography as an encyclopaedic knowledge of places is illustrated when a newspaper rings up its local department of geography to find out how many towns there are in the world called after Newcastle, or when readers write in to settle bets as to which is the world's longest river.

People also have an idea that geography has something to do with maps. Less cynically than Swift:

So geographers, in Afric-maps
With savage-pictures fill their gaps
And o'er unhabitable downs
Place elephants for want of towns

Geographers are thought to be people who know how to draw maps and are somehow associated with the Ordnance Survey or the US Coast and Geodetic Survey.

A third view is that geographers write travel descriptions – a reasonable belief for anyone who reads reviews of the year's books and sees that most of those listed under 'geography' are accounts of exciting expeditions to the Amazon, sailing trips around the world or something similar.

Each of these three popular opinions as to what geography is has some truth in it. The names and locations of towns are facts for geographers of the same order as dates are facts for historians. They are the basic building blocks of the subject, but they are not the subject itself. The map, which represents a collection of such data, is the geographers most useful specific resource.

Different types of thematic maps are also important means of expression in geographical research, along with tables, diagrams and written accounts. The art of visual expression is much more closely associated with geography than with other social and natural sciences. Observations recorded during travel and fieldwork still provide essential data for geographers. A cultivation of the power of observation is therefore an important objective in the education of a geographer. Geographical training should develop the ability to 'see geographically', to observe and interpret a natural or cultural landscape in the field and/or through the study of maps, aerial photographs and other visual representations. Travel writers often lack this ability to observe and interpret. Admittedly, many people have had their initial interest in geography aroused through reading travel stories in their youth. But those who later trained as geographers eventually came to find this type of light reading unsatisfactory because of its lack of systematic observation.

Exploration and the cosmographic tradition

Before the present century, voyages of discovery and the mapping of formerly unknown lands were, however, closely associated with geography. Wayne K. Davies (1972, p.11), for instance, maintains that geography enjoyed its strongest relative position among the sciences during the so-called 'golden age' of exploration from the fifteenth to the nineteenth centuries. This was not due to the academic status of the subject during this period, but to the work of a number of people who were actively involved with the mapping and description of the new lands being discovered. To the extent that they were working scientifically they would, however, be better described as *cosmographers* rather than geographers. Cosmography, as termed by Schmithüsen (1976, p. 10) included not only geography and cartography but also natural sciences like biology, geology and geophysics and social sciences like anthropology, which only achieved their independent academic standing towards the end of the nineteenth century. Exploration, and all these other fields of cosmographic activity, were also regarded as being part of geography by the general public because they were carried out, to a large extent, under the auspices of the geographical societies.

The founders of these geographical societies were enthusiastic scientists and others who sought to widen the support given to research and to expeditions. The societies were supported by prominent members of the middle classes. They also received help from governments during the period of colonial expansion at the end of the century. Although forerunners of these societies existed during the sixteenth and seventeenth centuries the first modern geographical society was founded as the Société de Géographie de Paris in 1821. In rapid succession came the Gesellschaft für Erdkunde zu Berlin in 1828, the Royal Geographical Society in London in 1830, then societies in

Mexico (1833), Frankfurt (1836), Brazil (1838), the Imperial Russian Geographical Society in St Petersburg (1845), and the American Geographical Society in 1852. By 1885 nearly 100 geographical societies with an estimated membership of over 50,000 were spread across the world (Freeman, 1961, pp. 52–3).

The most important work of these societies was their support for expeditions and their publication of yearbooks and journals, which included maps and other material from expeditions. Many of the societies also supported colonial expansion by their respective countries. Some, such as the societies at Nancy and Montpellier, supported local studies in their home areas. At Nancy, barely 10 km from the Franco-German frontier of 1871, the Société Géographique de L'Est pursued studies supporting the return of Alsace–Lorraine to France. During this period the geographical societies held an important public position because of their commitment to exploration and popular political causes. Their meetings attracted great public interest, especially when one of the well-known explorers returned to give an account of his discoveries and adventures.

The activity of the geographical societies was in marked contrast to the development of academic geography at that time. In the 1880s there were fewer than twenty university teachers in geography in the whole world and there were far fewer registered geography students than members of geographical societies. The universities were reluctant to give geography status as an academic discipline largely because of the cosmographic nature of the investigations promoted by geographical societies. The information brought back by explorers helped to build up new disciplines at the universities, particularly in the natural sciences. Many scientists working in these disciplines, however, only regarded the geographical societies as umbrella organizations for their data collecting activities. In many cases geography was introduced as a university discipline against more or less active opposition from the universities. In Germany, for instance, geography was made a university discipline at all the Prussian universities by a governmental decree of 1874. Professorships in geography were actually wished on the universities in the belief that they would promote the education of better schoolteachers. Geography had been introduced as a broad school subject in the new educational programmes which had replaced the traditional classical curriculum.

Some academics argued that geography was not a science and was only sustained by borrowing from others (Schültz, 1980, p. 65). In Britain, the initiative to establish geography as an academic discipline came from the Royal Geographical Society, which showed a growing interest in education from the 1860s onward. The Society urged the need to establish chairs in geography at Oxford and Cambridge, pointing out that chairs had been or were being established in German, Swiss and French universities. But the proposals were only taken up by the universities in 1887, when the Royal Geographical Society offered to cover the main part of the costs involved in establishing lectureships at Oxford and Cambridge.

Geography thus developed as an academic discipline partly on the basis of a cosmographic philosophy which was developed to give coherence to the different activities of the geographical societies. Gradually theoretical studies made an increasing contribution to the advancement of a specific geographical methodology for the analysis of spatial distributions and correlations. The chief emphasis remained on geography as a science of synthesis (as in the Keltie Report [1886]). Later chapters of this book will show that geographical synthesis is not an easy task. Some even argue that it is impossible. We will, however, leave these critics for the time being, and present some of the features that characterize geography as a science of synthesis.

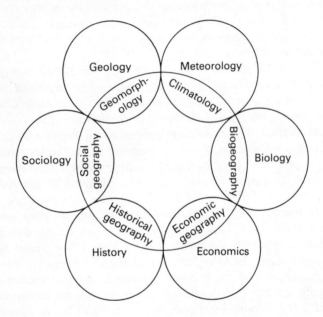

Figure 1.1 The circumference of geography (adapted from Fenneman, 1919)

The organizational plan of geography

Firstly, a student immediately notices that geography has no obvious place in the traditional classification of the sciences by faculty. Some parts of geography have their strongest affiliations with mathematics and natural sciences, others with history, philosophy and social sciences. Other sciences study distinctive types of phenomena: geologists study rocks, botanists plants, sociologists social groups, and so on. The work of geographers involves several types of phenomena, each already studied by another science. Are geographers therefore, 'jacks of all trades and master of none'?

Some geographers argue that the subject matter is shared with other disciplines but is treated in a different way for geographical purposes. Others affirm that the subject matter of geography is exclusive; geographers alone study places. All geographers will however agree with Ackerman (1958, p 8) that the fundamental approach in geography 'is the differentiation of the content of space on the Earth's surface and the analysis of space relations within the same universe.'

To clarify this point we may analyse the position of geography as seen by Fenneman (1919) (Figure 1.1). The diagram expresses the conception that sciences overlap and that each one of the overlapping zones, which also represent specialized, *systematic branches of geography,* belong equally to some other science. The question is whether geography occupies anything more than these overlapping zones. Is anything left in the centre that is specifically geographical? What would be missing if the geography of an area were written by a group of scientists who each contributed his own chapter: the geologist writing about the rocks, the botanist about the plant life, the meteorologist about climate, the demographer about population conditions and the economist about economic conditions? Such an account would surely fail to consider the overall interaction between phenomena. It is easy to see, for example, that the relationship between climate and soil type must have an important bearing on conditions of agricultural production and that the development of industry in an area may not be due only to economic factors but also to the natural resources of the area, its population potential and its historical and political development. Fenneman concluded that the interaction of all these factors can primarily be studied within definite areas or regions, and argued that geography should cultivate its core, *regional geography,* 'as a safeguard against absorption by other sciences'. Regional geography is defined as the study of areas in their total composition or complexity. In most cases, regional geography would, however, focus on the relationship between humanity and its habitat or another theme that makes an illuminating presentation of the region possible.

While there is still some truth in the assessment that many geographers have lost their geographical identity to alien subjects when working on the periphery, Fenneman's fear of absorption by other disciplines seems rather strange today. Instead of illustrating the robbers trying to disintegrate our discipline, Figure 1.1 may be used to demonstrate the point made by Ackerman (1958, p. 3), that geography is 'a mother discipline' from which other specialized disciplines like geodesy, meteorology, soil science, plant ecology and regional science have emerged. Geography has become an outward-looking discipline that has frequently created new specializations. This multidisciplinary perspective may be regarded both as our *raison d'être* and our life-raft in the sea of knowledge (Capelle, 1979, p.65). If the periphery seems interesting, why not explore it; this will only widen the 'circle of geography'.

Minshull (1970, p. 28) considers that 'many of the subjects from which geography is said to borrow just do not exist'. The systematic branches of human geography especially, are breaking much new ground. Admittedly, useful knowledge from other disciplines can be fitted to the procedures used in geography but no other specific procedures are designed or followed in order to reveal the intricacies of space relations. The only other science concerned mainly with space relations is astronomy, which has a different universe to treat. Biology and economics have also treated space relations but in a much more limited way than geography has.

Economic geographers, for instance, start with the spatial distribution of different forms of economic activity and try to explain this distribution, while economists are generally less interested in spatial distribution preferring to concentrate on the factors which determine economic development on the macro scale.

There is even in general a difference between the botanist specializing in plant distribution and a geographer interested in vegetation. In most cases, the geographer will concentrate on vegetation types and their distribution, and will delimit the topic with its importance to human geography somewhere at the back of his mind. The botanist, on the other hand, will be more interested in the distribution of single plant species or grouping of species; vegetation as part of the landscape picture and its importance to man recedes into the background; rare and inconspicuous flowers are often of greater interest to him than common and landscape-forming trees.

Geography exits in order to study variations in phenomena from place to place, and its value as an academic discipline depends on the extent to which it can clarify the connections between different features of the same area. The central *geographical* question is 'Why is it like this here?'

Joseph Schmithüsen in his *Allgemeine Geosynergetik* (1976), attempts to establish a philosophical base for geography as a science, arguing that scientific research is based upon four different categories of basic reasoning, which are characterized by the following pairs of concepts: total-general, partial-general, partial-special and total-special (Figure 1.2). *Total-general* reasoning implies a holistic understanding of objects with the intention of making general statements. The questions asked are about the nature or essence of the objectives of science. This is the type of reasoning undertaken by the philosophers of science.

Partial-general reasoning implies a study of the parts as such, with the ultimate aim of presenting general statements, like laws in physics. Scientific reasoning in physics thus corresponds to B in Figure 1.2. *Partial-special* reasoning is concerned with the understanding of individual phenomena, such as 'why was Hadrian's Wall built across Britain?' This form of reasoning is also termed *idiographic*. *Total-special* reasoning tries to understand the

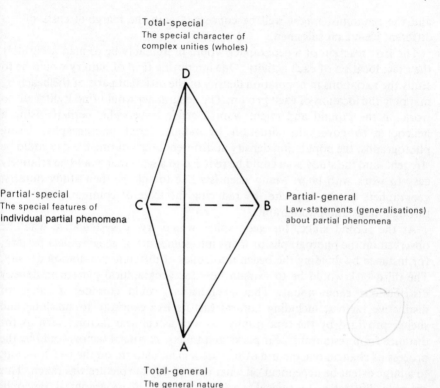

Figure 1.2 The four categories of basic reasoning (after Schmithüsen, 1976). The use of the tetrahedron stresses that it is not necessary to choose only one of the four categories of basic reasoning. Most scientific reasoning involves more than one category

particular features of complex unities, for example, landscapes or regions in geography.

According to Schmithüsen (1976, p. 22) the methodological peculiarity of geography is that it seeks to understand the complexities that exist together in a part of the earth in its spatial integration. This is the basis of geography as an independent science. No other discipline concerns itself with the earth's surface and its spatial parts in their totality; with the association of phenomena in space.

Peter Haggett (1983) illustrate the geographical viewpoint by discussing the starting points of different scientists who might all be studying the same beach full of people bathing and sunning themselves. The geologist would be interested in the sand particles and the zoologist in the marine life along the shore. The sociologist might study the behaviour of the groups using the beach and the economist might well be concerned with the marginal costs of the different ice-cream salesmen.

The first reaction of a geographer would presumably be to map accurately the exact location of each activity. One interesting field of inquiry would be to study the variations in population density of the different parts of the beach by mapping the location of each person. The geographer would find it difficult to work on the ground and might want a general oversight, perhaps using a helicopter to cover the situation by taking aerial photographs. Using photographs, the population density at different hours during the day could be 'frozen', and the study area could be reduced to a scale that would be relatively easy to work with later. Many scientists like to enlarge their study objects; geographers do the opposite, by reducing the scale of complex phenomena through maps and photographs.

At the second stage, the geographer would try to systematize what he observed on the photographs or maps into some sort of geographical pattern, for instance by dividing the beach into zones of different population density. The third task would be to explain how the geographical pattern in density distributions came about. That explanation would consider a range of distinctive factors, including natural factors like exposure to sunshine and shelter provided by the topography, as well as cultural factors, such as the distance from restaurants, car parks and toilets. A crucial factor would be the process of change; one picture of the 'settlement pattern' on the beach would, to a large extent be dependent on what time of day the picture was taken. This example illustrates the typical working sequence in geographical research: *localization–geographical pattern–explanation*. We start to locate phenomena in space and use different mapping methods in order to discover specific geographical patterns, which we set out to explain. As geographical patterns in general change through time, an understanding of the processes of change is crucial to the explanation of a specific geographical pattern.

All the phenomena which have a recognizable spatial distribution or can be shown on a map are basically of geographical interest, but many are of little significance. It is, however, impossible to say unambiguously which of the phenomena are of no significance. This has to be decided by the circumstances of each case. In most cases, for example, the distribution of Mormons in a region would have little geographical interest, but where, as in parts of the American West, their distribution becomes dominant or has contributed to the cultural and economic development of the area, then it becomes significant.

In research it is not always necessary to take account of all the factors of geographic interest. The research worker might restrict him/herself to the distribution pattern of only one geographical phenomenon and try to find an explanation for it. He/she might try to make valid generalizations about the distribution of settlements in the landscape. He/she might postulate a close relationship between population density and the distance between towns. In this case he/she is specializing in settlement geography, a systematic branch not mentioned in Figure 1.2.

The number of branches of systematic geography could be argued indefinitely. In 1919 Fenneman even included 'mathematical geography', which has long been regarded as part of astronomy. Uhlig (1971, p. 15) limits the field of geographical inquiry to five aspects of the physical environment and five aspects of human life (Figure 1.3). Uhlig uses the term *social*

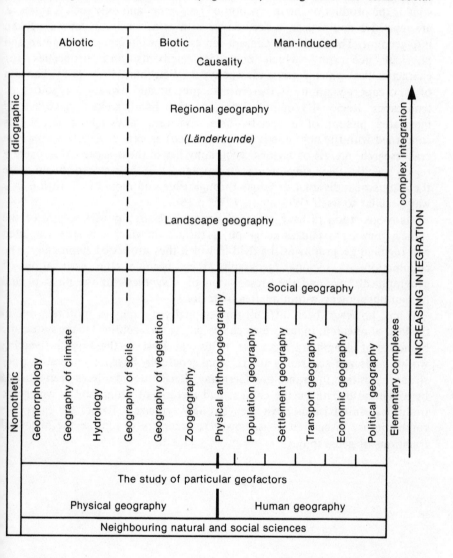

Figure 1.3 An organizational plan of geography (after Uhlig, 1971; Weichhart, 1975)

geography in the German sense of integrative human geography rather than in the Anglo-American usage as a specialized branch of human geography. Of more significance is Uhlig's location of *landscape geography* at a higher level of integration than the systematic branches. In the German geographical tradition, landscape geography *(Landschaftskunde)* forms a transition or bridge between systematic geography and regional geography *(Länderkunde)* which is the most complex form of geographical integration. The landscape is seen as the product of the interaction of *geofactors* and only such features as are repetitive and appear in accordance with certain rules or laws are taken into account. The landscape concept represents an integration of human and physical geography which considers elements and properties (or characteristics) which form landscape types (Weichhart, 1975, p. 9). The aim of landscape geography is therefore to present and explain a typology of landscapes. Regional geography, on the other hand, seeks to give a total integrated picture of a specific area. Whereas landscape geography is concerned with the nomothetic (law-controlled) aspects of a certain area, the real research interest of regional geography lies in those aspects that make a region specific. Such *singular* aspects have arisen in the course of history, are the results of individual decisions through time and mould each region in a way peculiar to itself (Weichhart, 1975, p.16).

Many geographers have regarded regional geography as the core of the subject, viewing systematic geography as the area in which laws are formulated and regional geography as the field in which they are tested empirically. The culmination of regional geography then becomes the verification of geographical laws and the presentation of a *synthesis* of the physical and human phenomena within an area or region.

It has, however, been difficult for regional geography to fulfil this role in the field of research. In fact, research has largely been confined to the systematic branches of geography since the 1930s – at least in the English-speaking world; landscape geography and regional geography have maintained a rather stronger position in France and Germany. Recent decades have been marked by a general debate on the content and method of geography in which the traditional subdivisions have been strongly criticized. Before we enter this contemporary discussion, it is, however, necessary to look at the historical traditions of geography.

2 The Foundation of Geography

Geography in the Ancient World

Interest in geographical problems, and writings on subjects we can recognize as geographical, began long before the introduction of the subject into universities. In fact it is difficult to imagine how there were ever people who did not think geographically, who never considered the conditions under which they lived, and never wondered how people lived in other places. In this sense geographical thinking is older than the term 'geography', which was first used by scholars at the Museum in Alexandria about 300 BC.

The ancient Greeks made the first major contribution to the development of the subject. Scholarly writers produced *topographical descriptions* of places in the known world, discussing both natural conditions and the culture and way of life of the people who lived there. The best known of these was Herodotus (*c.* 485–425 BC). He was first and foremost a historian, and is indeed often regarded as the father of history but he placed historical events in a geographical setting; some of his writings are truly geographical in character. He not only described geographical phenomena, as, for example, the annual flow of the Nile, but also attempted to explain them.

Herodotus had no interest in those mathematical and astronomical problems that later became associated with geography – the measurement of the circumference of the earth and the establishment of exact locations for places. He accepted the Homeric view of the earth as a flat disc over which the sun travelled in an arc from east to west. The belief that the earth was a sphere was discussed in Herodotus' time but it was Aristotle, about a century after Herodotus, who produced observational evidence for a spherical form of the earth. The scholars at the Museum in Alexandria were then able to establish the foundations for the calculation of latitude, longitude and the size of the earth.

Eratosthenes (276–194 BC), who was chief librarian at the museum, succeeded in calculating the circumference of the earth with remarkable precision. He actually measured the distance from Syene (Aswan) to Alexandria and estimated it to be one-fiftieth of the circumference of the earth by observations of the elevation of the sun. Of equal importance was his development of systems of co-ordinates for the world, i.e. latitude and longitude, which he used to locate places and to measure distances. This made it possible for him to draw the first passably accurate map.

Eratosthenes' cartographical work was later developed by his students and successors at the Museum in Alexandria. Ptolemy (AD 90–168) wrote a major work in eight volumes which is now known as *Ptolemy's Geography*. The first volume explained the principles for calculating the dimensions of the earth, its division into degrees, calculations of latitude and longitude, and a discussion of map projections. The eighth volume contained maps of different parts of the world. Other volumes included tables of latitude and longitude for 4,000 places.

Although it was widely known how to calculate geographical latitude from the altitude of the sun in Ptolemy's time, calculations had only been made for a handful of places. The calculation of longitude was then only possible by estimating the length of journeys from one place to another and so many of Ptolemy's locations for places were erroneous. His biggest mistake was to underestimate the size of the earth, rejecting the almost correct estimate of Eratosthenes in favour of a reckoning made by Posidonius in about 100 BC. Posidonious reckoned the circumference of the earth to be 180,000 stadii (a stadium can be taken to represent 157.5m), against Eratosthenes' estimates of 252,000 stadii. Because calculations of longitude had to be based on rather unreliable travel distances, Ptolemy's otherwise remarkably accurate map of the known world included too many degrees of longitude. The map extended from a prime meridian in the Canary Islands to a 180 degree meridian which crossed inner China. The actual distance between these places is only 120 degrees.

The topographical tradition of Greek geography, represented by Herodotus, was carried forward into Roman times. Strabo (64 BC–AD 20) wrote a work of seventeen volumes called *Geographica*. This was largely an encyclopaedic description of the known world whose chief value was that it preserved for posterity many writings which he annotated and cited. *Geographica* also included attempts to explain cultural distinctiveness, types of governments and customs in particular places. The significance of natural conditions for cultural development was discussed in relation to a number of places, especially in the description of Italy.

Middle Ages and Renaissance

The Middle Ages were a dark period for the development of science in Europe. At best, scholars made accurate but sterile copies of the works of the ancients, rejecting anything which did not conform with the dogmas of the Church. Such an intellectual environment stifled any development of scientific analysis. Concepts of the world which had been developed in ancient times were reshaped to conform to the teaching of the Church. The earth became a flat disc with Jerusalem at its centre.

Ancient learning was, however, carefully preserved in the Islamic countries at the Arab universities of Spain, North Africa and the Middle East. Arab traders travelled widely and gathered information which could be used by scholars to fill in the gaps on Ptolemy's original map. The best known of these travellers was Ibn Batuta (1304-1368) who travelled as far east as Peking in China, and sailed far south of the equator along the east coast of Africa. This particular trip showed that Aristotle had been wrong in believing that it was too hot for human habitation in what the Greeks had called the 'torrid zone'. But already by the twelfth century, Al Idrisi (1099-1180) had shown that the Greek division of the world into five climatic zones (two cold, two temperate and one torrid) did not correspond to reality and had suggested a more sophisticated world climatic system. Al Muqaddasi (945-988) was the most eminent Arab geographer of the Middle Ages according to Scholten (1980). Before his time, geographers had generally based their topographical descriptions on compilations of second-hand sources. Muqaddasi was a pioneer of fieldwork and states in his book *The Best Divisions of the Study of Climate* that he will not present anything as fact to his readers unless he has seen it with his own eyes. His book was based on extensive travels within the Islamic world.

The last great Islamic geographer of the Middle Ages was Ibn Khaldun (1332-1406). He established the foundation for historical geography in those of his writings which analysed the rise and fall of empires. He suggested that warlike nomads often founded large states, but after a while the nomads were absorbed by their permanently settled subjects. As peasants and townsmen, the rulers lost their warlike spirit and eventually their kingdoms fell apart. Ibn Khaldun both predicted and lived to see the collapse of the Islamic state he lived in. At the fall of Damascus in 1400 he actually met Tamerlane, the conqueror and devastator. It was unfortunate that the works of the Arab scholars were not translated into Latin or any West European language until the nineteenth century; as a result, the Europeans were unable to make use of their observations.

The journeys undertaken by Europeans during the Middle Ages made little significant contribution to the development of geographical knowledge. Around AD 1000 the Norsemen sailed across the North Atlanic to Greenland and North America but the Sagas of these adventures were only passed on by word of mouth and written down long afterwards in isolated Iceland.

Meanwhile, exploration and learning flourished in China. Actually Europe and India were 'discovered' by Chinese travellers long before Europeans reached the Orient. In the period between the second century BC and the fifteenth century AD, Chinese culture was the most efficient in the world in applying knowledge of nature to useful purposes. The study of geography was advanced well beyond anything known in Europe at this time; among other things, the Chinese used co-ordinates and triangulation to produce beautiful maps of China and neighbouring countries. When, however, the Italian Marco Polo (1254–1322) wrote an account of his travels to China describing the high level of Chinese learning, his book was widely discounted as a fictitious adventure.

The Renaissance brought about a renewed interest in the geographical knowledge of ancient times. Copies of Ptolemy's *Geography* that had been preserved in Byzantium (Istanbul) were discovered and brought to Venice where they were translated into Latin in about 1410 and made a great impact on contemporary scholars (Bagrow, 1945). Columbus and other expeditionary leaders relied on Ptolemy's calculations (p.12), but some of their more famous discoveries disproved the latter's calculations of longitude and changed the world picture he had established. There were new developments in cartography – new projections, especially that of Mercator in 1569, were invented; the first globes were made, and new world maps were published.

In addition to this there was a revival in another branch of ancient geography, that of topographic description. Large numbers of accounts of voyages provided raw material for encyclopaedic works on the geography of the world. The jumble of information related to place names included in such *topographies*, where notes on natural and physical conditions were juxtaposed beside miscellaneous information on folklore, etymology and history, places them outside the field of science as we understand it today. The popularity of these works in their own time might well puzzle us until we realize that we

> are often prisoners of contemporary logic and cannot see those qualities of old works which cannot be integrated into our system ...at the time it had just as much relevance as what continues to interest us today: it was part of what the episteme of the time indicated was knowledge.
>
> (Claval, 1980, p. 379)

Varenius and Kant

Strabo made a rough definition of the study of geography when he said that

> wide learning, which alone makes it possible to undertake a work on geography, is possessed solely by the man who has investigated things both human and divine... The utility of geography... regards knowledge both of the heavens and of things on land and sea, animals, plants, fruits, and everything else to be seen in various regions – the utility of geography, I say, presupposes in the geographer the same philosopher, the man who busies himself with the investigation of the art of life, that is, of happiness.
>
> (cited by Fischer *et al.*, 1969, p. 16)

Strabo considered that geographers should study both human activities and natural conditions.

This dualism within the subject is still characteristic of geography. Some writers have regarded it as the essential justification for the role of geography, while others have argued for a division of the subject into physical and human geography on the ground that the respective methodologies of physical and human geography must be different. In studies of natural phenomena, including climate, geology and land forms, it is possible to use the methods of the natural sciences and to draw conclusions with a large measure of scientific precision. The methods of natural science, however, do not lend themselves very well to the study of social and cultural phenomena. Our generalizations about human groups must be limited in time and space, and must relate to statements of probability rather than certainty.

Bernhard Varenius (1622–50), whose *Geographia Generalis* was published in Amsterdam in 1650, was one of the first scholars to suggest these essential differences in the character of physical and human geography. His book includes much material which today would be treated as mathematical geography or as astronomy. The *Geographia Generalis* is divided into three parts: (1) the absolute or terrestrial section, which describes the shape and size of the earth and the physical geography of continents, seas and the atmosphere; (2) the relative or cosmic section, which treats the relations between the earth and other heavenly bodies, especially the sun and its influence on world climate; and (3) the comparative section, which discusses the location of different places in relation to each other and the principles of navigation.

Varenius intended that the *Geographia Generalis* should be followed by what he called, in his foreword to the book, 'special' geography in which descriptions of particular places should be based upon (1) 'celestial conditions,' including climates and climatic zones; (2) terrestrial conditions with descriptions of relief, vegetation and animal life; and also (3) human conditions including trade, settlement and forms of government in each country. In fact he showed little enthusiasm to embark on the study of human geography as it was not possible to treat it in an exact way. He explained that he had included this last group of conditions as a concession to traditional approaches to the subject. Unfortunately, he did not have the opportunity to write on special geography since he died at the early age of 28 (Lange, 1961).

Varenius made two major contributions to the development of geography. Firstly, he brought together contemporary knowledge of astronomy and cartography and subjected the different theories of his day to sound critical analysis. Secondly, his partition of geography into *general* and *special* sections originated what we now call systematic and regional geography. *Geographia Generalis* dealt with the whole world as a unit, but was restricted to physical conditions which could be understood through natural laws. Special geography was primarily intended as a description of individual countries and world regions. It was difficult to establish 'laws' in the special (regional) part for the explanation must be descriptive where people are involved. Preston James (1972, p. 124) points out that the general (systematic) and special (regional) parts of Varenius' work complement each other, and that Varenius saw general and special geography as two mutually interdependent parts of a whole.

The lectures on physical geography given by Immanuel Kant (1724–1804) in Königsberg were of great significance for the later development of geography. The course, which was given more than forty times, was one of his most popular. It was not a course on physical geography as we now understand it, but also studied the races of human beings, their physical activities on the earth and natural conditions in the widest sense of the term. For Kant himself geography represented only an approach to the empirical knowledge which was necessary for his philosophical research,

> But, finding the subject inadequately developed and organised, he devoted a great deal of attention to the assembly and organization of materials from a wide variety of sources, and also to the consideration of a number of specific problems – for example, the deflection of wind direction resulting from the Earth's rotation.
>
> (Hartshorne, 1939, p. 38)

Kant provided a philosophical foundation for the belief that the subject has a significant scientific contribution to make. He pointed out that there are two different ways of grouping or classifying empirical phenomena for the purpose of studying them: either in accordance with their nature, or in accordance with their position in time and place. The former is a *logical* classification, the latter a physical one. Logical classification lays the foundations for the *systematic sciences* – the study of animals is zoology, that of the rocks is geology, that of social groups is sociology, and so on. *Physical classification* gives the scientific basis for history and geography, history studies the phenomena that follow one after the other in time *(chronological science),* while geography studies phenomena belonging to the same place *(chorological science).* History and geography are both essential sciences, standing alongside the systematic sciences. Without them, humanity cannot achieve a full understanding of the world.

Kant gave geography a central position in the sciences: geographers have often reiterated his views to justify the existence of the subject and its special character amongst the sciences. Alfred Hettner (1859–1941) who did most to redevelop Kant's thought, admitted (1927, p. 115) that for a long time he had not paid sufficient attention to Kant's exposition of geography but had later rejoiced to discover a close correspondence between the conclusions of the great philosopher and his own. The American geographer Richard Hartshorne closely followed Hettner in his *Nature of Geography* (1939), considering that Kant's approach led towards a satisfactory understanding of the nature of geography and answered all its basic questions.

Today it is widely considered to be impossible, and to some extent philosophically untenable, to draw such sharp divisions between the 'sciences' as Kant did. Understanding of geographical situations is always improved when we consider their development over time. Just as there are geographers who wish to study the cultural landscapes of former times without necessarily using their knowledge to illuminate contemporary conditions, so historians cannot neglect the study of differences between places. Here the individual sciences overlap each other.

Hettner (1927, pp. 131–2) considered that the biggest difference between history and geography

> does not lie in that geography sets out to study a given time, namely the present, but that in geography the time aspect recedes into the background. Geography does not study development in time as such – although this particular methodological rule is often broken – geographers cut through reality at a distinct point in time and only consider historical developments in so far as they are necessary to explain the situation at that chosen point in time.

During the period between the death of Kant in 1804 and Hettner's book in 1927, this 'methodological rule' had not only been broken but almost systematically opposed, since Kant's philosophical guidelines for the subject had been virtually forgotten until Hettner and Hartshorne resurrected them. In the nineteenth century, geographical research was closely associated with the study of process, that is, the development of phenomena over time in geographical space.

The classical period

While Kant gave geography a philosophical basis it was Alexander von Humboldt (1769–1859) and Carl Ritter (1779–1859) who laid the scientific foundations for geography as a branch of knowledge. These two men had many views in common and were united in their criticism of the casual and unsystematic treatment of geographical data by their predecessors. The similarity of their opinions was not accidental – Ritter regarded himself as a student of Humboldt, and Humboldt described Ritter as 'his old friend'. They differed markedly, however, in temperament and character.

Humboldt was the last of the great polymaths. Penck (1928, p. 31) regarded him as a *cosmographer* rather than a geographer. He mastered a number of disciplines and put all his energy (and fortune) into travel and research in order to understand the whole complex system of the universe. In his great work *Kosmos,* with its subtitle *Sketch of a Physical Description of the World,* he attempted to assemble all the contemporary knowledge of the material world. *Kosmos* was published (1845–62) in five volumes at the end of his life, while the results from his long and important jouneys in Latin America (1799–1804) had been published in thirty volumes in Paris (1805–34).

Humboldt had a gift for exceptionally sharp observation, and in fieldwork he was unsurpassed. His books and letters demonstrate that nothing escaped his observation. This, together with his training in geology, is shown in a letter he wrote to a Russian minister after a visit to the Urals: 'The Ural Mountains are a true El Dorado,' he wrote, 'and I am confident, from the analogy they present to the geological conformation of Brazil, that diamonds will be discovered in the gold and platinum washings of the Urals.' A few days later, diamonds were actually discovered (Tatham, 1951, p. 55). Humboldt was primarily interested in the natural sciences. He undertook a large number of altitudinal measurements during his travels and drew height profiles of the continents. These measurements were used in his studies of climatic and vegetation zones which were of basic importance for later research in biogeography and climatology. He also wrote regional accounts of Mexico and Cuba that are still of interest at the present day (Schmieder, 1964).

In contrast to most other natural scientists of his day, Humboldt was not so much interested in discoveries of new species and in collections for natural science museums as in the understanding of connectivities in the world of nature – a scientific approach he called *'physikalische Geographie'*. This must not be confused with the more limited concept of *'physical geography'* as used today. The relations between the vegetable and animal kingdoms and also humankind with geographical conditions of climate, topography and altitude were central to Humboldt's interests. In his search for *'Oeconomia Naturae'*, we find some of the roots of modern ecological thinking. His work is much more free of environmental determinism than the much later studies of Ratzel and Semple (see pp. 31–32)

Humboldt transferred Kant's idea of a threefold division of all the sciences to the natural sciences, dividing them into (1) *Physiography* or description of nature; (2) *Historia telluria,* the geological history of the earth; and (3) *Geonosia* or *physikalische Geographie* (Beck, 1982, p. 90). Humboldt did not wish to confine his research to any one of these subdivisions. As a *cosmographer,* he was not interested in becoming a specialist in either history or geography. Geography and the natural sciences were not then institutionalized and specialized disciplines. Humboldt and Ritter would barely have understood the later division of science into *disciplines,* the specialized fields of work of scientific institutions or the interminable discussions about the nature or limitations of specific disciplines. They were both in this sense cosmographers, although their field of inquiry differed.

Ritter's recognition as a geographer dates from the publication of the first two volumes of his *Erdkunde,* a volume on Africa and a volume on Asia, in 1817–18. The second edition was published in nineteen enlarged volumes in 1822–59. In 1820 he was established as the first professor of geography in Berlin, on the initiative of leading politicians. Although Ritter travelled widely in Europe, he spent relatively more time in his study than did Humboldt. The two men complemented each other in that Ritter was chiefly concerned with studies in human geography, and stood somewhat apart from the rapidly advancing research front of the natural sciences. It would be wrong to describe him as a crude determinist (see p. 3) as some commentators have done. He believed, as did Vidal de la Blache much later, that 'the earth and its inhabitants stand in the closest reciprocal relations, and one cannot be truly presented in all its relationships without the other. Hence history and geography must always remain inseparable. Land affects the inhabitants and the inhabitants the land' (cited by Tatham, 1951, p. 44).

This implied that the individual region or continent had a unity, a *Ganzheit* (which may be translated as a 'whole'), which it was the task of the geographer to study. This entity was something more than the sum of its parts – more than the totality of topographical, climatic, ethnic and other circumstances. Ritter's views were shaped by his deeply religious outlook and by the accepted natural philosophy of his time. His ideas on the 'wholeness' of things were in accordance with the writings of the German 'idealist' philosopher Georg W. F. Hegel (1770–1831), whose attitudes amounted to an attempt to comprehend the entire universe, to know the infinite and to see all things in God (Chisholm, 1975, p. 33). The scientific stance of Ritter, like Immanuel Kant before him, was *teleological* (Greek *teleos* = purpose). Teleology seeks to understand events in relation to their underlying purposes. Teleological explanations are therefore often regarded as the opposite of *mechanical* explanations, where the phenomena and observations are understood as outcomes of prime causes – such as the 'laws of nature' (see p. 54). Ritter studied the workings of nature in order to understand the purpose behind its order. His view of science sprang from his firm belief in God as the planner of the Universe. He regarded the Earth as an educational model for man, where nature had a God-given *purpose* which was to show the way for man's development. He did not regard the shape of continents as accidental but rather as determined by God, so that their form and location enabled them to play the role designed by God for the development of man.

Ritter's approach to knowledge was strongly criticized later; Hettner (1927, p. 87) said that Ritter's views were in accordance with the spirit of his time and this reinforced their influence on his generation. This influence, however, was bound to decline when Darwin's *Origin of Species* inaugurated a new philosophy of science.

Ritter combined a basic teleological standpoint with a most critical scientific precision. 'My system builds on facts, not on philosophical arguments', he said in a letter. The collection of facts was not an end in itself; the systematization and comparison of data, region by region, would lead to a recognition of unity in apparent diversity. The plans of God, which give purpose and meaning, could only be discovered by taking into account all facts and relationships in the world as objectively as possible. In this he followed the advice of Immanuel Kant that the scientist must, on one hand, continue to explore the universe along mechanistic lines, and should never abandon this approach, yet on the other hand should bear in mind that organic life can best be understood by minds like ours in terms of the principle of natural teleology (Greene, 1957, p. 68)

Ritter's significance as a scientist lies in his thorough and critical study of sources and in his ability to systematize extensive material, and in these respects his work is in the same tradition as that of Humboldt. While earlier regional descriptions had consisted to a large extent of the accumulation of unsystematized data about particular places, Humboldt and Ritter effected a clear structuring of such material and, through deliberate research into both the similarities and the differences between countries and regions, sought to compare the different parts of the world with each other.

Ritter was, says Hassinger (1919, p. 66), 'the founder of the comparative method in regional geography, the victor over every dead aggregate presentation of geographical knowledge. He gave our science unity and coherence' through his use of historical development as its leading thread. Ritter himself, however, regarded Humboldt as the founder of the *comparative method* (Schültz, 1980, p. 44). The basis for Ritter's comparative studies was the physical layout of the land, the area and character of river basins for example. In this way he could present a land classification or a set of physical regions. The most important part of his work, however, would be to explain the relationships between humanity and nature in the different regions through the history of humankind. Ritter believed that thorough research into the historical development of culture and its relations to physical regions would demonstrate the physical layout of the land as God's educational home for humankind. He therefore made historical development in geographical space the main theme of his educational endeavours. Geography followed this tradition for a long time afterwards, including the period of its institutionalization as a specific discipline.

Subsequent writers have commented on the differences between the religious and scientific outlooks of Humboldt and Ritter and have somewhat exaggerated them. Both men laid great stress on the unity of nature. They both believed that the ultimate aim of research was to clarify this unity, and, in this respect, were in accord with the idealistic philosophies of their time. Humboldt did not pursue *idealism* as far as Ritter, for his concept of the unity of nature was more aesthetic than religious. In this respect he had more in common with Goethe than with Ritter. Unlike Ritter, he saw no reason to explain unity and order in nature as a God-given system to further man's development. Humboldt was strongly engaged in the gradual development of natural science and his greatest contributions lay in the field of *systematic* physical geography. Many regard him as the founder of biogeography and climatology. Ritter was to a considerable extent a *regional* geographer.

The geography Ritter and Humboldt represented was designated as 'classical' by Hartshorne (1939) because it dominated the foundation – or perhaps we should rather say the pre-foundation – period of the subject, since the institutionalization of the discipline came later.

From cosmography to an institutionalized discipline

No geographers, before or since, have enjoyed a more central position in science and society than Humboldt and Ritter. It might have been expected that this position would have led to a real breakthrough for geography as a scientific discipine in Germany. Quite the contrary: with the death of both Humboldt and Ritter in 1859 the classical period came to an end with no real successors to take up the heritage. The personal professorship held by Ritter ceased with his death and new university chairs in geography were not established until much later.

An important reason for this lack of progress was the cosmographic character of the achievements of Ritter and Humboldt. By this time, geographical societies were flourishing but the field of 'geography' was still not related to a specific discipline and remained an umbrella concept for a variety of expeditions and other activities within the natural and social sciences. In the latter part of the nineteenth century, however the universities effected the disciplinary division of the sciences. Earlier *universalistic* philosophies were also gradually replaced by a scientific philosophy which emphasized natural laws and causality (partial-general reasoning in Figure 1.2, p. 7) and found it difficult to accommodate a universalistic geography as a scientific discipline. The year 1859, in which both Humboldt and Ritter died, also saw the publication of Charles Darwin's *Origin of Species,* which provided much of the basis for the new ways of scientific reasoning.

The lack of new chairs in geography was also partly due to the fact that the discipline expounded by Ritter was considered by influential academics as merely a subdivision of history or, at best, as a subsidiary subject to it. In his zeal to demonstrate that the earth is a school for humanity, Ritter had become more and more interested in its historical development: his more influential students concentrated on historical research to an even greater extent. In many schools of geography, especially in France, the subject came to be very closely associated with history. In Germany, geography was a widespread school subject by 1850, taught in most cases as an auxiliary subject to history. However, the early introduction of compulsory elementary education in Germany and Switzerland, based on modern pedagogical principles, made the development of academic geography possible. By 1875 there were geography chairs at three Swiss universities (Capel, 1981, p. 59).

It was after the Franco-Prussian War of 1870–1 that influential politicians in Prussia realized that geography could also serve an important political purpose as a contemporary discipline. Geographical education could be used to reinforce and popularize the idea of the nation-state, a commendable objective at that time, and also provide people with a better understanding of the economic and political possiblities of world trade and development. To achieve these goals, it was necessary to provide a better education for geography teachers. For this reason, in 1874, the Prussian government decided to establish chairs of geography in all the Prussian universities. By 1880, ten professors had been appointed. In other European countries geography was established as a university discipline for more or less the same reasons. While both history and geography could serve to develop nationalistic sentiments, the relative position of these two subjects in the educational system largely came to depend on the degree to which either seemed more useful in building up the idea of a national identity. In Germany, with its long history of shifting borders and divisions into small states, geographical patterns associated with the German-speaking lands seemed to be very significant and so geography was heavily stressed. Norway, on the other hand, developed its educational system during the union of the crowns with Sweden (1814–1905) and had no disputed borders. Under these circumstances a national awakening was fostered by teaching about the glorious history of Viking times and the precious liberal constitution of 1814, so history predominated over geography. Finland, which also experienced a union of crowns, in this case with Tsarist Russia, lacked a clearly discernible glorious past and geography developed as a relatively important subject. A pioneer research work of great political importance in the liberation process, the *Atlas of Finland,* first edited in 1899, stressed the uniqueness of the Finnish lands.

In France, it was claimed that German teachers had won the war of 1871–2. School reform was therefore needed in order to replace the old classical curriculum. This reform introduced the new natural sciences with geography among them. During the 1870s, a handful of chairs of geography were established at French universities, the most significant appointment was that of the young Paul Vidal de la Blache (1845–1918) to the chair at Paris in 1877 (Capel, 1981, p. 60).

In Britain, the first personal chair of geography was held by Captain James Machonochie at University College, London from 1833 until 1836. Permanent university teaching dates from the appointment of Halford J. Mackinder to a readership at Oxford in 1887 with the financial support of the Royal Geographical Society. Mackinder became an outstanding promoter of geography at universities and also in schools. In 1893, together with a group of schoolmasters, he founded the Geographical Association, which did much to encourage and improve geographical education. In 1910, Mackinder was elected to Parliament but remained an important father-figure in British geography. The first British geography *department* was established at Oxford in 1900 but geography only achieved a firm footing at Cambridge after 1908, mainly through the continued financial support of the Royal Geographical Society. During a period of thirty-five years, the Society invested about £7,250 in the Cambridge project and £11,000 at Oxford (Stoddart), 1986, pp. 83–125). 'Hence we have the paradox that in the 1880s and 1890s British geography emerged as a scientific discipline without the benefit of aid from strictly scientific men' (Stoddart, 1986, p. 67).

The reluctant and somewhat hostile attitudes in the universities towards the establishment of geography as an academic discipline were largely due to the rapid growth of the systematic sciences and the increasing need to specialize in scientific work. The image of geography as an all-embracing cosmographic subject did not fit the academic development of the period. Influential academics argued that the fields of geographical inquiry were already covered by existing disciplines. The historian, Edward A. Freeman, could not understand how geography could be recognized as an independent university discipline when 'on the one hand a great deal belongs to history, but on the other the geologists lay claim to much of its material' (reference by Keltie, 1886). McKenny Hughes, a professor of geology at Cambridge, argued that his geology department did all the necessary lecturing and fieldwork in physical geography already. In a university, students should specialize either in history, geology or zoology, drawing on a knowledge of geography already imparted at school (Stoddart, 1986, p. 70).

The Keltie Report of 1886 provided, however, a powerful and comprehensive documentation of the academic and practical value of geography.

It is through geography alone that the links can be seen that connect physical, historical and political conditions; and it is thus that geography claims the position of a science distinct from the rest, and of singular practical importance ...scientific geography may be defined as the study of local correlations.

(Keltie, 1886, p. 71)

In the USA, individual university teachers of geography included William Morris Davies (1850-1934), who began teaching at Harvard in 1878. The first geography department was established in Chicago in 1903. By the First World War, the discipline was firmly established at a number of North American universities, notably Harvard, Yale, Teachers College (Columbia University), the Wharton School (University of Pennsylvania) and Chicago.

The *institutionalization* of geography meant that national examinations with national standards were organized and the discipline had to be defined as a subject area with a defined content. This 'new geography', for which syllabuses and reading lists had to be drawn up, led to the *professionalization* of people calling themselves geographers. New professional journals were founded, like the *Geographical Journal* in Britain, *Annales de Géographie* in France and the *Annals of the Association of American Geographers*. The new academic geography gradually distanced itself from the geographical societies as the university geographers developed a scientific base the societies lacked. This divergence was, in some cases, widened by the attitudes of prominent members of the societies. The chairman of the Finnish Geographical Society, for instance, maintained the cosmographic view that geography was a collection of different sciences but not a science in itself. This view was, of course strongly repudiated by the Finnish professors of geography (Granö 1986). In the new academic journals, which had often been founded almost in opposition to the journals of the geographical societies, geographers set out to justify the new science by defining its long traditions, its utility and special methods and to delimit geography unequivocally from neighbouring disciplines. A more important function of the academic journals was to publish research that could be used as exemplary models by students.

The 'new geography' drew on some ideas from Humboldt and Ritter but was also influenced both by developments within the natural sciences which followed the Darwinian breakthrough and the political milieu of the period.

Anarchists and Darwinists

The most able of Ritter's disciples was the French geographer Elisée Réclus (1830–1905), who was less concerned with history and teleological thinking than most of the others. He achieved recognition with a work of systematic physical geography called *La Terre* (1866–7), but is best remembered for his nineteen-volume regional geography *Nouvelle Géographie Universelle* (1875–94). The clarity and accuracy of this work made it much more popular than Ritter's *Erdkunde,* which had been its exemplar in many respects, but which also contained many obscure passages. Réclus's work became a model for a range of encyclopaedic studies of the geography of the world and of particular countries.

Réclus was probably the most productive geographer of all time. At the end of his life he also wrote *L'Homme et la Terre* (mostly published posthumously in 1905–8) which may be described as a social geography comprising a broad brush historical presentation of humanity's life on earth and its use of its resources. Réclus also wrote travel handbooks and articles. Although Réclus was the greatest French geographer of his time, he never held a university chair in France and had to earn his living from his writings. Although most of his books were published by Hachette in Paris he was obliged to live abroad in exile because of his political activities and could not directly influence the development of French academic geography.

Réclus was first and foremost an uncomprising idealist. He was expelled from the seminary at Montauban in his very first year, because he supported the ideals of the 1848 revolution. In 1851 he went to Berlin to study theology, but began to attend the popular lectures of Carl Ritter, which awakened his interest in geography. Returning to France in the autumn of 1851, Réclus resumed his political activity. Resisting the *coup d'état* of Napoleon III, he was obliged to flee to England with his brother (Dunbar, 1981, p. 155). Réclus also undertook extensive journeys in North and South America, travelling more in order to observe than to do research. Sustained research was, in fact beyond his means for Réclus had to make a living from the meagre wages he could earn as a tutor and worker *en route.* In 1857, he returned to France and befriended the leading *anarchist,* Michael Bakunin (1814–76). From that time onwards, Réclus belonged to the inner circle of the secret anarchist association *Fraternité Internationale.* In 1871, he took an active part in the Paris Commune but was captured during the first days of fighting. He was held in prison for almost a year. A sentence of deportation to New Caledonia was commuted to ten years' banishment as a result of the active intercession from geographical societies and such leading personalities as Charles Darwin. He chose to settle in Switzerland in his exile. Although Réclus had been promised a readership in geography in the Université Libre in Brussels in 1892, the university reneged on the appointment for fear of demonstrations after an outbreak of anarchist violence in France in the autumn of 1893. A committee of support for Réclus started to collect money and eventually founded the New University of Brussels where Réclus was professor for the last eleven years of his life, refusing to take any salary since his modest needs could be satisfied by the income from his books.

Réclus's books, including his major work, *Nouvelle Géographie Universelle,* showed little evidence of his political beliefs. For this reason they attracted a large, middle-class readership and provided politicians and leading members of the geographical societies with a model for the geography they wished to introduce as a subject in schools and universities. So Réclus had an important indirect influence on the institutionalization of geography at a time when most academics saw geography only in its role as a natural science. Like Ritter, Réclus was particularly interested in the human aspects of geography. He had a sharp eye for the inequalities of the human condition around the world, and made this a central theme of his books. He was also the first European geographer to support the ideas of the American geographer George Parkins Marsh. Marsh had written *Man and Nature, or Physical Geography as Modified by Human Action* in 1864, describing his book as 'a little volume showing that whereas Ritter and Guyot [a student of Ritter who emigrated to the USA] think that the earth made man, man, in fact made the earth' (cited by Beck, 1982, p. 148). Marsh suggested that man had destroyed many natural resources and landscapes throughout history and called for a better management of natural resources. In his very first work, *La terre* (1866–7), Réclus acknowledged his debt to Marsh.

Réclus's political views were more directly expressed in his last work, *L'Homme et la Terre,* which introduced the concept of *social geography.* As Réclus devoted his political life to social justice, social conditions were always discussed in his books. He had made a special study of social geography and his inclusion in a travel guide of a description of poverty and relief among the poor of London broke new ground (Beck, 1982, p. 135).

Réclus also established a connection between geography and modern town planning and sociology. He influenced and had close contacts with Fréderic le Play, the French sociologist, and Sir Patrick Geddes, the Scottish biologist, social scientist and planner. Geddes, although no anarchist, became a close friend of Réclus in the last decade of the latter's life. He spread Réclus's ideas in Britain and was most interested in his ideas on social geography which he found a suitable basis for the development of his work on applied research and planning (see p. 42). We have laid considerable emphasis on the life and work of Réclus in order to demonstrate that the old masters still have something to say to us today. The urge for social relevance in geographical work was not invented in our time; it was present in the life and work of the anarchist geographers one hundred years ago. Today Réclus and his anarchist friend and fellow-geographer, Count Peter Kropotkin (1842–1921), have aroused renewed interest. The Russian nobleman became famous for his research into the physical geography of Northern Europe and Siberia and was a welcome speaker among the geographical societies of Western Europe. Kropotkin also gave Réclus ample help with the sections of *Nouvelle Géographie Universelle* that dealt with Siberia and Eastern Europe.

Kropotkin voiced his political opinions much more directly than Réclus. He tried to revolutionize the discipline of geography in a number of ways. He presented theories of geographical education, the relations between man and nature and of decentralization, which were clearly aimed at discouraging the use of geographical research for exploitative and imperialistic purposes (Breitbart, 1981, p. 150). He voiced the modern view that geographical education is ideally suited to promote a sense of mutual respect between nations and people (Kropotkin, 1885, p. 942). Kropotkin's political ideas had developed while he was travelling in Siberia during the 1860s. He was impressed by the spirit of equality and self-sufficiency of the Russian peasants but disheartened by the negative effects of political centralization and social inequality. In 1871, Kropotkin became an active advocate of social anarchism and had to go into exile. From that time onwards he devoted his life to two revolutions: one in social and economic relations, the other in the discipline of geography itself. Kropotkin' *social anarchism* sought to demonstrate that people had a capacity to develop a better society on a co-operative basis, provided that the structures of domination and subordination were taken away. He believed that centralized institutions inhibit the development of a co-operative personality, promote inequality and limit economic progress (Breitbart, 1981, p. 138). He advocated small-scale economic activity within and between regions, which, he thought, could produce economies of scale superior to those produced by large-scale industry. Such arguments are advanced today by the 'green' movements and by economists such as Schumacher in *Small Is Beautiful* (1974). Kropotkin suggested that large city-regions should be disaggregated into small, more or less self-sufficient townships within which living, working and recreational space might be integrated. Such ideas were later put into practice by the 'garden city' movement led by Ebenezer Howard, Lewis Mumford and Patrick Geddes.

Most significantly for his time, Kropotkin strongly opposed the dominant interpretation of Darwin's *Origin of Species* (1859) which saw nature as an immense battlefield upon which there is nothing but an incessant struggle for life and the extermination of the weak by the strong. He strongly opposed the *social Darwinist* views of the popular philosopher Herbert Spencer (1820–1903). Spencer envisaged human societies as closely resembling animal organisms which must engage in constant struggle in order to survive in particular environments. Politically, Spencer was a liberal, believing that the 'fittest individuals' would survive best in a free enterprise system, and thus lead civilization forward. In his 'general law of evolution' Spencer claimed that all evolution is characterized by concentration, differentiation and determination. Kropotkin, on the other hand, wrote (1924, p. vii), 'I failed to find, although I was eagerly looking for it, that bitter struggle for the means of existence between animals of the same species.' The struggle for existence may be hard, but it is not carried out by individuals, rather by groups of individuals co-operating with each other. In the development of civilization, as in the quest for survival, Kropotkin believed that mutual aid within small, self-contained communities was the best workable solution.

This discussion has shown that, during the late nineteenth century, it was thought to be important to learn from nature how to shape human societies. The influence of *Darwinism* was strongly felt, not only on social thinking but on the development of science as such. It is also interesting to note that the ideas of Carl Ritter were, by this time, best advocated by his anarchist pupils, with the views of the social Darwinists standing in marked contrast. Both Réclus and Kropotkin stressed and developed the idea that geography as a discipline should encompass both man and nature. Kropotkin was a close friend of Scott Keltie, the secretary of the Royal Geographical Society, and he strongly supported the arguments used to establish geography as a university discipline in Britain (Keltie, 1886).

There are good reasons to maintain that, alongside the Bible, no book has had a more profound influence on our ways of thinking than Charles Darwin's *Origin of Species* (1859). Stoddart (1966) suggests that the following four main themes from Darwin's work can be traced in later geographical research: (1) Change through time or *evolution,* a general concept of gradual or even transition from lower or simpler to higher or more complicated forms. Darwin used the terms evolution and development essentially in the same sense. (2) Association and organization – humanity as part of a living ecological organism. (3) Struggle and natural selection. (4) The randomness, or chance character of variations in nature. The concept of change over time is, for instance, found in Davis's cyclic system for the development of a landscape through the stages of youth, maturity and old age, which Davis himself described as evolution. The French school of regional geography also took up the study of evolution within the cultural landscape.

The ideas of association and organization – which Darwin had inherited from earlier philosophers and scientists – have been rather tenacious in geographical research. The influential German geographer, Friedrich Ratzel (1844–1904) discusses in his *Political Geography* (1897), 'the state as an organism attached to the land'. Although this *organism* analogy was derived from the natural sciences, its roots may also be traced in the earlier idealist philosophy and the idea of *Ganzheit* or 'whole' as used by Ritter (p. 19). The *region,* that particular field of study for geographers, has been regarded as a unique functional complex, which, despite a steady stream of material and energy, is in apparent equilibrium and constitutes a 'whole' which is more than the sum of its parts. This understanding of the region is found in the French school of regional geography and it is also apparent in more recent university textbooks (Broek and Webb, 1973, pp. 14–15). The idea of the region as an organic unity pervaded British geography in the first half of this century. Andrew John Herbertson (1865–1915) used the term 'macro-organism' for the 'complex entity' of physical and organic elements of the earth's surface (Stoddart, 1966, p. 691).

The concept of struggle and selection, which had parallels in the contemporary political ideas of both economic liberals and Marxists, is reflected in subsequent geographical research, although no agreement was reached as to whether variation and development occurred by chance or were determined. This reflects a certain ambiguity in Darwin's thought. In later revisions of his work Darwin abandoned the issue of random variation and chance, partly because he failed to discover the laws he had earlier believed to govern chance variations, and partly as a response to churchmen who sought to reconcile evolutionary process with fundamental direction.

It was significant that the new scientific method that came to dominate research was in marked contrast to the teleological thinking of the 'classical' period that had supported and sustained the pursuit of a cosmographic science. It was no longer the objective of science to be witness to the existence of God or to find in His grand plan the *final causes* or purposes of what was observed. Scientists sought to determine the laws of nature as *prime causes* which might explain observed reality. This change in viewpoint gradually led to the replacement of *inductive* reasoning by *hypothetic-deductive* reasoning. Hypothetic-deductive reasoning sets up *hypotheses* to see how far they can explain observed reality. If and when the testing of these hypotheses yields positive results, scientists are on the way to formulating *scientific laws* (see p. 52). Scientists were now generally agreed that religion could not provide explanations for natural phenomena: some theologians were even prepared to accept that the Bible was not an authoritative source on scientific matters. Discussion as to whether or not there was a thought or a God behind the laws of nature, or whether natural laws were the means of development towards a designed end, came to be regarded as unscientific. Questions of belief and questions of knowledge now occupied two different realms, with science concerning itself with causes rather than purposes.

The increasing belief in the inherent value of science led to a considerable growth in research into the natural sciences.

Geomorphology and physiography provide academic respect

It was primarily a group of natural scientists with interests in physical geography who won academic respect for the subject during the latter half of the nineteenth century. A start had been made in Britain by the first prominent woman geographer, Mary Somerville (1780–1872), whose *Physical Geography* had been published in 1848. This was a book, that gave, without illustrations, detailed descriptions of the topography of each continent, and of the distribution of plants, animals and human beings. The book was not a simple physical geography since it included the works of human beings but more of an exercise in the *cosmographic* tradition.

As a result of the work of Darwin, *geology* and *biology* became the most ambitious branches of the natural sciences. *Geology* was important because it could, with the aid of a *palaeontology,* which interprets fossils, clarify the evolution of plant and animal species. These sciences had been elements within cosmographic geography and their independent development, leading to the establishment of university chairs, was a threat to the universalistic claims of geography. Some opportunities were also created for geography and these were first appreciated by the German, Oscar Peschel (1826-1875). In a scientifically weak book, called *New Problems of Comparative Geography as a Search for a Morphology of the Earth's Surface* (1870), Peschel chose the right moment to propose that geographers should study the *morphology* of the earth's surface. Like Ritter, he was interested in the significance of land forms for the development of human beings, but he did not share Ritter's religious outlook, being more concerned with causes and effects as illustrated by the methods of the natural sciences.

Geologists had set themselves such huge tasks, including the development of geological time-scales, the systematic mapping of rock types and the analysis of fossils, that they found it difficult to cope with the morphology of the earth's surface in addition. Here was a field where geography could carve out a place for itself as a scientific discipline. The study of land forms became the leading field of research for most of the professors appointed to geography chairs in the latter half of the nineteenth century. The biological elements in nature subsequently came to play a relatively small role in the teaching of geography in Britain and North America, so that *physical geography* is a more appropriate description of what was taught than the term *natural geography*.

One important reason for the 'geologification' of geography during the 1870s and 1880s was that the new professors needed academic qualifications, preferably doctorates. Friederich Ratzel (1844-1904) said: 'they told me when I returned from my expeditions that they needed geographers'. So he organized all the material he had collected on the Chinese migration to the USA as quickly as possible and wrote it up as a doctoral thesis which gained him in the chair of geography at Munich in 1875 (Jean Brunhes [1912], after a discussion with Ratzel in 1904).

At the same time there were many academics with scientific training in geology. Ferdinand von Richtoven (1833-1905) was a well-known geologist and explorer when he was offered the chair of geography in Bonn. Although he did not want to exclude humanity from his teaching of geography, he made the study of land forms the main research field for himself and his students. Even more influential in this development was Albrecht Penck (1858-1945), a dominating figure in German geography. Internationally, his influence could only be compared to that of the American, William Morris Davies (1850–1934) with whom he was in close contact, despite their very different interpretations of the cycle of erosion (Martin, 1985, p. 224). Penck, like von Richtoven, was a geologist by training, but he was primarily interested in the quaternary period and worked on the identification of *glacial periods* and on *glacial morphology* in general. Early in life, Penck developed his glacial theory, which he used to explain many of the land forms of northern Europe. His main work (1901–9) was on the glacial periods in the Alps and their effects on quaternary sedimentation. His identification of the four glacial periods (Günz, Mindel, Riss and Wurm), was a major step in the development of glacial geomorphology. Having been advised by a geologist friend to take his doctorate in geography, Penck was, at 27, appointed to a chair of physical geography in Vienna. He founded an influential school of geography there but in 1906 moved to Berlin, where he occupied a dominant position until his death.

In the Scandinavian countries the work of Penck had a major impact and, for a long time, academic geographers were primarily concerned with the study of the effects of glacial periods on the landscape. The leading professors, generally the first to be appointed, were geomorphologists. Another important contributor to geomorphological research was the Serbian geographer Jovan Cvijic (1865–1927). His work on the *karst phenomena* in the limestone regions of his homeland introduced Serbo-Croat words like *dolina* and *polje* into the scientific vocabulary (Freeman, 1980, p. 19).

In Britain, no work was more influential in changing the teaching of geography at all levels than T. H. Huxley's *Physiography,* first published in 1877. At this time the term *geomorphology* had not yet been invented and only *morphology* was in general use. *Physiography* has a much wider meaning; it may be defined as a 'description of nature', ecompassing the systematic sciences of botany, geology and zoology. One reason for the success of Huxley's book was its demonstration of better and more interesting ways of learning, linked directly with the pupil's own experience. The book begins with the Thames at London Bridge and, working from the local and familiar to the unfamiliar, it ends with the earth as a planet. The characteristic of the book is its emphasis on experimentation and local studies. The idea that geography can only be learned through local studies, field courses and excursions is to a large degree derived from the educational principles of Huxley.

Physical geography (renamed physiography after 1877) became a very popular school subject during the last third of the nineteenth century accounting for some 10 per cent of the examination papers sat in English and Welsh schools during that time (Stoddart, 1975, p. 26). Physiography was now regarded as an integral, if not the most important part of geography.

As more specialized earth sciences became established, physiography as a comprehensive subject eventually vanished from the syllabuses. Within geography, its place was filled by the new science of *geomorphology,* which was introduced to Britain in 1895. The American, William Morris Davis 1850–1934) became a leading personality in the development of geomorphology, although he preferred the term physiography himself. His organizing principle was not simple causality, but rather the idea of regular change of form through time, as systemized in his scheme of the *cycle of erosion.*

The success of physical geography, variously termed 'physiography', 'morphology' or 'geomorphology', led the German Georg Gerland to suggest in 1887 that the study of cultural phenomena should be separated from geography. He supported this view on the logical grounds that geography is the science of the earth and that a science should be developed on the basis of natural scientific methods. Scientific methods, as defined, could not be used to study cultural phenomena.

Developments in physical geography provided the main innovations in geography during the latter part of the nineteenth century. Gerland's statements indicated how far the pendulum had swung in this direction and his arguments may have led many to conclude that geography had moved out of balance.

Environmental determinism and possibilism

Geographical research after Darwin was primarily concerned with recognizing the laws of nature. Nature was studied with open eyes, seeking as objectively as possible to identify the forces of processes that governed the formation of valleys, uplands and coastlines. A more restricted view was taken of human activity, the relationships between nature and humanity were considered to be of primary interest. Humanity's achievements were to be explained as consequences of natural conditions. In this respect there are links with Herbert Spencer (1820–1903) and his *social Darwinism* (see p. 26).

Friedrich Ratzel, widely recognized as the founder of human geography, was strongly influenced by such ideas. The first volume of his chief work, published in 1882, was entitled *Anthropogeography, or Outline of the Influences of the Geographical Environment upon History.* In this volume, which sought to develop the new methods of natural science within human geography, Ratzel stressed the extent to which humanity lives under nature's laws. He regarded cultural forms as having been adapted and determined by natural conditions. Although he may be criticized today for his determinism, we should recognize that Ratzel broke new ground in demonstrating that cultural as well as natural phenomena can be subjected to systematic study. Before his time human geography had largely confined itself to regional studies.

Environmentalism is evident in other work of Ratzel, particularly in his *Political Geography* (1897). In this book, the establishment of states is seen as an evolutionary necessity; Ratzel explains the growth of political unities in terms of organic growth (Uhlig, 1967). These ideas quite clearly influenced his Swedish pupil Rudolf Kjellén, who became a propounder of geopolitics. Kjellén simplified and popularized Ratzel's ideas, maintaining that states follow the principle of the 'survival of the fittest' and have an independent existence over and above that of their citizens. These ideas were readily accepted and followed up by Karl Haushofer (1869-1946), who, as a geographer, tried to build up geographical arguments for a German right of domination over neighbouring peoples. Geopolitics became an important part of Nazi ideology. While it is unfair to hold Ratzel responsible for this much later development, we must be aware of the connections between environmental determinism, nationalism and racism (Peet, 1985).

Ratzel somewhat modified his environmental determinism in his later work. The second volume of Anthropogeographie (1891) discussed the concentration and distribution of population settlement forms, migrations and the diffusion of cultural characteristics. He did not merely explain phenomena in human geography in terms of natural conditions, but stressed the significance of the historical development and cultural background of populations. At one point he even declared (as quoted by Broek, 1965, p. 18): 'I could perhaps understand New England without knowing the land, but never without knowing the Puritan immigrants.'

In scientific circles, however, the first volume of Anthropogeographie had a much greater impact than the second volume. Ratzel's American disciple Ellen Churchill Semple (1863-1932) in particular laid great significance on the deterministic opinions of Ratzel in her teaching at American universities. One of her own major works was entitled Influences of Geographical Environment (1911). Ellen Semple and others of the same way of thinking, including the geomorphologist William Morris Davis, came to dominate geography in America until the 1930s and had an influence over American school geography for much longer. Peet (1985, p. 317) argues that the popularity of Semple and her followers depended not so much on the brilliance of their ideas as on the extent to which environmentalism served significant socio-political objective including the perceived right of American settlers to dominate American Indian and Spanish-American societies and other US imperialist goals in the Western Hemisphere.

Two influential geographers who carried on the study of the effects of the environment until the middle of the twentieth century were Ellsworth Hungtingdon, who related the rise of civilization in the mid-latitudes and the lack of development in the tropics to climatic conditions, and Griffith Taylor 'whose determinist views so angered politicians interested in the settlement of outback Australia that he was virtually hounded out of his homeland' (Johnston, 1987, p. 37). Taylor moved to the USA in 1928 and later to Canada; he insisted that he was not an old-fashioned determinist, but based his views on scientific knowledge of the environment. In 1951 Taylor could state with satisfaction, 'Thirty years ago I predicted the future settlement-pattern in Australia. At Canberra (in 1948) it was very gratifying to be assured by the various members of the scientific research groups there, that my deductions (based purely on the environment) were completely justified' (1951, p. 7). At the age of 70 Taylor returned to Sydney, was welcomed as a national hero and was even commemorated with his picture on a stamp. This example shows that a scientifically based *environmental determinism* might have some merit.

Up to the middle of the twentieth century, school textbooks in most countries included strong elements of crude environmental determinism in their selection of topics. A type of commercial geography was popular which laid considerable emphasis on raw material supplies and little on the distribution of entrepreneurial skills and institutions. The influence of physical geography on transport routes was greatly overstressed and oversimplified.

Geographical research in Germany soon reacted against crude environmental determinism. We have seen that Ratzel modified his earlier approach. Alfred Hettner (1859–41) was the most significant contributor to further development. Hettner was the first German to enter university with the declared aim of becoming a geographer. What intrigued him about geography was the idea of humanity's dependence upon nature (Beck, 1982, p. 215). But gradually he modified his environmentalism and in 1907 declared that as far as we restrict discussion to the influence of nature upon human beings, we are only dealing with possibilities, not certainties. In his monumental presentation of the history, content and methodology of geography *'Die Geographie, ihre Geschichte, ihr Wesen und ihre Methoden'* (1927) Hettner asserted that the geographical systhesis is distorted when nature is regarded as dominant and humanity as subsidiary. Through this book and his editorship of *Geographische Zeitschrift,* Hettner became the most influential philosopher of geography. He maintained that the primary cultural task of geography is to build a bridge over the gap that had opened during the latter part of the nineteenth century between the natural sciences and the humanities. He stressed that geography must maintain Kant's concept of a chorological science – that is, a subject that studies things that are mutually co-ordinated, but not subordinated, in places. Regional geography *(Länderkunde)* was therefore the crucial part of geography. As Hettner moved away from environmentalism, he became more and more strongly opposed to the development of geopolitics and particularly to the notion that there is some correlation between race and culture (Schultz, 1980)

The view that 'there are no necessities, only possibilities' was strongly urged by the French historian Lucien Febvre (1922), who termed this approach *possibilism* and contrasted it strongly with environmental determinism. Febvre invented the term, but the development of the possibilist way of thinking had started earlier and is especially associated with the geographers Paul Vidal de la Blache (1845–1918) and Jean Brunhes (1869–1930) in France. Later, Isaiah

Bowman (1878–1950) and Carl Sauer (1889–1975) became active advocates o
possibilism in the USA. The possibilists did not deny that there were natura
limits to the activities of humanity but emphasized the significance o
humanity's choices of activity rather than the natural limitations to it.

The French school of regional geography

Paul Vidal de la Blache (1845–1918) is regarded as the founder of moder
French geography. Vidal started his academic career as a student of classic
and history. It is not clear why he transferred his interests to geography, bu
the fact remains that, when he was appointed to a chair in history an
geography at Nancy in 1873 (when only 28) he sought permission to teac
geography alone. Andrews (1986) links this to the transformation of th
curriculum in the secondary school system, which was initiated at the sam
time. Better geography teachers were needed and it seems that Vidal graspe
this opportunity at the right moment. He became *professeur* and holder of th
chair in geography (alone) at Nancy in 1875, when he had attained th
minimum age of 30, which was required for the title. The chair at Nancy set a
example for the Ministry of Education, who became convinced of th
desirability of naming chairs in geography alone rather than following th
long-standing tradition of combined chairs in history and geography. Som
years later, Vidal moved to Paris and became the father figure of Frenc
geography.

Vidal had the clearest insight into the weakness of deterministic arguments
realizing the futility of setting humanity's natural surroundings in oppositio
to its social milieu and of regarding one as dominating the other. H
considered it even less useful to tackle these relationships along systemati
lines in the hope of discovering general laws governing the relationship
between human beings and nature.

According to Vidal, it is unreasonable to draw boundaries between natura
and cultural phenomena; they should be regarded as united and inseparable
In an area of human settlement, nature changes significantly because of th
presence of human beings, and these changes are greatest where the level o
material culture of the community is highest. The animal and plant life o
France during the nineteenth century, for example, was quite different fror
what it would have been had the country not been inhabited by human being
for centuries. It becomes impossible to study the natural landscape a
something separate from the cultural landscape. Each community adjusts t
prevailing natural conditions in its own way, and the result of the adjustmen
may reflect centuries of development. Each single small community therefor
has characterisitics which will not be found in other places, even in place
where the natural conditions are practically the same. In the course of tim
humanity and nature adapt to each other like a snail and its shell. In fact, th
relationship between humanity and nature becomes so intimate that it is nc

possible to distinguish the influence of humanity on nature from that of nature on humanity. The two influences fuse.

The area over which such an intimate relationship between human beings and nature has developed through the centuries constitutes a *region*. The study of such regions, each one of which is unique, should be the task of the geographer. Vidal therefore argued for regional geography and against systematic geography as the core of the discipline.

Vidal's method, which was inductive and historical, was best suited to regions that were 'local' in the sense of being somewhat isolated from the world around them and dominated by an agricultural way of life. These circumstances favoured the development of local traditions in architecture, agricultural practices and the general way of life; the communities lived in such a close association with nature that they might be self-sufficient in the majority of goods. Vidal advised geographers to carry out research in folk museums and collections and to investigate agricultural equipment used in the past in order to study the individuality of development of the region.

Vidal used the following illustration in order to underline the long associations between the major factors governing the development of a community (1903, p. 386): while the surface of a shallow lake is being swept by a gust of wind, the water is disturbed and confused but after a few minutes the contours of the bottom of the lake can clearly be seen again. In the same way, war, pestilence and civil strife can interrupt the development of a region and bring chaos for a while, but when the crisis is over the fundamental developments reassert themselves. Changes can come in such a community, and Vidal pointed out many developments which had taken place in the French regions during the centuries preceding the French Revolution. These developments had taken place within a stable framework of interaction between human beings and nature.

Vidal's characterization fitted fairly well those virtually unchanged communities in Europe with which he was most familiar. These had been agricultural societies throughout the Middle Ages and well into recent times, having essentially local interests and interaction patterns resulting from a long interplay between humanity and nature. In certain circumstances, and for certain members of the small upper classes, their contact field was national rather than local, but in general Vidal's concepts were appropriate. Ironically, however, he was describing a rapidly disappearing phenomenon. His method is still well suited to the study of the historical geography of Europe up to the Industrial Revolution and also for the study of those parts of the world where society depends on subsistence economies. As Wrigley (1965, p. 9) pointed out, however, Vidal's method is not so well suited to the study of regions that experienced the Industrial Revolution of the nineteenth century.

Towards the end of his career, Vidal was well aware of this situation. This is most evident in *La France de l'Est* (1917), in many ways his most original work, which studied the development of the landscapes and agricultural societies in Alsace and Lorraine over a period of two thousand years. A considerable portion of the book, which is arranged chronologically, is devoted to changes that preceded the French Revolution of 1789. The revolution produced a great ripple in the picture, but afterwards the main lines of development reasserted themselves. After a particular point in the nineteenth century, however (Vidal identified the year 1846 himself), the finely balanced interplay between humanity and nature was profoundly disturbed. The surface of the lake was, as it were, whipped up by something more significant and persistent than the earlier gusts. Eventually the visible contours of the bottom of the lake were reshaped. The building of canals and railways, together with the reformation of the Alsatian woollen industry, initiated the decline of the traditional local, self-sufficient economy. Industry was developed on the basis of new cheap and rapid means of transport and could mass-produce goods for a wider market. These developments reduced the value of the regional method in a growing number of areas.

Vidal regretted these developments, which he could not avoid observing. He considered that much of the best in French life was vanishing with the self-sufficient economy but his stature as a scholar enabled him to suggest possible new approaches for further research. In the future, he suggested (1917, p. 163), we should study the economic interplay between a region and the city centre that dominates it, rather than the interplay of natural and cultural elements. Despite the breakdown of the self-sufficient regional economy, Vidal's work has been and still is a great inspiration to a vital tradition in geography, that of the *regional monograph*.

The French regional monographs began to function as models for geographers around the world. At the Institute of Geography at Belgrade University, for instance, under the inspiring leadership of Jovan Cvijic, twenty-five monographs on the regions of Serbia were produced in the years before the First World War. These investigations made Serbia one of the best-studied countries of the world, and were also instrumental in the creation of modern Yugoslavia at the Paris Peace Conference in 1919. In Britain, regional monographs were widely admired. They were studied and produced in the Oxford School of Geography and later introduced into the newer universities by Roxby and others (Buttimer, 1983, p. 91).

Landscapes and regions

Vidal de la Blache is only one, if the most significant, of the founders of regional geography. There are other directions and methods in regional geography, although their discussion and classification has been rather neglected by English-speaking geographers. In Germany and France, where regional geography has been regarded as the core of the subject until quite recently, contributions have been much more extenstive in this field. German learning has a long tradition of classification and systematization, and we can turn to Fochler-Hauke's *Geographie* (1959, pp. 251–61) for a review of the different approaches to regional geography.

In doing so we must first clarify the concepts 'region' and 'landscape' and their German counterparts. The two German words *Land* and *Landschaft* may both be translated as 'region', but *Land* is a definite unit – a county or a country normally defined by its administrative borders. *Länderkunde* is the art of describing such definite units, as in regional monographs like Demangeon's *Picardie* (1905) – regional geography in its traditional sense. The word *Landschaft,* literally analogous to the English word 'landscape' also means a 'scientifically defined geographical region' in German . A *Landschaft* may be either a specific unit area or type of area. *Landschaftskunde,* which concerns both the study of such small unique areas and the delimitation and classification of different types of regions, straddles regional and systematic geography. Hannerberg (1968, pp. 132–3) considers that *Landschaftskunde* may be taken over by the systematic branches of geography, while *Länderkunde* remains as regional geography in its own right. With this background in mind we now turn to the five approaches to *Landschaftskunde* as distinguished by Fochler-Hauke: landscape morphology, landscape ecology, landscape, chronology, regionalization and landscape classification (or systematization). We shall have a closer look at the first three of these.

Landscape chronology might seem to include French regional geography, with its use of development over time as a device to present regional synthesis. But this approach must be regarded as a method of regional geography or *Länderkunde,* and not as an approach to *Landschaftskunde.*

Landscape chronology more particularly concerns the specific scientific work of reconstructing former landscape types, for instance on the basis of relict elements in the contemporary landscape. The use of aerial photographs to detect the ridge and furrow patterns of ancient fields, as first analysed by Mead (1954), and the study of the lost villages of medieval England (Beresford, 1951), are examples of research that might be used to reconstruct a chronology of shifting landscape types through history. As a research theme this might seem rather thematic and restricted, but it is possible to make the study of shifting landscape types the leading thread in a fully-fledged regional presentation.

In this category we may include the type of geographical study described by Derwent Whittlesey (1929) as *sequent occupance*. Sequent occupance studies the ways in which each culture uses a region in its own way. This is demonstrated in America where most regions experienced a sudden change from the Indian to the European culture, and in many parts of Europe which progressed from agrarian to industrial cultures. Sequent occupance stresses the stages in the development of a region, not, as in the France of Vidal de la Blache, through studies of local differentiation as a result of the long continued and largely undisturbed interplay of man and nature over the centuries, but by emphasizing how easily shifts in regional character can take place.

The concept of *landscape ecology* is less understood in the Anglo-American world, but has been particularly well developed in Germany. Carl Troll (1899–1975), who introduced the concept, defined landscape ecology as the complex of causal and reciprocal connections between biological communities (*Biozönosen*) and their environment in a particular landscape section (according to Leser, 1980, p. 53). Troll did not regard this as a systematic branch of geography, but as an approach to an integrating study of landscapes, for which he introduced and developed the art of aerial photography interpretation. His work placed biological and climatological conditions in a central position within German landscape research; the role of geomorphology being relatively reduced. Troll regarded landscape ecology as a unifying approach to the natural science part of geography, with social geography playing a similar role on the human geography side. Uhlig (1973) (see Figure 1.3, p. 9) also used social geography as a term for the integrated approach to the human side, but employs a new concept, *geo-ecology* to represent the landscape ecology of Troll. Uhlig and other German geographers would reserve the term 'landscape ecology' for the study of humanity and nature on a higher integrative level, but even on this scale it takes its inspiration mainly from the natural sciences and particularly from ecology.

While in German the term 'landscape ecology' is fairly clearly defined, in the Anglo-American world it is often confused with terms like *human ecology* and *ecological analysis*. Ecological analysis has been proposed by Haggett in his textbook *Geography; A Modern Synthesis* (1972) as one of the three approaches to modern integrated geography (Figure 5.11, p. 156).

The Anglo-American terms 'human ecology' and 'ecological analysis' have a stronger emphasis on human geography than the German term 'landscape ecology'. There are historical connections in the Anglo-American usage with the school of *urban ecology* that was founded by the Chicago sociologists in the 1920s and concerned itself with the social and functional development and division of urban areas. In such a broad context, 'human ecology' and 'ecological analysis' could also be thought of as encompassing the functional approach in regional geography, which has developed in order to study the relationships between centres and their surrounding areas.

Landscape morphology is a form of regional geography that was particularly well developed in Germany between the wars. Otto Schlüter, who played a central role in its development, asserted as early as 1906 that geographers should consider the form and spatial structure created by visible phenomena on the surface of the earth as their unifying theme. Mountains, rivers, pastures, forests, roads, canals, gardens, fields, villages and towns within a restricted viewpoint form a unity in the eyes of the geographer: this visible picture is the object of his study. Those who try to include too much in the field of their vision cannot cope with it all, maintains Schlüter (1920), who therefore argues against the all-encompassing *chorological geography* advocated by Hettner.

Schlüter does not regard non-material geographical patterns, such as economic, racial, psychological and political conditions, as being of primary geographical interest. They should be studied as part of the explanation of material distributions. The French scholar Jean Brunhes illustrated this view when he said that we should study the earth as if we were sitting in a balloon and looking down upon it. We should analyse the landscape and the characteristic interplay of observable phenomena there. The visible landscape is a result both of natural conditions and forces and a manifestation of the work of humanity. The landscape itself creates a synthesis, there is no longer a gap between physical geography and the geography of humanity, both have the same object – the visible landscape – and there is also close contact in terms of methods. Because of this, says Leo Waibel (1933), the landscape morphological approach represents an advance for geography, although the field of inquiry is thereby greatly narrowed.

Landscape morphologists argued as to how much their field of inquiry should be limited. Should they consider, for example, humanity's movements and the transport of goods and services? Many landscape morphologists considered that these activities should not be objects of study, they might only be considered as explanatory factors in so far as they contribute to an understanding of the evolution and character of the landscape. According to Schlüter, however, the cultural landscape includes not only the routes and route patterns, but also the men and the goods that move along them.

Alfred Hettner was opposed to Schlüter's limitation of geographical study to the visible landscape. He was (as described by Dickinson, 1969, p. 132) 'concerned with the uniqueness of areas, whether this uniqueness was evident in the visible landscape or not. He recognized the focal interest of landscape, but refused to recognize the limits set by it on the study of the human facts in space.'

Hettner maintained the universalistic character of geography on the basis of his evaluations of the philosophy of science. He considered landscapes to be very small länder and, for this reason, regarded attempts to study visible landscapes as a restriction of the scope of regional geography. He argued (1929) that it is 'against the logic of science to permit the picture, i.e. the appearances, to be the decisive factor in defining the subject ... They exclude thereby exactly those features which have been the pre-eminent concern of geography in the past (human life, nationality, state, partially even the economy) and ... still are.' Hettner presented his länderkundliches schema as a guideline for a chorological regional presentation, starting with physical features and concluding with population. The presentation of thematic maps, juxtaposed 'on top of each other', makes some sort of integration possible, but it is quite clear that Hettner did not convincingly solve the problem of regional synthesis. His dominance of the geographical scene was perhaps greater abroad, through his follower Richard Hartshorne, than at home in

Germany.

In Germany, the different types of landscape geography did not supercede regional geography as Hettner had feared but came to be developed as a bridge between systematic and regional geography. Bobek and Schmithüsen (1949) suggested that landscape could be seen as the integrative product of the *geofactors* of the systematic branches (Figure 1.3, p. 9) through which only such features which appear in an orderly and regular fashion are taken into account. Practical methods were presented by Hermann Lautensach (1886–1971) in his *Formanwandelanalyse,* which he used in his regional work on the Iberian Peninsula and Korea. The *Formanwandel* or 'variation of geographical form' is seen as a function of four basic *location types:*

(1)   Location in relation to latitude (north–south).
(2)   Central-peripheral location within continents and seas.
(3)   Longitudinal (east–west) location within continents or seas.
(4)   Hypsometric location (in relation to relief).

A synthesis of geographical forms within a country, for instance, makes it possible to define regional types and, from then on, proceed to a study of man's adaptation to, and influence on nature within the different location types. Lautensach's method may be described as *landscape ecology* rather than *landscape morphology,* since it leans heavily on climatology and biogeography. In general, however, the Germans accept many transitions between landscape morphology and landscape ecology, so that most recent research in this field cannot easily be placed in either category. Methods have been developed by Schmithüsen, among others, to build up broader regional types through the delimitation of small units called *Fliese,* or 'mosaic tiles' of landscape (Uhlig, 1967 – see Figure 2.1).

Landscape morphology received its widest following on the European continent. In the USA Carl Sauer gave a basic evaluation of the new direction in his *Morphology of Landscape* (1925) but, apart from this, landscape morphology attracted little interest in the New World. In 1939 Robert E. Dickinson described landscape geography as the most important new line of growth within the subject and blamed its lack of development in Britain on lack of interest in it by British scholars. In fact, landscape morphology was only developed by a limited number of British geographers although it provided an objective for several courses in cartography and in the interpretation of aerial photographs.

Regional studies in Britain

'There is fully as much confusion over the meaning of the words "regional studies" as there is over the German Word *Landschaft,'* states James (1972, p. 267), with special reference to British geography. *Regional* studies have at least three different connotations in Britain. Firstly, there are regional studies

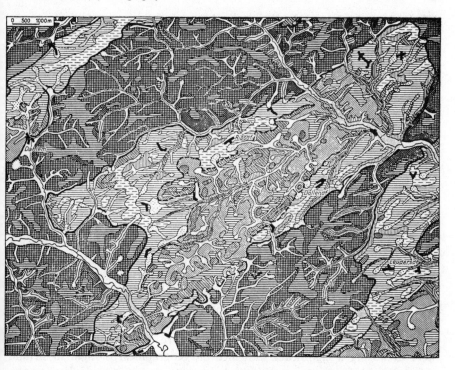

Figure 2.1 An example of cartographic techniques in landscape morphology. Characteristically used by German geographers to build up broader landscape types from a mosaic of local types (after Paffen, 1955)

that amount to descriptions of segments of the earth's surface, broadly synonymous with regional geography or *Länderkunde* as we have defined it above. Secondly, there are regional studies which seek to divide the surface of the earth into either homogeneous or functional areas to varying size, which we have termed *regionalization*. Thirdly, regional studies may denote regional specialization, when an individual geographer devotes a large part of his/her life to study different aspects of some part of the world (a good example is Percy M. Roxby of Liverpool, who built up a formidable expertise on China).

Regional studies in Britain were influenced by Vidal de la Blache and other French regional geographers, but to an even greater extent by the French sociologist Frédéric Le Play (1806–82) through his influential Scottish follower Sir Patrick Geddes (1854–1932). As a starting point for the study of social phenomena in different parts of the world, Le Play carried out research on family lifestyles and family budgets. He recognized that family life depended on the means of obtaining subsistence, that is, work, while the character of the latter is largely determined by the nature of the environment, that is place.

This leads to the famous Le Play formula which is basic to his ideas - place, work, family - which Geddes transformed into the slogan *place, work, folk* as basic concepts in the study of cities and regions.

Although not a geographer himself, Geddes had a major influence on British geography, especially in the fields of regional survey, regionalization and applied geography. Field study - observation and recording in the field - was basic to Geddes's teaching. This led on to what he called 'regional survey', embracing place, work and folk (alternatively described as geography, economics and anthropology, or as environment, function and organism -Dickinson, 1969, p. 204). Geddes and his followers established the Le Play Society, which grew out of the Sociological Society in order to foster regional surveys. Geddes saw an important application of regional survey in *regional planning,* comparing the regional surveyor to an old family doctor who could interpret specialist knowledge and apply it to the actual condition of the individual patient, which he would know intimately. As a man of radical views, Geddes was rather impatient with geographers who defined their subject as a *descriptive science,* which tells us what is. Geography should rather be an *applied science* that tells us what ought to be (Stevenson, 1978, p. 57). In this way, visionary planners - and we must mention Ebenezer Howard with his models of suburban land use and funtional structure that were developed in order to plan garden cities (Howard, 1902) in this connection - were exercising a significant influence on geographical thought in Britain before World War I, laying the foundations for studies in applied geography that have continued ever since.

Geddes also influenced the study of regionalization. Andrew J. Herbertson (1865-1915), who was an assistant to Geddes in Dundee, and later taught geography at Oxford, presented a scheme for a division of the world into natural regions, based on an association of surface features, climate and vegetation. A more direct application of Geddes's ideas occurs in the work of Charles B. Fawcett (1883-1952). In this book *The Provinces of England* (1919), which attracted considerable attention, he proposed a federal structure of twelve autonomous provinces for England.

> All six principles of the division were clearly inspired by Geddesian regionalism, particularly so in the organisation of each province round a "definite capital which should be the real focus of regional life," that provincial boundaries should "be drawn near watersheds, rather than across valleys," and that "the grouping of areas must pay regard to local patriotism and tradition".
>
> (Stevenson, 1978, p. 59)

Fawcett translated the somewhat obscure ideas of Geddes into a workable form, and made one of the first identifications of *functional regions*. It is also interesting to note that the use of the catchment area of a stream (which served as an emblem for the Le Play Society) as a basis for regional divisions is still regarded as rather versatile by modern geographers (see Haggett, 1972, pp. 61-2). The main translator of Geddesian thought into geography, Herbert

J. Fleure (1877–1969) found, however, that the grand systematization of society and environment into 'valley sections' was too rigid. Nevertheless, by expanding, qualifying and developing Geddes's ideas, Fleure rendered them accessible and acceptable to geography. Like Herbertson, he also worked on the definition of global scale regions.

One concept derived from the work of Geddes was that of the regional survey of potential land quality and land use as a basic input to plans for economic development. On his own initiative, L. Dudley Stamp (1898–1966) organized and directed the first British Land Utilization Survey during the 1930s, employing some 22,000 schoolchildren in the mapping of *land use* on a scale of 1/2,500 in their home district under the supervision of school and university teachers. When World War II began in 1939 the vital importance of the maps was quickly appreciated as essential data for the programme of expansion of food production necessitated by the German blockade. At the International Geographical Congress in Lisbon (1949), Stamp suggested the establishment of a World Land Use Survey. The idea was adopted and an international commission under the IGU (the International Geographical Union) was set up to supervise the work.

The first Land Use Survey eventually formed the basis for an official agricultural regionalization of Britain. The economic depression of the 1930s accentuated the effects of longer-term economic changes that were creating marked divergences of economic prosperity and distress between the sub-regions of Britain. Geographers contributed to national and local studies of these prosperous and 'depressed' areas – although description predominated over analysis at this stage – and, during the 1940s, were widely involved in the planning of post-war reconstruction.

In recent years, there has been an increasing interest in the cultural landscape in connection with regional planning, perhaps as a reaction against the uniformity of most modern buildings and other landscape features. The ease with which a landscape may be disfigured through modern technology has awakened a concern for the care of landscape. The uncontrolled building of houses and cabins has created so many eyesores that the need has been recognized for an active policy of landscape protection. This concept includes both aesthetic and economic aspects. This was pointed out by Steers in his book *The Coastline of England and Wales* (1946), which gave a clear indication of the major planning problems of coasts, including the notorious bungalow and camp-site development which had been permitted during the inter-war years (Freeman, 1980, p. 53).

J. H. Appleton (1975) and others have demonstrated the importance of an educated perception of landscape if many of the attractions of long-settled countries like lowland Britain are to be preserved. The rapid growth of industrial archaeology, especially as a hobby of educated laymen in Europe, also illustrates a persistent general belief in the importance of preserving something of the visual culture of the past. Robert Newcomb (1979) calls for a 'planning of the past', and gives suggestions for active use of historic features, in order to make a preservation of at least relics of historic landscapes and townscapes possible.

The demand for area planning in districts, counties and regions has also increased interest in studies of the cultural landscape. In Norway, for instance, the book *Mountain Regions and Recreation (Fjellbygd og feriefjell)* (Sømme, 1965), the result of research into the effects of the recreational use of upland areas, is an example of a modern landscape study that attempts to provide a sound basis for new planning laws.

Several other regionalization projects sought to delimit single-attribute regions such as industrial, climatic, vegetational, morphological and social regions.

> Each had its links with the relevant systematic sciences – social geography with sociology, for example The key differentiating factor between the two was the geographers' focus on the region, the specialist's single attribute region and the synthesisers multi attribute region.
>
> (Johnston, 1987, p. 40)

Whereas much effort between the wars was put into the development of methods of defining multi-attribute regions, systematic studies in various specialisms gradually claimed the attention of the great majority of British geographers.

Even those who regard all forms of regional geography as blind alleys concede that they will continue to exist within geography. E. A. Wrigley (1965, p. 13) put it this way:

> The regional period of geographic methodology like the 'classical' (including determinism) has left many traces, some of which will perhaps prove permanent, on the methods used in organising and presenting geographical material. Any discipline is both the product and the victim of its own past successes and these were two of the most important successes thrown up by geographical scholarship.

The widespread hold of regional geography in the past has discouraged many geographers from seeking general relationships and theories, and has led them to decry the formulation of geographical laws and models. Rejecting the general theories of the determinists, they sought refuge in regional methodologies where each area is unique and somewhat exceptional and must be studied as such. Many still consider that geographers should continue with *idiographical* methods, that is, the description of unique phenomena and unique regions.

Amongst this regional school it has been suggested that geography is as much an art as science. Geographers, in common with other 'arts' scholars, should emphasize literary quality. Jan Broek (1965, p. 21) puts it this way: 'The humanities stress real persons and cases rather than models, quality rather than quantity, evaluation and evocation rather than calculation, beauty and wisdom rather than information. Geography shares these attitudes to some extent.'

The idiographic method and the humanistic way of thinking within the subject began to be strongly criticized in the 1950s. A new and dynamic school was developed and new methods brought into use. There was much talk of paradigm crises and revolution. We shall see what this implies in the next chapter, which attempts to bring together the threads from this chapter and to present 'the quantitative revolution' in its historical connection.

3 Paradigms and Revolutions

'Geography is concerned to provide accurate, orderly, and rational description and interpretation of the variable character of the earth's surface.' (Hartshorne, 1959, p. 21)

'A traditionally held view – that geography is concerned with giving man an orderly description of his world – makes clear the challenge faced by contemporary geographers... The contemporary stress is on geography as the study of spatial organisation expressed as patterns and processes.'   (Taafe, 1970, pp. 5–6)

'Geography can be regarded as a science concerned with the rational development, and testing, of theories that explain and predict the spatial distribution and location of various characteristics on the surface of the earth.'   (Yeates, 1968, p. 1)

While geographers would be in general agreement that major changes took place in every aspect of geographical thought during the 1950s and 1960s, there is no general consensus as to what degree the many innovations that took place during those decades will be of lasting value nor on their effect on the future of geography as an academic discipline. The quotations above illustrate the divergent views expressed during this period.

Hartshorne and Yeates seem to differ widely in their prescription of methods but find more common ground in their definitions of the objectives of geographical research. While both are concerned with the variation of phenomena over the surface of the earth, Hartshorne visualizes geography as an *idiographic science* with its main emphasis on the description and elucidation of individual phenomena because they are unique; Yeates considers geography to be a *nomothetic* (law-giving) science that requires the development and testing of theories and models through hypothetic–deductive methods in order to develop geographical laws (pp. 52–4).

Taafe implies that geography had changed by 1970, or was in the process of changing from an idiographic to a nomothetic science. Explanatory model-once thought to be satisfactory were discredited by a large number of geographers. John D. Adams (1968, p. 6) said that

> geography is currently in the throes of a paradigm crisis. Instead of asking the traditional question 'Is it geography?' or 'What is geography?' geographers are now asking 'What should geography be?' If a satisfactory answer is not found to the latter question the next question is likely to be 'Is geography relevant?'

It is clear from Chapter 2 that this was not the first crisis phase in the development of geography. Ritter's teleological framework did not satisfy the determinists: views that were scientifically acceptable to Ratzel and Semple were too deterministic for Vidal and Hartshorne.

Kuhn's paradigms

Perhaps Thomas S. Kuhn (1962, 1970a) is right to claim that science is not a well-regulated activity where each generation automatically builds upon the results achieved by earlier workers, but a process of varying tension in which tranquil periods, characterized by a steady accretion of knowledge, are separated by crises which can lead to upheavel within disciplines and breaks in continuity. Even Hettner (1930, p. 356) pointed out 'that a science does not always follow a straight line of development, but often zig-zags on its road to higher professionalization. This development often corresponds to changes in generations among its professional practitioners. It would be a bad thing if a new generation had no new thoughts.' Hettner however, upheld the importance of historical continuity to his colleagues. 'A science should not suddenly be changed into something quite different from what it has been before' (1929, p. 279).

Such veneration of the past is rejected by Kuhn, who argues that fundamental changes are often necessary in order to enable science to progress. Further, while it is possible to determine objectively whether an explanatory framework is satisfactory and reasonable *within* a specific scientific tradition, we must choose *between* different scientific traditions, and this choice is subjective. We must select what Kuhn calls *paradigms* (models or exemplars) for our science.

Kuhn defines paradigms (1962, 1970a, p. viii) as 'universally recognised scientific achievements that for some time provide model problems and solutions to a community of practitioners'. Haggett (1983, p. 21) defines a paradigm as 'a kind of supermodel. It provides intuitive or inductive rules about the kinds of phenomena scientists should investigate and the best methods of investigation.' A paradigm is a theory of scientific tasks and methods that regulates the research, for example, of most geographers, or, where there is a conflict between paradigms, by a group of geographers. The paradigm tells researchers what they should be looking for and which methods are, in this case 'geographical'.

Kuhn did not provide an altogether clear definition of the paradigm concept in the first place. Mastermann (1970) identifies no less than twenty-one discrete definitions of the concept. In addition, the paradigm concept has later been used by a large number of scholars who may not have paid very close attention to Kuhn's statements and have attached a multiplicity of meanings to them. As Mair (1986) has pointed out, Kuhn later clarified some ambiguities and accepted that he had conflated two conceptually distinct, though empirically inseparable, types of paradigm. In the second edition of his book Kuhn (1962, 1970a) argued that the most basic function of a paradigm is as an *exemplar*, a concrete problem solution within a discipline that serves as a model for successive scientists. Such exemplars generally tie a scientific theory together by an example of a successful and striking application. 'For example,' says Putnam (1981, p. 69), 'once the law of universal gravitation had been put forward and one had the example of Newton's derivation of Kepler's laws together with the example of, say, a planetary orbit or two, then one had a paradigm.' The most important paradigms are those that generate whole new fields of scientific endeavour. The whole subject of celestial mechanics has been generated from the Newtonian paradigm. Paradigms in the sense of 'exemplars' may not always have this all-embracing effect, but will guide research as they are presented to students as models they should try to copy. An example from geography would be the regional monographs written by Vidal de la Blache and some of his contemporaries, which established examples for a long-standing tradition.

Because Kuhn had used the history of theoretical physics and the more striking discoveries within that field as the basis of his presentation of the paradigm concept, the assumption was made that a paradigm shift would involve an all-embracing change within a discipline. In a later version of his book, (1970a), Kuhn admitted that many 'exemplars' would have minor effects and only impinge upon the work of smaller groups within a discipline.

The other meaning of paradigm accepted by Kuhn is a *disciplinary matrix* – 'the entire constellation of beliefs, values, techniques and so on shared by a member of a given community' (1970a, p. 175). A disciplinary matrix may be shared by all members of a discipline, while at the same time they are working with different 'exemplars' in their everyday research (Mair, 1986, p. 352). It is in its sense of disciplinary matrix that the term paradigm has most commonly been applied in the context of geography. Although this implies, as Mair points out, a simplification, we will use the term 'paradigm' here to infer a disciplinary matrix in attempting to interpret the history of geography in (simplified) Kuhnian terms.

The development of science consists, according to the simplified Kuhnian model, of a series of phases (Figure 3.1). A branch of science, beginning as a comparatively restricted philosophical problem region, becomes the subject for more thorough and systematic study. This first phase, the *pre-paradigm period*, is marked by conflicts between several distinct schools which grow

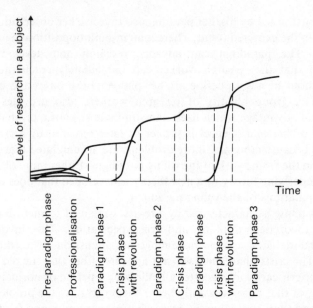

Figure 3.1 A graphical interpretation of Kuhn's theory of the development of science (after Henriksen, 1973)

round individual scientists. If we take paradigm to mean *exemplar,* this phase should perhaps rather be called the *multi-paradigmatic period,* as each school of thought develops its own model solutions. During this period there is full communication between all schools of thought and also with other scientists and laymen.

The development from the multi-paradigmatic period to the stage of scientific maturity or *professionalization* has taken place at quite different historic dates amongst different sciences. Kuhn argues that mathematics and astronomy left this phase in antiquity, whereas in parts of the social sciences the transition may still be occurring today. The transition begins when the question as to what a specific science is about becomes acute. This happened in geography when a university degree in the discipline was needed in order to qualify as a geography teacher in high school. A disciplinary matrix had to be defined for such a degree course which would also secure and demarcate the domain of geography against other university disciplines. One of the conflicting schools of thought will often begin to dominate the others in so far as it seems to be the best suited to win academic esteem for the discipline. A paradigm is established that leads to concentrated research within a clearly distinguishable problem area, an activity described as *normal science.*

To bring a normal research problem to a conclusion is to achieve anticipated results in a new way; Kuhn called this *puzzle-solving* because of its similarity to the solving of a jigsaw or crossword puzzles. The perception of the research worker is constrained by his/her paradigm so that his/her observation of dat is attracted to the expected result. There is an in-built opposition to unexpecte discoveries. The paradigm can advance research and develop researc economy in that the research worker can immediately reach the researc frontier without having to define his/her philosophical bases and underlyin concepts. The group identity of research workers also provides a stron psychological advantage which itself can stimulate scientific productivity.

A period of 'normal science' is sooner or later replaced by a *crisis phas* This occurs because more and more problems are accumulated that cannot b solved within the framework of the ruling paradigm. Either more observatior shake the underlying theory or a new theory is developed that does not accor with the stipulations of the ruling paradigm.

The crisis phase is characterized by a re-assessment of former observation data, new theoretical thinking and free speculation. This involves bas philosophical debates and a thoroughgoing discussion of methodologic questions. The crisis phase ends when it appears either that the old paradig can solve the critical problems after all, allowing a period of normal science t be resumed, or that no significantly better theory to solve the problems can t developed and that, consequently, research must continue for a further peric within the old paradigm. Otherwise the crisis phase ends when a new paradig attracts a growing number of researchers.

The acceptance of a new disciplinary matrix inaugurates a *revolutiona phase*. This involves a break in the continuity of research, with thoroughgoing reconstruction of the theoretical structure of a research fiel rather than a steady development and accumulation of knowledge. Th acceptance of a new paradigm is also revolutionary because it attracts th allegiance of the younger research workers in opposition to establishe scientists. The new scientific 'reason' seldom triumphs by convincing i opponents, but succeeds as they die and a new generation takes over. Young workers who do not conform to the newly accepted paradigm are ignored t its followers. Researchers are continually forced to ask themselves whether th type of puzzle-solving they are doing is the 'right' one.

The exchange of one paradigm for another is not a wholly ration transaction. The new paradigm will generally provide solutions for th problems that the old one found difficult to resolve, but may not answer all th questions that were fairly easy to solve before. It is seldom possible to argu from logic that the new paradigm is better than the old. Even if a ne paradigm can buttress itself with empirical and logical proofs, its origin choice was basically subjective – an act of faith. Aesthetic considerations m influence the choice of a new paradigm, which may be regarded as simpler more beautiful.

Kuhn's picture of scientific activity is not wholly attractive. Our faith in th objectivity of research is weakened when we consider how subjective th choice of paradigms can be and experience the often protracted opposition some scientific workers to the establishment of new explanatory models. Few research workers welcome a general debate on the subjectivity of research in case it may lead to the evaporation of respect and financial support. On the other hand, as suggested by Peter Taylor (1976, p. 132), the youngest research workers at the bottom of the very formal academic hierachy have a clear vested interest in changing the existing scientific ideology and thereby taking over from their elders.

The simplified Kuhnian model has given the new prophets a very effective weapon against the disciplinary matrix of a scientific 'Establishment'. They do not need to justify their research as objective in itself; it is enough if they declare it to be objective within the subjective framework they have chosen. This can give rise to particular conflicts amongst social scientists because it is easy to equate the choice of a paradigm with the adoption of a value judgement. The ultimate conclusion may be that only those who affirm the same general outlook on the world and have similar political beliefs are competent to evaluate a piece of scientific research.

Critics of Kuhn

Few geographers, says Bird (1977), have noticed that the concept of a paradigm ruling a community is very close to that of a dogma, which must be adhered to if a person is to be accounted orthodox. This is in line with the views of Karl Popper, the scientific methodologist who has most effectively criticized Kuhn. Popper (1970) maintains that an active and progressive science will be in a constant state of revolution. While acknowledging that Kuhn has demonstrated the existence of 'normal science' and 'paradigms', Popper deplores these periods as dangers to scientific progress. Normal science is established when uncritical scientists accept the leading dogmas of their day and espouse some newly fashionable but formally revolutionary theory. Popper fears that if these kinds of scientists were to predominate, it would be the end of science. Dubbing 'normal science' the 'myth of the framework', Popper asserted that one of the most important roles of the scientist is to break down myths. Given that we are always trapped within theoretical frameworks to some extent, we can break out of them at any moment if we act as true scientists. An active science will be in a state of *permanent revolution* (Bird, 1975).

Some scientists have identified Popper's concept of a 'permanent revolution' as a prescription for what science should be rather than as a description of how it is actually practised. Kuhn (1970b) declares that Popper's demand for a 'permanent revolution' is built on assumptions that are just as unreal as attempts to square the circle.

Paul Feyerabend rejects the Kuhnian model of alternating periods of 'normal science' and 'revolution' as historically false. He maintains that even in theoretical physics, which Kuhn (1962, 1970a) used as his example, there have always been alternative basic theories that could act as 'exemplars'. Sciences do not show a chronological shift between periods of normal science and periods of pluralism. The historical development of a science might best be described by synthesizing the models of Popper and Kuhn. The discussion between Kuhn, Popper and Feyerabend depends on their different ideas as to how a scientist works and how scientific theories and laws are established.

Is scientific verification possible?

Francis Bacon (1561-1626) defined the *inductive* route to scientific explanation (Figure 3.2). A scientist starts with a range of sense-perceptions that he works up conceptually and verbally into a number of loosely arranged concepts and descriptions that we like to call facts. Next, certain definitions are necessary in order to organize the data. Afterwards the facts are evaluated and arranged in relation to the definitions.

The ordering and classification of data is often the chief activity of science in the early stages of its development. These first classifications may have only a weak explanatory function. Continuing study of the interaction between classes and groups of phenomena reveals a number of regularities; such regularities and laws may be called *inductive laws* since they are derived from the observations of a large number of single instances.

Here we must clarify what a *scientific law* is. Braithwaite (1953, p. 12) defines a law as 'a generalisation of unrestricted range in time and space', in other words, a generalization with universal validity. With this definition we can distinguish between empirical generalizations and laws. An empirical generalization is valid for a specific time and place but a law is universal. James (1972, p. 473) maintains that a law within Braithwaite's' rigorous definition can hardly be formulated on the basis of geographical evidence. The only truly universal laws are those of physics and chemistry, although even in physics there are elements of uncertainty that make probability calculations necessary. Harvey (1969, p. 31) gives the concept of law a much wider significance and postulates a threefold hierarchy of scientific statements from *factual statements* or systematized descriptions, through a middle tier of *empirical generalizations* or laws, to universal *theoretical laws*. We will use the expression 'law' in the wider sense adopted by Harvey. A scientist hopes to be able to link together a number of inductive laws that will include the relationships and association between the established laws. From this material he hopes to formulate general and overriding laws. The weakness of the inductive method is that the processes of ordering and structuring data are not independent of the theory that is ultimately constructed. The *a priori* establishment of a system of classification is an essentially similar operation to the setting up of an *a priori* theory.

Carl Ritter used the inductive method as a framework for his presentation of

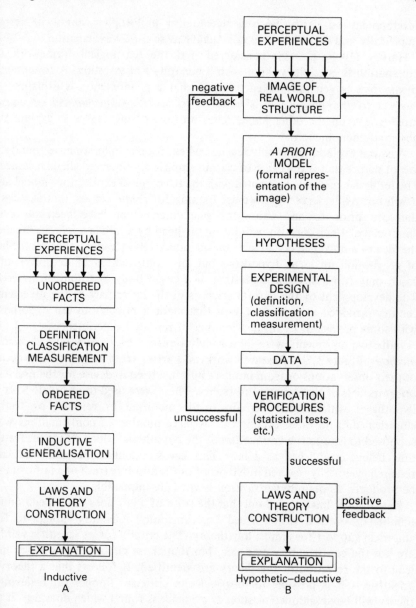

Figure 3.2 Inductive (Baconian) and hypothetic–deductive routes to scientific explanation (from Harvey, 1969)

data and as a means to arrive at some simple empirical generalizations. From his material he hoped to gather evidence about the overriding principles in God's plan for humankind-which he regarded as the underlying purpose of development on earth. Such a teleological philosophy cannot be tested empirically and therefore does not qualify as scientific explanation.

Harvey (1969, p. 438) considered that the teleological framework of explanation is possible without such a metaphysical assertion. A *teleological explanation* is generally taken to mean that a phenomenon is explained in relation to the purpose it is believed to serve. A *mechanical* or *causal explanation,* on the other hand, relies on pre-existing causes to explain the observed phenomenon.

A causal explanation is only reached when, for example, we have found the law of nature that is the cause of certain empirically observed single instances. The inductive model is associated with the teleological explanatory model and it will not really serve when we are looking for *prime causes,* that is, cause that are prior to and cause the phenomena that have been observed empirically. When Newton 'was hit on the head by a falling apple' he grasped the idea of a universal law of gravitation inductively. He could then set the law of gravitation up as an hypothesis but any confirmation of its universality could only come through the testing of a larger body of empirical material. The development of the natural sciences in the latter part of the nineteenth century provided the technical tools that made it possible to test hypotheses with some precision, by using a number of repeated experiments.

Inductive arguments were increasingly replaced by *hypothetic – deductive methods* (Figure 3.2b). Research workers, starting from an inductive ordering of their observations or from intuitive insights, tried to devise for themselves *priori* models of the structure of reality. These were used to postulate a set of hypotheses which could be confirmed, modified or rejected by testing empirical data through experiment. A large number of confirmations were supposed to lead to the *verification* of the hypothesis, which was then, for the time being, established as a law. This law stood until the results of later research eventually rejected it. No proof of the absolute truth of a law can ever be produced as definite verification is virtually impossible.

Karl Popper has pointed out that the truth of a law does not depend on the number of times it is confirmed experimentally; it is easy enough to find empirical support for almost any theory. The criteria for its scientific validity are not the confirmatory evidence, but that those circumstances which may lead to the rejection of the theory are identified. It follows that a theory scientific if it is possible to *falsify.* Kuhn criticizes Popper for believing theory will be abandoned as soon as evidence is found which does not fit the theory. Kuhn maintains that all theories will eventually be confronted with some data which do not fit. A fundamental theory is not rejected if individual research data do not fit it, for if it were, then all theories would have to rejected. Up to now the history of science does not record any theory which has not eventually been confronted by contradictory circumstances (instances of falsification). According to Kuhn, a fundamental theory is only rejected when a new theory is put forward which is *believed* to be superior (Johansson, 1973).

Feyerabend adds that scientific development is much more *irrational* than Popper's scheme of falsification allows. Alongside straightforward arguments, the proponents of new theories have also often used propaganda and psychological tricks. Feyerabend does not believe that we would have had any science as we know it today if the principles of verification or falsification had been followed in every detail. Perhaps our world view would have still been geocentric. For Galilei stuck to his heliocentric world view although he could not find empirical proofs which would falsify the geocentric view. Feyerabend supports the view that the development of scientific knowledge follows an irrational, almost anarchic path, along which almost anything goes, as far as methodology is concerned (Åquist, 1981, p. 11).

Kuhn does not accept Feyerabend's views on the irrationalities of scientific progress. He denies intending to present scientific theories as intuitive and mystical; more appropriate for psychological analysis than for logical and methodological codification. On the contrary, Kuhn asserts that every scientist must gather as much rational proof in support of a new theory as possible and to be precise and honest in his work. This approach reflects the underlying values of science and scientific choice of theories rather than providing a blueprint as to how a scientific theory should be chosen and defended.

In spite of Kuhn's own statements, many observers believe, with Feyerabend, that the paradigm theory seems to suggest an element of irrationality in the course of scientific progress. It is an important part of Kuhn's approach that *data are dependent on theory*. All observations presuppose a certain conceptual apparatus by which the sense perceptions, or empirical verifications, can be arranged. For example, the categories of language divide the reality in a particular way and will also guide our interpretations of our observations. Expectations and former ideas, that is, the hypothesis which have been set up, guide the interpretation of the data to a large extent. In its extreme form, this argument may lead us to believe that knowledge is a reflection of our ideas and has a rather slight relation to empirical data.

The alternative to such *relativistic* theories of knowledge is to line up with those who believe that that verification is possible through the hypothetical – deductive method, or to agree with Popper's belief in *falsification*. Maybe it is possible to reconcile these contradictions by maintaining that the discussion takes place on two different levels. The debate may have been based on a pseudo-disagreement. Popper has proposed an ideal way to carry out research. We might work towards this ideal but be unable to follow all the rules. Kuhn, on the other hand, describes how scientific work is normally carried out.

The hypothetic–deductive method has been recognized as the characteristic method of the natural sciences and for a long time was accepted by most research workers as the only method that was scientific. It was developed to its fullest extent in physics. In biology and geology the hypothetic–deductive method was less strongly developed than in chemistry and physics because of the type of the questions which must be answered and the nature of the empirical data studied in these disciplines. It is characteristic of the phenomena studied in physics that they are quantifiable. The phenomena of theoretical physics are, however, much more 'abstract' than those studied by biologists and geologists. As neutrons and atomic nuclei cannot be directly observed, measurement has provided a theoretical supposition of their existence. Theoretical physics operates in an abstract milieu, seeking unity and association through mathematical hypotheses and postulates. Physics has been able to develop into a model-building theoretical science precisely because it works with abstract and quantifiable phenomena and not because its phenomena are concrete and quantifiable. Geology and the systematic sections of biology study concrete phenomena which have a known position in time and space. They do not manifest themselves directly as quantities and theory plays a less important role in studying them. The same can be said about the phenomena studied in history, geography and the social sciences. It is significant, however, that psychology and the social sciences that study not so clearly identifiable social phenomena display stronger tendencies to theorizing.

The transfer of natural science methods into the social sciences has, however, brought about a vigorous debate among social scientists that will be discussed in more detail in Chapter 4. There may be similar problems in transferring the paradigm concept. Kuhn was trained as a physicist. His theory largely derives from a study of the history of physics. How far is the history of physics relevant to the less theoretical and quantitative sciences? To answer this question we will now look at the history of geography in the light of Kuhn's (simplified) model.

Changing paradigms in geography

Bird (1977) argued that Kuhn has been the most influential scientific methodologist as far as geography is concerned. Mair (1986) suggests that geographers influenced by Kuhn form two groups. First there are those who have used Kuhn to legitimize their propaganda for a 'paradigm change' within the discipline and a weapon against the scientific 'Establishment' see pp. 70, 76). Secondly, several historiographers of the subject have tried to apply a (simplified) Kuhnian model to the development of geographical thought (see, among others, Widberg, 1978; Schultz, 1980; Harvey and Holly, 1981; Schramke (1975); Johnston, 1983b; Martin, 1985). The paradigm school has taken on a life of its own out of Kuhn's control, and as such has been regarded as a useful 'exemplar' or model or teaching framework for histories of geography. We will use the paradigm model here in this latter sense but it is important to realize that few historians of geography have identified the same paradigms and revolutions. Some may have exaggerated the frequency of paradigm shifts, as when Taylor (1976, p. 141) identifies seven revolutions in geography within thirty years.

Figure 3.3 attempts to systematize the theoretical development of geography. It gives an incomplete and oversimplified picture, as only the main concepts in the development of the subject have been shown. These concepts have changed in significance and connotation over the course of time. In Kuhn's terminology (Figure 3.1), geography was in the pre-paradigm phase until the time of Darwin. Kant did not found a school of geography but clarified the role of the subject and its position in relation to other sciences. Geography was, for him, a chorological and descriptive science distinct from the systematic sciences and from history.

Ritter did not emphasize the distinctive roles of geography and history, but studied developments over time, linking history with geography in his work. In this respect Ritter and his school disagreed with Kant. Ritter was, however, the first geographer to give a clear description of his method. His account conforms to Francis Bacon's classical model of how a scientist works (Figure 3.2a) but because of his teleological outlook, the first apparently active school of geography did not lead the subject into the first phase of a paradigm. The contemporary developments of Darwinism led to the rejection of ideas which might have developed into a paradigm.

Neef (1982, p. 241) may be right in suggesting that it was at this time that the most important revolution took place within geography, as the universities subdivided their faculties into separate disciplines and a *cosmographic* way of thinking was replaced by the *causal explanations* characteristic of the developing natural sciences.

It should be emphasized that Darwinism did not represent a complete break with the major ideas upon which Ritter's geography had been founded. The study of development over time continued to be regarded as very important and, although it is doubtful whether Darwin supported it or not, a deterministic explanatory framework was strengthened. The conflict with Ritter was not about the deterministic explanatory model but about the forces that shaped development. After Darwin, scientists were looking for the laws which controlled nature (and for materially conditioned social laws) so, to a considerable extent, they adopted a nomothetic or law-making approach.

In order to make geography acceptable as a science during the latter half of the nineteenth century, the newly appointed professors of geography tried to develop the discipline as a nomothetic science. The hypothetic–deductive method was, however, not applied in a strict sense; we may agree with Minshull (1970, p. 81) that determinists as well as geomorphologists stated the generalizations first and then gave a few highly selected examples as proof. Geographers could not test hypotheses by verification procedures involving a

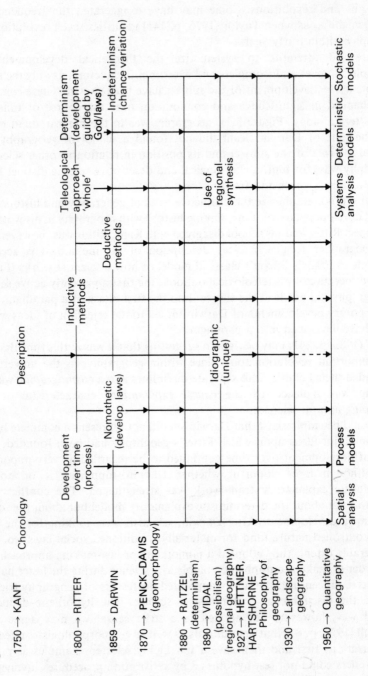

Figure 3.3 Ideas in geography 1750–1950 – two centuries of development

The column headings across the top of the figure read:

Chorology — Description — Inductive methods — Teleological approach 'whole' — Determinism (development guided by God/laws) — Indeterminism (chance variation)

Development over time (process) — Nomothetic (develop laws) — Deductive methods

Spatial analysis — Process models — Systems analysis — Deterministic models — Stochastic models

Idiographic (unique) — Use of regional synthesis

The timeline entries down the left-hand side read:

1750 → KANT
1800 → RITTER
1859 → DARWIN
1870 → PENCK–DAVIS (geomorphology)
1880 → RATZEL (determinism)
1890 → VIDAL (possibilism) (regional geography)
1927 → HETTNER, HARTSHORNE Philosophy of geography
1930 → Landscape geography
1950 → Quantitative geography

number of repeated experiments, as could physicists. Statistical tests that might play the same role as experiments were not then sufficiently developed to cope with the complex geographical material.

Geomorphology and *determinism* may be said to represent the first paradigm phase in geography. This paradigm was effective for geomorphology – it lasted for a good half-century and advanced the scientific reputation of the whole subject through the accumulation of scientific information until alternative explanations began to be put forward. While geomorphology expanded through the accumulation of relevant knowledge, the other branches of geography experienced a series of crisis phases. For this reason we can leave geomorphology aside and concentrate on developments in human geography.

Determinism had a short life as the dominating paradigm in human geography. It was challenged by possibilists and by the French school of regional geographers who stressed that man has free will and participates in the development of each landscape in a unique historical process. On the methodological front geographers trained themselves to concentrate on the study of the unique single region. This automatically limited the development of theory (as normally understood in science) and made the hypothetic-deductive method redundant. The appropriate method would be to try and *understand* a society and its habitat through field study of the ways of life and attitudes of mind of the inhabitants of the area concerned. This method, in the form of *participating observation,* characterizes the work of many social anthropologists today.

In practice, however, possibilists and regional geographers were somewhat freer in their choice of methods. Fieldwork was, however regarded as of the utmost importance. Vidal de la Blache based his *Tableau de la Géographie de la France* (1903) on studies in each *département*. Albert Demangeon walked every lane in Picardy before publishing his regional monograph on that *pays* in 1905. Such fieldwork was not, however, sufficient for geographers who wished to work on a macro scale and to collect data from large regions. They needed material from written sources and from official statistics. Their handling of these data, their organization, classification and analysis, approached the inductive method very closely. They also sought general causal relationships but were rather unwilling to identify them as 'laws'.

Although possibilists reacted against the simple explanatory models of the determinists, they developed further many ideas derived from Darwinism. They took over Darwin's ideas about struggle and selection although they also held that chance and human will played an important role in development. While possibilism could be said to establish a new paradigm, this did not immediately defeat its predecessor. Partly because of the strong position of geomorphology and physical geography, the deterministic explanatory model survived side by side with possibilism.

For a long time, however, geographers continued to stress the central position of *regional geography* within the subject. Georges Chabot declared in 1950 that 'Regional geography is the centre around which everything converges' (Chabot, 1950, p. 137). It is, however fairly obvious that the greatest advances in geographical research during the last sixty years have taken place within *systematic geography*. In geomorphology, biogeography, economic geography, population geography and many other branches of the subject, a range of new theories and methods have been developed while research has developed strongly. During the inter-war period, even landscape ecology and landscape morphology were subdivided. Many specialist studies were made of urban morphology, while research into the morphology or rural settlements was separated from general studies of agrarian cultural landscapes.

Regional geography flourished in countries like France, where geography was closely associated with history in school and university teaching and where the educational system fostered a national self-image of sturdy peasantry and cultured townsfolk. Regional studies were also important to the academic leaders of emergent nations in central and eastern Europe who were seeking to establish and preserve the uniqueness of their national heritage, not just through the native language, but also by studying a whole range of traditional relationships to their land, which had survived centuries of foreign domination.

While the peace settlement of 1919–21 created many new nation-states in Europe, arguments over their boundaries between the 'winners' and 'losers' of the First World War continued to draw extensively on local historical and geographical relationships. After 1945 the economic revival of western and northern Europe from prosperity to affluence has, however, been associated with the growth of essentially similar urban industries and services, organized and controlled at national or even international level. 'Regions' have come to be defined in strictly economic terms: 'regional policies' are devised to help areas that lag behind the national norm of economic growth. The communist parties which came to power in Russia (in 1917), in eastern and central Europe, and in China (after 1945) have also, in their different ways, been more concerned with changing society than in preserving (and therefore studying) traditional local characteristics. The study of relations between the indigenous inhabitants and their territories has had even less relevance in North America, southern Africa and Australasia, where the destiny of the European settlers, as they saw it, was to occupy the country and to reorganize it in a wholly new and much more productive way.

In the USA, Edward A. Ackerman (1911–73) argued that, 'taken as a whole, those geographers who had mastered some systematic field before the war were notably more successful in wartime research than those with a regional background only' (1945, p. 129). He went on to point out ways in which emphasis upon systematic methods would serve geography best in the future. His analysis, although an immediate impact is difficult to trace, encouraged the subsequent move towards training on the systematic side (White, 1974, p. 301).

Another reason for the limited progress of regional geography lay in the basic philosophy of the subject held by Hettner and Hartshorne. While both regarded the *regional* geographical *synthesis* as central to geography, they discouraged historical methods of analysis, basing themselves on Kant's view of geography as a chorological science. Hartshorne was strongly criticized, by Carl Sauer among others who, within a year of the publication of *The Nature of Geography* in 1940, said 'Hartshorne... directs his dialectics against historical geography, giving it tolerance only at the outer fringes of the subject... Perhaps in future years the period from Barrow's *Geography as Human Ecology* (1923) to Hartshorne's latest resumé will be remembered as that of the Great Retreat' (Sauer, 1963, p. 352).

The advantages of historical explanatory models have been appreciated especially by historical geographers and geomorphologists. Accordingly, historical explanations have been used by certain schools of thought within geography up to the present day.

The concept of the subject developed by Kant, Hettner and Hartshorne was, however, adopted by a large majority of human geographers from the 1930s until the 1960s. This, if anything, could be regarded as a paradigm. The disadvantage was that it did not lead to a universally accepted method of chorological regional description. Neither Hettner's *Länderkundliches Schema* nor Hartshorne's identification of regions through 'comparison of maps depicting the areal expressions of individual phenomena, or of interrelated phenomena' (1939, p. 462) solved the methodological problems of regional synthesis convincingly.

Schlüter and his followers, however, provided a firm methodological basis for the study of the cultural landscape by developing methods of *landscape morphology* (see pp. 38–39). The diffusion of landscape morphology to the Anglo-American world was hampered by political developments in inter-war Germany. Furthermore, the majority of geographers, including the influential Hettner, regarded these methods as being too restricted in scope for geography as a whole, since landscape morphology restricted its analysis to the visible landscape but a proper regional synthesis also includes the 'invisible' transactions of social and economic life.

Kuhn's model fits the development of geographical science only superficially. As we have followed the development of the subject, we have seen how new paradigms, in the sense of 'disciplinary matrices' have, to some extent, included ideas from the older paradigms. New paradigms therefore lose in clarity and value as a guide for research until, in the end, more and more people define geography as what geographers do. Despite the impressions we may get from simplified accounts (for instance Wrigley, 1965), a closer look at the history of geography reveals that complete revolutions

have not taken place; paradigms, or what may be more appropriately termed
schools of thought, continue to exist side by side.

An idiographic or nomothetic science?

Another reason for paradigm shifts being more apparent than real is that each
new generation of workers, or each individual trying to change the scientific
tradition of his discipline, will tend to ascribe a more fundamental significance
to their own findings and ideas than they really have. A characteristic
oversimplification of the views held by the immediately previous generation,
or, rather, by the leading personalities of the current tradition, is
demonstrated a number of times in the history of geography.

A rather good example is the vigorous criticism of Hartshorne presented by
Fred Schaefer (1953) in *Exceptionalism in Geography*. Schaefer attacked the
'exceptionalist' view of the Kant–Hettner–Hartshorne tradition; the view that
geography is quite different from all other sciences, methodologically unique
because it studies unique phenomena (regions), and therefore is a idiographic
rather than a nomothetic discipline.

> Hartshorne, like all vigorous thinkers, is quite consistent. With respect to uniqueness
> he says that "While this margin is present in every field of science, to greater or lesser
> extent, the degree to which phenomena are unique is not only greater in geography
> than in many other sciences, but the unique is of very first practical importance."
> Hence generalizations in the form of laws are useless, if not impossible, and any
> prediction in geography is of insignificant value. For Kant geography is description
> for Hartshorne it is "naive science" or, if we accept this meaning of science, naive
> description.
>
> (Schaefer, 1953, p. 239)

Schaefer maintained that objects in geography are not more unique than
objects in other disciplines and that a science searches for laws. Having
eliminated some of the arguments against the concept of a rigorous scientific
geography, Schaefer sought to set down the kinds of laws geographers ought
to seek, and also urged them to study systematic rather than regional
geography.

Hartshorne (1955) delivered a very strong counter-attack on Schaefer in
which he maintained: 'The title and organization of the critique lead the reader
to follow the theme of an apparent major issue, "exceptionalism", which
proves to be non-existent. Several of the subordinate issues likewise are found
to be unreal' (Hartshorne, 1955, p. 242). Hartshorne admitted to having used
the words idiographic and nomothetic, but rejected the idea that different
sciences can be distinguished as being either idiographic or nomothetic. These
two aspects of scientific approach are present in all branches of knowledge
(1955, p. 231). As early as 1925 Sauer suggested that although geographers had
earlier been devoted to descriptions of unique places as such, they had also
been trying to formulate generalizations and empirical laws.

Both Hettner and Hartshorne made a distinction between systematic geography, which seeks to formulate empirical generalizations or laws, and the study of the unique in regional geography, whereby generalizations are tested so that subsequent theories may be improved. Hartshorne (1959, p. 121) suggests that geographical studies show 'a gradational range along a continuum from those which analyse the most elementary complex integrations in areal variation within small areas'. James (1972, p. 468) emphasizes that there is no such thing as a 'real region'. The region exists only as an intellectual concept which is useful for a particular purpose. Later critics have read a much more metaphysical significance into the concepts 'unique' and 'region' than the geographers who were practising between the wars intended. Incorrect quotations from Hettner and Hartshorne have however gained an amazingly wide acceptance. 'It is discouraging to find some writers who continue to accuse Hettner and his followers of defining geography as essentially idiographic, thereby obscuring the underlying continuity of geographic thought' (James, 1972, p. 228). James thus maintains that what we call *the quantitative 'revolution'* did not represent such a major change in direction as many think.

It can hardly be denied, however, that a significant change in the type of research undertaken by geographers took place in the 1950s and 1960s. The inter-war generation of geographers had been sceptical of the formulation of general and theoretical laws, partly as a reaction against the crudities of environmental determinism. It was only after World War II that such theoretical issues as the study of diffusion models and location theory, and also the search for geometrical models to explain geographical patterns, came to occupy a dominating position in the subject.

The quantitative revolution

Location theory, as taught today, originates from economic theory. The classic location theories, including Johan Heinrich von Thünen's work on the use of areas in agriculture (1826) and Alfred Weber's study of industrial location (1909), are economic theories. Later economists, including Ohlin, Hoover, Lösch and Isard, have developed our understanding of the areal and regional aspects of economic activity.

Walter Christaller (1893–1969) was the first geographer to make a major contribution to location theory with his famous thesis *Die Zentralen Orte in Süddeutschland* (1933), translated by Baskin as *Central Places in Southern Germany* (1966). Christaller, who had studied economics under Weber, declared in 1968 that his work was inspired by economic theory. His supervisor when he was working on *Die Zentralen Orte* was Robert Gradmann, a geographer who had himself made an outstanding regional study of southern Germany (1931), which, however, closely followed the current idiographic tradition in German *Länderkunde*. Although Christaller's thesis was accepted, his work was not acclaimed during the 1930s and when Carl Troll (1947) wrote a review of what had been going on in German geography between the wars, he did not even mention him. In Kuhn's terminology, Christaller's attempt to explain the pattern and hierarchy of central places by a general theoretical model was not acceptable within the reigning paradigm. Christaller never held an official teaching position in geography.

Eventually Christaller gained a following, notably in North America and Sweden when it was realized that his *central place theory* could be applied to the planning of new central places and service establishments, as well as to the delimitation of administrative units. Central place theory had its first real application after the Second World War in the planning of the newly reclaimed Nord Oost Polder in the Netherlands (Figure 3.4). Edward Ullman was one of the first American geographers to draw attention to Christaller's work (Ullman, 1941) as American geographers began to develop the theoretical models of urban structures and also of cities as central places which had been devised earlier by economists and urban sociologists (Harris and Ullman 1945) Guelke (1978, p. 45) points out that after the Second World War the North American 'universities were expected to produce problem-solvers or social technologists in order to run increasingly complex economies, and the geographers were not slow in adopting' theory building and modelling methods which might promote the status of their science in these fields. Through a very well-balanced and clear account of geography as a fundamental research discipline Edward A. Ackerman (1958) encouraged students to concentrate their attention on systematic geography, cultural processes and quantification. A range of different statistical methods was gradually brought into use in several systematic branches of geography enabling the development of more refined theories and models.

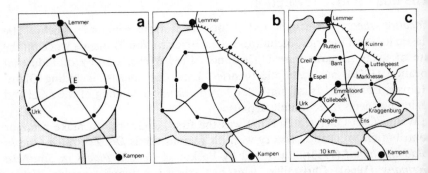

Figure 3.4   Christaller's central place theory applied in the planning of the settlement in the north-east polder in the Netherlands (from Meijer, 1981, p. 30)

     a. Geometrical diagram of the proposed settlement pattern
     b. Plan with five new villages around the town Emmeloord
     c. The revised plan as carried out

This acceleration of theoretical work was especially marked in institutions led by geographers who had studied the natural sciences, especially physics and statistics, and/or where there were good contacts with developments in theoretical economic literature. The frontier between economics and geography became very productive in new ideas and techniques during the 1950s at several American universities.

A seminar for Ph.D. students in the use of mathematical statistics conducted by William L. Garrison at the University of Washington, Seattle, from 1955 onwards was of particular significance. Garrison and his co-workers were mainly interested in urban and economic geography, into which they introduced location theory based on concepts from economics with associated mathematical methods and statistical procedures (Garrison, 1959–60). Many of the students from Seattle became leaders of the 'new' geography in the USA during the 1960s, including Brian J. L. Berry, William Bunge and Richard Morrill. Both Berry and Garrison later moved to work in the Chicago area. Berry had much to do with the development of the geography department at the University of Chicago into a leading centre of theoretical geography. There was a simultaneous development of quantitative geography at the universities of Iowa (where Schaefer had taught until his death in 1953) and Wisconsin.

It is possible, as Johnston (1987) maintains, to recognize four schools of quantitative geography in the United States. Three were developed in the departments of geography in the universities of Washington, Wisconsin and Iowa, with Washington as the most prominent centre of innovation. The fourth, 'social physics' school, developed independently, drawing its inspiration from physics rather than economics. Its leaders were John Q. Stewart, an astronomer at Princeton University, and William Warntz, a graduate in geography from the University of Pennsylvania (who was later employed as a research associate by the American Geographical Society).

In the 1920s American sociologists had postulated that the movement of persons between two urban centres would be proportional to the product of their populations and inversely proportional to the square of the distance between them, but it was Stewart who pointed out the *isomorphic* (equal form or structure) relationship between this empirical generalization and Newton's law of gravitation. Thereafter this concept became known as the *gravity model*. Stewart's ideas about isomorphic relations between social behaviour and the laws of physics were introduced to geographers by a paper in the *Geographical Review* as early as 1947. Here Stewart stated that human beings obey mathematical rules resembling in a general way some of the primitive "laws" of physics' (Stewart, 1947, p. 485). Warntz, working with Stewart, also borrowed analogy models from physics in his studies of population potentials (Warntz, 1959, 1964). He suggested that the mathematics of population potential is the same as that which describes a gravitational field, a magnetic potential field and an electrostatic potential field (James, 1972, p. 517).

The work of Christaller, August Lösch and others was introduced into
Sweden by Edgar Kant, an Estonian geographer who had tested their theorie
in his homeland before taking refuge in Lund after the Second World Wa
(Kant, 1946, 1951). His research assistant in 1945-6 was Torsten Hägerstrand
a brilliant young geographer, who was also working on migration processes
Through his contacts with the Swedish ethnologist Sigfrid Svensson, who ha
made a number of studies of the relations between innovation and tradition i
rural areas using the currently accepted methodology, Hägerstrand becam
interested in the possibilities of investigating the process of innovation with th
aid of mathematical and statistical methods. In focusing on the *proces*
Hägerstrand made a clear break with the current regional tradition. Hi
dissertation *Innovations-förloppet ur korologisk synpunkt* (1953, late
translated by Pred [1967] as *Innovation Diffusion as a Spatial Process,*
examined the diffusion (or spread) of several innovations among th
population of a part of central Sweden. Some of these innovations concerne
agricultural practices, such as bovine tuberculosis control and pastur
improvement, and others were more general, such as car ownershi
Hägerstrand's work is less important for its empirical findings than for i
general analysis of the diffusion process. He stated himself that although th
material used to throw light on the process relates to a single area, this shou
be regarded as a regrettable necessity, rather than a methodological subtlet
(Hägerstrand, 1953, 1967, p. 1). With the aid of the so-called 'Monte Car
simulation', which involves the use of random samples from a know
probability distribution, he was able to construct a general *stochastic* model c
the process of diffusion. Stochastic literally means at random; stochastic c
probability models are based on mathematical probability theory and bui
random variables into their structure. Models may be classified as eithe
stochastic or *deterministic*. In deterministic models the development of som
system in time and space can be completely predicted, provided that a set c
initial conditions and relationships is known.

The stochastic Hägerstrand model enabled the spread of innovation to b
simulated and later tested against empirical study. It was demonstrated th
the form of distribution at one stage in the process would influen
distribution forms at subsequent stages. Such a model *could* therefore be c
use to planners in support of future innovations they wished to bring abou

The department of geography at Lund University soon became renowned a
a centre of theoretical geography, attracting scholars from many countrie
Almost from the beginning there were contacts between Lund and Seattl
Hägerstrand taught in Seattle in 1959 and Morrill studied with him in Lun
where his work on migration and the growth of urban settlement (Morril
1965) was presented.

In the years that followed, Hägerstrand's technical and statistic
procedures attracted more attention than his analyses (1953, pp. 169 ff.) c
individual fields of information and their change through time. He regarde

the study of such information fields as basic to the deeper understanding of the processes of diffusion. During the 1960s Hägerstrand went on to make detailed studies of individual behaviour, using three-dimensional models to portray the movement of individuals in time and space. An important feature of *time–space geography* is that time and space are both regarded as resources that constrain activity. Individuals have different possibilities of movement in space, conditioned by their economic status and technical possessions, but time imposes limitations on everyone. Subsequent studies in time–space geography, which have been carried out actively at Lund and elsewhere throughout the 1970s and are summarized in Carlstein *et al.* (1978), have shed much new light on patterns of diffusion and other geographical aspects of human behaviour.

Quantitative geography spread over the world from the innovative centres, but it did not have the same impact in all countries. Christaller's work had aroused little interest in his home country, Germany. His theories had to take a detour into the English-speaking world, from whence they returned steeped in the 'new geography' – to be fully appreciated. Initial forms of quantification, such as the use of frequency distribution scattergrams, parameters and index numbers, were first applied around 1960. The introduction of *factor analysis,* notably in a classificatory study of Swiss cantons by Steiner (1965) was the real introduction to quantitative geography for most German-speaking geographers. The philosophical implications of the quantitative school were first presented by Dietrich Bartels in his book *Zur wissenschaftsteoretischen Grundlegung einer Geographie des Menschen* (1968). But since he proposed that physical and human geography should be separated, his ideas fell upon more or less stony ground. The concept of a united geography was upheld by both tradition and institutional unity.

Another reason why quantitative human geography did not have as strong an impact in Germany was that West German geographers followed Troll's appeal in *Erdkunde* (1947) and accepted the principle that worldwide research should be a normal component of an academic career. Virtually all established geographers were attracted to employ their talents abroad, leaving their graduate students to cultivate research at home. Research abroad undoubtedly contributed to an international reputation, particularly through the application of German methods of detailed landscape studies and cartographical work. German geographers also found that their existing techniques were well adapted to research abroad, particularly in the Third World where the statistical basis for quantitative analysis were sparse or unreliable. It is still the case that German research abroad generally follows the line of 'traditional' geography while quantitative techniques have progressed better at home, especially in applied human geography.

There was marked opposition among established geographers to learning and teaching quantitative methods and a reluctance to open professional journals to contributions the editiors did not understand. 'There was something electrifying about tilting with the dragons of the establishment' says Morrill (1984, p. 59), and for this reason the young generation of quantitative geographers had the feeling of being revolutionaries. In the USA the lack of publication outlets led to the establishment of a theoretically oriented journal, *Geographical Analysis* (Morrill, 1984, p. 65).

In 1963, a Canadian geographer, Ian Burton, arguing that the quantitative revolution was over and had been for some time, cited the rate at which schools of geography in North America were adding courses in quantitative methods to their requirements for graduate degrees. It must be stated, however, that the theoretical development within the subject was not felt as a revolution by most geographers and that many 'revolutionaries' were at pains to emphasize continuity in the ultimate objectives of human geography. The use of statistics for the making of relatively precise statements was generally accepted, although the related use of mathematics in modelling received much less attention (Johnston, 1978).

Most research workers regarded advanced statistical methods as being useful in some branches of the discipline: other branches, notably historical and cultural geography, felt less need for new techniques. Leonard Guelke (1977b, p. 3) claimed that 'To an extent that is not widely recognised, the move to quantification took place within the basic framework of geography put forward by Hartshorne in *The Nature of Geography.*' In many geography departments the works of both Hartshorne and Garrison were on the students' reading lists, but philosophical and methodological differences between them were not an issue in teaching up to the mid-1960s; Schaefer's viewpoints had been forgotten.

Johnston (1987, p. 66) points out that the leaders of the quantitative school did not study the philosophy that they were adopting very deeply, apart from references to the works of Gustav Bergmann, a philosopher and close friend of Schaefer who had actually read the galley proofs for Schaefer's paper on 'exceptionalism' (Schaefer, 1953) in some of the papers of the Iowa group and William Bunge's thesis *Theoretical Geography* (1962, new edition, 1966). Bunge, who had worked at Iowa for a short period, extended the arguments of Schaefer, to the effect that geography is the science of spatial relations and interrelations, geometry is the mathematics of space, and so geometry is the language of geography. The *chorological* viewpoint, emphasizing the character of and interrelationships between specific places or regions was rejected in favour of a geography based on *spatial analysis* which stressed the geometric arrangement and the patterns of phenomena. 'The study of the where of things, their spatial distribution, which the regional, chorological view considered as a deviation, was presented as the core of the geographic enterprise' (Sack, 1974, p. 444).

The major advances towards a unifying methodological and philosophical basis for the quantitative school were made in the 1960s by British geographers, notably Peter Haggett, Richard Chorley and David Harvey.

Locational Analysis in Human Geography by Peter Haggett was published in 1965. The importance of this book lay in its overview of much new theoretical work in the subject. Haggett (1965, pp. 14–15) used the diagram reproduced in Figure 3.5 to illustrate the argument that there are three traditional subject associations of geography: with the earth sciences (geology and biology), with the social sciences and with the geometrical sciences.

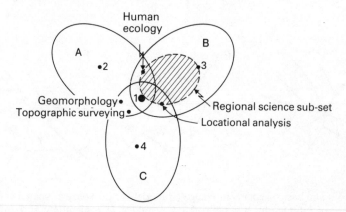

Figure 3.5   Geography and its associated subjects (adapted from Haggett, 1965) A   earth sciences, B   social sciences, C   political sciences.

The geometrical tradition, the ancient basis of the subject, is now probably the weakest of the three, he maintained. 'Much of the most exciting geographical work in the 1960s is emerging from applications of higher order geometrics... Geometry not only offers a chance of welding aspects of human and physical geography into a new working partnership, but revives the central role of cartography in relation to the two' (Haggett, 1965, pp. 15–16).

At the heart of geography as a science is the distributional view. Geography is a *discipline in distance.* When we discuss space it is not the container-space 'that frames the totality of a landscape; we prefer to think of space as a system of distance relationships between objects' (Hard, 1973, p. 184). The study of spatial arrangements may be summarized in Haggett's (1965) diagram (Figure 3.6) of spatial structures. The sketch may be seen as a disaggregation of *functional regions* like those established around central places in a Christaller model, into five geometrical elements (movements, channels, nodes, hierarchies and surfaces). A sixth element, diffusion, was added later (Haggett, Cliff and Frey, 1977). In contrast to the traditional system of self-sustained regions, the primary element in a modern society is the need and desire for interaction between places which results in a pattern of *movements.* These might be studied as geometric pattern of straight lines between points, but in fact most movements are channelled along particular route corridors, such as roads. So we can study the patterns of *channels,* which, together with *nodes* represent an organization network. The *hierarchy* represents the relative

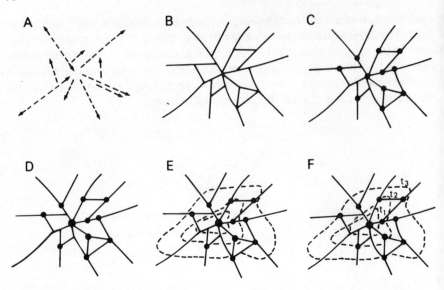

Figure 3.6   The basic elements in Haggett's model for the study of spatial systems: A
= interaction; B = networks; C = nodes; D = hierarchy; E = surfaces; F
= diffusion

importance of the nodes and the *surfaces* represent the system of land use as
exemplified by the work of von Thünen. Patterns of human occupance are,
however not static. The process of change in time therefore involves *spatial
diffusion* as developed by Hägerstrand.

Haggett's book led to a fundamental debate within the subject. The
arguments presented by Kuhn (1962, 1970a) on paradigm shifts within the
world of science were applied to the debate. Thus Chorley and Haggett (1967,
p. 39) stated that they had looked at the traditional paradigmatic model of
geography and had found that it was largely classificatory and under severe
stress. They suggested that geography should adopt an alternative *model-
based* paradigm, and so made it clear that the new development within the
subject not only represented a wider range of methods, but demanded a
fundamental paradigm shift. Each geographer was given the choice between
the traditional and the new model-based paradigm. Model building was set up
as the aim of geographical investigation, a task to be performed with the aid of
quantitative methods and the use of computers to handle data. A *model* was
defined as an idealized or simplified representation of reality that seeks to
illuminate particular characteristics. The concept is a wide one – for Chorley
and Haggett (1967) a model was either a theory or a law or a hypothesis or a
structured idea.

The rapid development of model building and the use of quantitative
techniques could not have taken place without computers, but the computers

did not determine the development of either model building or quantitative methods. 'Model building preceded the invention of the computer in many sciences, but in a discipline like geography which handles such large quantities of data it would hardly have been possible to develop operational models worthy of the name without computers' (Aase, 1970, p. 23). This technological development had given the subject new possibilities that researchers had no hesitation in exploring.

Critics of quantification

The quantitative 'revolution' did not take place without opposition. Stamp (1966, p. 18) preferred to call the quantitative 'revolution' a 'civil war', and noted that quantification had many points in common with a political ideology; it was more or less a religion to its followers, 'its golden calf is the computer'. Broek (1965, p. 21) stated that 'there are more things between heaven and earth than can safely be entrusted with a computer'. Even Ackerman, one of the advocates of quantification, warned (1963, p. 432) that 'the danger of dead end and nonsense is not removed by "hardware" and symbolic logic'.

Stamp (1966, p. 19) pointed out that there are many fields of inquiry in which quantification may stultify rather than aid progress, because there will be a temptation to discard information that cannot be punched on a card or fed onto a magnetic tape; there is also a danger that ethical and aesthetic values will be ignored. Broek (1965, p. 79) voiced the opinion that the search for general laws, at a high level of abstraction, 'goes against the grain of geography because it removes place and time from our discipline'. Minshull (1970, p. 56) observed that the landscape was becoming a nuisance to some geographers, that many of the models will only apply to a flat, featureless surface, and warned that there was a real danger that these ideal generalizations about spatial relationships could be mistaken for statements about reality itself.

The hypothetic–deductive method implies that a hypothesis or model is made first. This is an excellent way of avoiding collecting facts for the sake of collecting facts, but Minshull (1970, p. 128) suspected there would be an overriding temptation not to test and destroy one's beautiful hypothesis or model but to prove it in a subjective way. In the knowledge that there are subjective elements in even the apparently objective sections of a verification procedure, such as classification (Johnston, 1968), this possibility is clearly present. Fred Lukermann, (1958) reacted especially to attempts by the social physics school to establish analogies with physics, maintaining that hypotheses derived by analogy cannot be tested: falsification is impossible. Robert Sack, a former associate of Lukermann at the University of Minnesota, criticized the view put forward by Bunge (1962) and Haggett (1965) that geography is a spatial science and that geometry is the language of geography, in a series of papers in the early 1970s. Sack (1972) maintained that space, time and matter cannot be separated analytically in a science concerned with providing explanations. The geographical landscape is continuously changing. The processes which have left historical relics and which are creating new inroads all the time must be taken into account as important explanatory factors. The laws of geometry are, however, static – they have no reference to time. The laws of geometry are sufficient to explain and predict geometries, so that if geography aimed only at analysis of points and lines on maps geometry could be sufficient as our language. But, 'We do not accept description of changes of its shape as an explanation of the growth of a city... Geometry alone, then, cannot answer geographic questions' (Sack, 1972, p. 72).

One clear deficiency of quantitative generalization, as Broek reminds us (Broek, 1965, p. 79), is that

> since massive quantitative data on human behaviour are only available for the advanced countries, and then only for at best a century, the theorists tend to construct their models from facts of the 'here and now,' virtually ignoring former times and other cultures. The procedure becomes invidious when one projects the model derived from one's own surroundings over the whole world as a universal truth and measures different situations in other countries as 'deviations' from the 'ideal' construct.

There is certainly a danger that models based on research within the Western cultural experience may be elevated into general truths. Brian Berry (1973b) came to the conclusion that a universal urban geography does not exist, and that urbanization cannot be dealt with as a universal process: 'we are dealing with several fundamentally different processes that have arisen out of differences in culture and time' (Berry, 1973b, p. xii). He divided the world into four universes: (1) North America and Australia, with their free market economies; (2) Western Europe, with its planned welfare economy; (3) the Third World, with its economy split between a traditional and modern sector, and (4) the socialist countries, with their rigidly planned economies. Each of these has its own urban geography, which again will change through time.

Haggett, Cliff and Frey (1977, p. 24) also noted that 'the Russian translation of the first edition of this book (Haggett, 1965) made clear how heavily the locational explanations were rooted in the classical economics of the capitalist world. Inevitably, the lopsidedness of the book will appeal to certain readers and condemn it to others.'

Whereas the adherents of the quantitative school could admit a certain lopsidedness in their approach by the late 1970s, their approach and argumentation had been far more orthodox at the end of the 1960s when it was thought that a definite choice between paradigms had to be made.

Absolute and relative space

Harvey (1969) argued that Kant's concept of geography as a chorological science was not tenable because it built on the assumption of *absolute space*. The concept of absolute space is tied to Euclidean geometry which is based on five *axiomatic* statements; the parallel postulate (which states that, given a straight line and a point outside it, there is only one straight line through that point parallel to the given line) is one of these. In the Euclidean system a straight line is defined as the path of the shortest distance between two points. In the nineteenth century, however, mathematicians including Carl Gauss, Nicolai Lobatschevsky and Bernhard Riemann showed how to construct a non-Euclidean geometry. Gauss, who gave his name to a celebrated orthomorphic map projection, observed that Euclidean geometry is relevant to two-dimensional space, but it is also possible to regard space as spherical, in which case the shortest line between two points is the arc of a great circle, and the parallel postulate does not apply. Riemann showed that hyperbolic, Euclidean and elliptic geometries were special cases of what came to be known as the geometry of 'Riemannian space'. The essential point of this approach is that the type of geometry required is a consequence of the rules adopted for making spatial measurements (Harvey, 1969, p. 201). It is also possible, given Riemann's general theory, to extend space to more than three dimensions; *n*-dimensional space can be discussed. It was left to Albert Einstein to provide an application of Riemannian general theory.

As science has accepted Einstein's theory of relativity, it has rejected the concept of absolute space. It is ironic, observes Harvey (1969, p. 209), that such influential geographers as Hettner and Hartshorne took their guidance from Kant, rather than from Gauss, who also directly made major contributions to the science of geography in his work with map projections. As a consequence the main current of philosophical opinion within geography in the first half of the twentieth century was based upon concepts other scientists had already rejected as untenable. We cannot identify any point that objectively represents 'now': both time and space are relative concepts. Nothing in the world of physics may be characterized as pure chorology or pure chronology; everything is process. Abler, Adams and Gould (1972, p. 72) express a similar viewpoint: 'The shift to a relative spatial context is still in progress and is probably the most fundamental change in the history of geography as it opens an almost infinite number of new worlds to explore and map.'

When it comes to practical methods, however, it is quite clear that absolute location on an isotropic surface is the most common way of viewing space. This is what ordinary maps portray, regardless of the problems created by the transformation through map projections of the spherical globe to a plane map.

Especially when mapping smaller areas, say a part of England, where a plane surface is a good approximation of the globe, the distortion created by projections is negligible. This is generally the scale at which geographers work. In a practical sense Euclidean space is rather useful, but it may be argued that 'faced by the seductive utility of Euclidean space we have allowed an interest in maps to become an obsession' (Forer, 1978, p. 233).

Two new basic lines of geographical research each give a central importance to concepts of *relative space*. Recent work in behavioural geography (see p. 82 for a discussion of the concept) minimizes the significance of space as it is mapped objectively, but emphasizes instead the importance of the perception of space. Spaces become relative because they are related to the perception of individuals. In location theory the builders of spatial models are also trying to use measures of relative rather than absolute location.

The main point is that most concepts of accessibility or isolation refer to distance measured in a special way, usually in terms of cost distance, time distance or mileage through a transportation network, and these distances are measured from special nodes or axes. One important aspect is that geographical features like settlement patterns, land-use, diffusion processes, etc. show a location and dynamics which to a large extent are due to their relative positions in space.

Pip Forer (1978, p. 235) observes that since distances in time, cost or even network mileage are partly artefacts of socioeconomic demands and technological progress, these types of spaces are naturally dynamic and truly relative. This leads him to the definition of *plastic space,* a space that is continuously changing its size and form. An illustration is given with his own time–space map of New Zealand (Figure 3.7) (Forer, 1978, p. 247).

This discussion leads to the following conclusions: the Kantian view of space is false and therefore it is not possible, on a philosophical basis, to define geography as a strictly chorological science and to contrast it with history, which is defined as the study of all phenomena organized according to the time dimension. On the same grounds we cannot argue that studies that emphasize process should be regarded as 'not geographical'. The line of argument proposed by Harvey leads to the conclusion that we cannot define the content and methods of geography from philosophical arguments. As Harvey observes (1969, p. 8), it means that every method is open for us to use, provided that we can show that its use is reasonable under the circumstances, but it also means that what may be termed the Kant-Hettner-Hartshorne paradigm for geography is torn down, without being replaced with a new, clear-cut paradigm. It is rather difficult to define a disciplinary matrix on a methodological basis alone, especially when all methods are open for use, provided they are reasonable under the circumstances. The increased use of computers and mathematical–statistical methods hardly represent a new

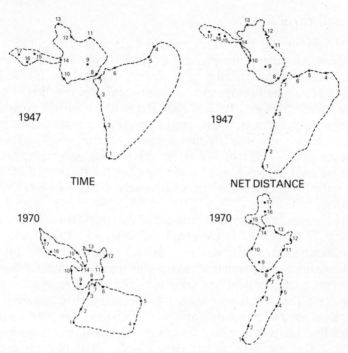

Figure 3.7 A demonstration of the plasticity of space. The four maps have been constructed from data on the New Zealand airline system and its changes from 1947 to 1970. The two maps on the left show how distance measured in time has changed as the airline network has grown and the speed of travel has increased. The maps on the right show how the net distance travelled has changed with the network (from Forer, 1978)

paradigm. It may be argued that Chorley and Haggett (1967) tried to establish a new paradigm with a model-based approach, but they refrained from excluding research with a traditional approach from geography. This meant that the model-based paradigm did not fulfil all the requirements for a disciplinary matrix.

The renewed discussion on the basic problems of the subject that followed in the wake of the quantitative 'revolution' may, however, be an appropriate sign of a crisis. Individual research workers felt themselves more or less obliged to take a stand and to clarify their own research situation so there was little opportunity for straightforward puzzle-solving. It may, however, be characteristic of social science that new paradigms do not become so well established as to enable a long period of normal science. Or rather, we may have reached a stage of mature science where we experience 'revolution in permanence' in the Popperian sense.

A 'critical' revolution?

In 1972 Haggett appeared confident that the quantitative school had taken the lead. 'Today the general acceptance of [quantitative] techniques, the more complete mathematical training of a new generation and the widespread availability of standard computers on campus make the conflicts of a decade ago seem unreal' (Haggett, 1972, p. 460). But he also made the point that 'the first years of over-enthusiastic pressing of quantitative methods on a reluctant profession have given way to the present phase in which mathematical methods are just one of many tools for approaching geographic problems'. 'Let one hundred flowers bloom' could easily be the watchword of the more relaxed early 1970s, when the quantitative school was well established and respected.

In the meantime, a new type of criticism of the quantitative 'revolution' was developing. In *Directions in Geography* (Chorley ed., 1973b) a number of geographers who, one way or another, had had some hand in the quantitative innovations, discussed possible directions the discipline might follow in the future. Many of the contributors suggested quite new directions for research, while others criticized different aspects of the quantitative approach openly. Harvey also became a notable apostate, declaring that 'the quantitative revolution has run its course, and diminishing marginal returns are apparently setting in ...Our paradigm is not coping well ...It is ripe for overthrow' (Harvey, 1973, pp. 128–9).

In retrospect it may be said that the 1960s can be characterized as an era of 'hard science', whereas in the 1970s there was much questioning of the law-seeking approach. Guelke (1977a, p. 385) concluded that 'the idea that a scientific discipline must necessarily have laws of its own is false. A discipline can be scientific if it uses or consumes laws from other areas.' Michael Chisholm (1975, pp. 123–5) noted that geographical 'laws' in general would not meet the exacting specifications needed to qualify as laws, since they are not generally verifiable. It would be more correct to talk of models and theories rather than laws in geography, a *theory* being defined as an articulated system of ideas or statements held as an explanation (Chisholm, 1975, pp. 123–6).

In his view the essential characteristic of central place theory, and other theories established by the quantitative school, is their *normative* character; the theoretical construct is not intended to show how the world is actually organized, but to demonstrate the patterns that would occur if reality were rational.

Descriptive, or what Chisholm called *positive,* theories seek to account for observed phenomena, as did, for example, Copernicus's theory of the motion of the planets around the sun. The urban rank–size relationship is one of the more famous regularities observed in geography, and may as such qualify as a positive theory, according to Chisholm (1975, p. 148). In positive theories the observations of discrepancies between the predicted state and actual states of the system may stimulate an advance or changes in the theory whereas the normative theory is used to create a world that is 'rational'. Normative theories are rather useful in social studies and in town and regional planning, in which many trained geographers found career outlets in the 1960s. The many *assignations* in this field, observes Olof Wärneryd (1977, p. 29), encouraged a situation in which geography lost contact with its earlier scientific traditions. As in other fields of social activity, there was a general belief in economic growth and economic theories: values embedded in these were not seriously debated.

Another problem was that many of the geographical models used in planning were static. For example, central place theory played a major role in many development programmes but little attention was given to the fact that functional space is dynamic and in more or less continual change.

An example from Sweden, discussed by Gunnar Olsson (1974), may clarify this point. In the 1960s Swedish geographers were engaged in a far-reaching reform of administrative and political districts, which was expressly intended to abolish spatial elements of social and economic inequality in the country. The new units were intended to be large enough to sustain the considerable burden of the welfare state. The methodology was to observe how the majority of people actually interacted in space and then to translate the observations into a Christaller-type model.

> Unnoticed by spectators and performers, the play was changed in the middle of the act. The *ought* of justice disappeared into the wings, invisibly stabbed by the *is* of the methodology. Exit man with his precise visions, hopes and fears. Enter Thiessen polygons with crude distance minimisations and cost-benefit ratios.
>
> (Olsson, 1974, p. 355)

No one thought to ask whether people wanted to change their observed interaction patterns or whether these patterns led to disadvantages for some groups.

The quantitative geography of the 1960s made use of theories from other sciences, notably economics, which were thought to give an objective description of society and how it functions. Models were constructed which gave an apparent explanation, but were misleading or directly fallacious in so far as they failed to recognize that the actual social situation might be amenable to change. Such models tend to support the existing conditions of society. This is particularly true of process models, which encourage us to believe that a trend, once ascertained, will continue to operate in the future. Thus a theory which appears to be positive or based on realistic description is translated into the purpose of the development through planning and political decision. During this sequence of events the theory becomes normative. In the Swedish example, a planning decision that had the objective of changing a social structure in fact led to the conservation of the structure because of the theories and methods used in the planning process. One conclusion that may be drawn from this is that the distinction between normative and positive theory may be useful in à scholastic sense, but the dichotomy may also be misleading as the same theory can be used both in a normative and a positive way.

Another conclusion, drawn by a number of geographers in the late 1960s, was that physical planning had not been as effective in fostering social change and equality as many people had hoped. For example, many of the land-use and transport plans that spread from North America to practically every large city in western and northern Europe, and in which many trained geographers had participated, seemed to have increased the segregation of social classes and to have sharpened differences in mobility between the car-owning and the car-less groups. In transport planning, the interaction pattern of the average family had been used as a guideline. Such 'deviant' travel patterns as those of old people with no access to a car had not been given much attention. The reason for this had been methodological; quantitative models were built to cope with aggregate and 'hard' data, that is, data easily expressed in numbers; 'soft' data, which concern human attitudes and deviations in behaviour, could not easily be handled in such models. But even research workers involved in aggregate studies were bound to wonder about the deviations from the 'normal'. This led to studies of the welfare of special groups of people such as old people and a growing concern for the position of the individual within a mass society.

The students of locational theory also had second thoughts as they came to realize that *economic man,* that decision-maker blessed with perfect predictive ability and knowledge of all cost factors, does not in fact exist. Locational decisions may be made on a rational basis, but this rationality relates 'to the environment as it is perceived by the decision-maker, which may be quite different from either "objective reality" or the world as seen by the researcher' (Johnston, 1987, p. 128). It was thus necessary to derive alternative theories to those based on economic man and to investigate the behaviour and perceptions of the decision-makers. There are a number of different research trends within present-day geography that stem from these observations. Figure 3.8 gives a simplified classification of those which have emerged since the Second World War. The 'traditional' and 'quantitative' schools have been dealt with earlier: *systems analysis* and *human ecology* will be dealt with in Chapter 5. Other trends within 'critical' geography will be briefly outlined below, while a discussion of the philosophical basis of 'critical' geography is postponed to the next chapter.

A new humanistic geography

A new concern for the individual has led some geographers to favour a revitalization of some of the methods of the traditional schools in geography

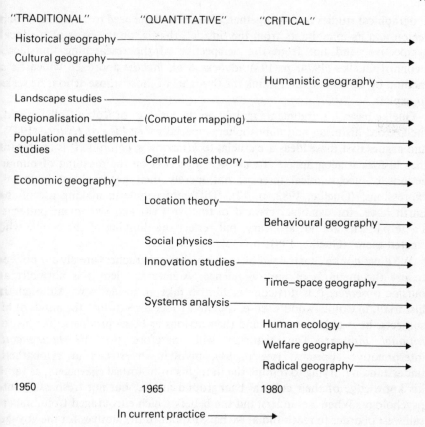

"TRADITIONAL"   "QUANTITATIVE"   "CRITICAL"

Historical geography ——————————————————————————→
Cultural geography ——————————————————————————→
                                    Humanistic geography ——————→
Landscape studies ——————————————————————————→
Regionalisation ————————(Computer mapping)————————————→
Population and settlement ——————————————————————————→
studies
                    Central place theory ——————————————→
Economic geography ——————————————————————————→
                    Location theory————————————————→
                                    Behavioural geography ——————→
                    Social physics————————————————→
                    Innovation studies ——————————————→
                                    Time–space geography————→
                    Systems analysis————————————————→
                                    Human ecology ——————→
                                    Welfare geography————→
                                    Radical geography————→
1950   1965   1980

In current practice ——————————→

Figure 3.8 Schools of human geography shortly after the mid-twentieth century. It
must be stressed that this classification should be treated with caution, for
the criteria for the classification are not consistent throughout the scheme.
While the 'traditional' schools are mainly classified on the basis of their
themes, most, but not all, of the 'quantitative' schools are classified in
terms of their type of theory. The 'critical' schools are a real mixture: some
are classified on the basis of their special methodology, while others owe
their position to a particular political approach. Systems analysis is better
regarded as a general method which might be useful to a number of
schools rather than as a school in itself. The expressions 'traditional',
'quantitative' and 'critical' are in inverted commas because the use of these
terms as labels is highly debatable – as is the grouping of schools under
each label.

including those of the French school of regional geography. This trend, which
may be seen as a new initiative by geographers who had not been involved in
the model-oriented approach of the 1950s and 1960s, emphasizes the need to
study unique events rather than the spuriously general. Anne Buttimer (1978,
. 73) argued along similar lines to Vidal de la Blache, that historical and

geographical studies belong together. She stressed the need to understand each region and its inhabitants from the 'inside', that is, on the basis of the local perspective, and not from the perspective of the researching 'outsider'. Leonard Guelke (1974, p. 193) advocated an *idealist* approach which 'is a method by which one can rethink the thoughts of those whose actions he seeks to explain.'

Guelke bases his arguments mainly on the writings of Robin Collingwood, the Oxford historian and philosopher, especially *The Idea of History* (1947), and argues that these ideas are crucial to *historical geography*. It is important that historical geographers 'focus their attention on the meaning of human actions of geographical interest, not merely their geographical [physical] expressions' (Guelke, 1982, p. 12). 'Different people in making use of the Earth have, for example, created distinctive field and settlement patterns. These patterns are not arbitrary, but reflect the thinking of the people who created them' (Guelke, 1981, p. 132).

We must not be constrained by the view that geographers are always obliged to use the methods of natural science. A natural scientist is normally an outside observer: it is difficult for him to take an inside view. Although an historian, in Collingwood's sense, is unable to see directly into the minds of his subjects, he is able to understand their actions as being products, like his, of *rational thought*. The historian will therefore use the *hermeneutic* interpretative approach (see p. 91), involving *verstehen* or sympathetic understanding, trying to rethink the thoughts of historical characters, as far as his knowledge of their cultural background allows, but not trespassing into psychology. When we understand the beliefs which encouraged Columbus to sail west in order to reach India, we have explained the motives for the voyage. It is not necessary to discuss why Columbus held those beliefs for that would take us into the realm of historical psychology.

Idealist thinkers restrict themselves to beliefs that are in some way *rational* and leave aside the emotional and psychological aspects of human behaviour. We cannot re-experience the emotional life of other people. An idealist approach does not, however, let us know for sure whether we have really succeeded in finding the true explanation of historical events. The idealist philosophy has elements in common with *phenomenology,* which has also been suggested as a useful approach for geographers. Unlike idealists, phenomenologists do not make sharp distinctions between intellectual and emotional life. The phenomenologist is more concerned with describing the life experience of the researcher. This description must inevitably be subjective because 'the approach fails to distinguish those elements of human existence that are open to subjective understanding and those that are not' (Guelke, 1981, p. 144). Whereas idealism accepts that there is a real world outside the individual's consciousness, phenomenologists argue that there is no objective world independent of man's experience; all knowledge proceeds from the

orld experience and cannot be independent of that world. One of the best-
known geographical phenomenologists, Yi-Fu Tuan, who has written a
amber of inspiring essays and books (1974, 1976, 1977, 1980), has stated
971) that geography is the mirror of man; to know the world is to know
aeself. The study of landscapes is the study of the essence of the societies that
ould them. Such study is clearly based in the humanities, rather than in
ocial and physical sciences. 'The model for the regional geographers of
amanist leaning is ...the Victorian novelist who strives to achieve a synthesis
the subjective and the objective' (Tuan, 1978, p. 204). Tuan prefers to use
e term *humanistic geography* for such studies, which are regarded here as
cluding both idealism and phenomenology.

In his book *Conceptions of Space in Social Thought* (1980) Robert David
ack rejected those conceptions of space which stem from the natural sciences
ad were the only ones used in 'quantitative' geography. He suggests that in
her modes of thought such as art, myth, magic, and the child's view of life,
ace may have very different meanings. 'If people see and/or evaluate things
ad space differently and "non-scientifically", then social science must
mehow represent and capture those meanings' (Sack, 1980, p. 8).

Such humanistic trends of thought may have been new to the English-
eaking world but can be related to significant traditions in both French and
erman geography. Ewald Banse, whom Hettner described as the *enfant
rrible* of geography, attacked the ruling disciplinary matrix of the subject as
rly as the 1920s, arguing that it only attempted to describe external reality.
order to understand the essence of things in depth, says Banse (1924, p. 58),
e science of geography should be redefined as an art. 'Only the unified
rspective of both the visible outer appearance and the inner core of things
nstitute real geography, which is a spiritual presentation of experienced
apressions.'

Nicholas Entrikin (1976, p. 616) makes the point that the humanist
proach is best understood as a form of criticism. However, as Johnson
987, p. 65) points out, we may also hold the view that "the human condition
n only be indicated by humanistic endeavour, for attitudes, impressions and
bjective relations to places (the 'sense of place') cannot be revealed by
ositivist research". This can provide insight on the essential structures of
aman relations to the environment.

The idealist approach may lead to some sort of rational explanation whereas
aenomenological research becomes very largely a personal matter, involving
tuition and imaginative interpretation (Johnston, 1986, p. 84). It is,
owever, clear that we will always use and need hermeneutic or interpretative
ethods in geography. Biilmann (1981) points out that even a map is an
terpretation of reality and has to be reinterpreted according to the purposes
each particular consultation.

Quantitative geography criticized from within

In contrast to humanistic geography, *behavioural geography* may be seen as developing criticism from within the 'quantitative' movement, starting fron disillusion with theories based upon the concept of 'economic man'. The root of behavioural geography are, however, much older. In Europe the Finnis geographer Johannes Gabriel Granö and his Estonian student Edgar Kan were attempting a behaviourist approach in the 1920s (Granö, 1929). Even i the USA, the behavioural and quantitative approaches were contemporar developments. The behavioural approach was taken up in the late 1950s an the 1960s by Gilbert White, then at the University of Chicago, and h associates, who made a series of investigations into the human response t natural hazards, guided by theories of decision-making and influenced b methods used in psychology and sociology. It was regarded as more importan to map the personal *perception* of the decision-maker than to describe th factual physical and economic conditions of the environment, since th decision-maker would act upon his own perceptions, and not on th environmental factors themselves (White, 1973). Julian Wolpert introduce behavioural geography to many human geographers through a paper in 196 which compared actual with potential labour productivity on farms in centr Sweden. He found that the sample farm population did not achieve prof maximization, nor were its goals solely directed to that objective. The farme were 'spatial satisfiers' rather than 'economic men'.

One other aspect of behavioural analysis has been the concept of the *ment map* of the environment. Mental mapping has been taken up by a number of workers, among them Rodney White and Peter Gould (1974). A somewh different approach to behavioural work is found in Allan Pred's (1967, 196 two-volume work *Behaviour and Location,* in which he tried to present a ambitious alternative to theory-building based on 'economic man'. Th *time–space geography* Hägerstrand established with his associates (see p. 6 may also be seen as a critique, not so much of the 'quantitative movement' of important aspects of social science research in general. In simple terms, provides a method of mapping spatial behaviour and at the same tin represents a reorientation of scale away from aggregate data towards studi of individual behaviour. More important is its introduction of a new econom theory in which time and space are regarded as scarce resources, the allocati of which form the basis of the social realities we study.

A corresponding concern for the individual within mass society is also bas to *welfare geography,* which developed as a special branch in the 1970s. Pa Knox (1975) stated that it was a fundamental objective for geography to m social and spatial variations in the quality of life. The study of such spat inequalities has been taken up by Bryan Coates and Eric Rawstron (197: Coates, Johnston and Knox (1977), Smith (1979), Morrill and Wohlenbe (1971), and a number of others. While some of this work represented t geographer as a 'delver and dovetailer', a provider of information, other examples, notably *The Geography of Poverty in the United States* (Morrill and Wohlenberg, 1971) also proposed both social and spatial policies for changing existing conditions.

Whereas welfare geography works in principle within the framework of the existing economic and social system, *radical geography,* which has become established more recently, calls for both revolutionary theory and revolutionary practice. Its aim is clearly voiced by Harvey in *Social Justice and the City* (1973, p. 137): 'Our objective is to eliminate ghettos. Therefore, the only valid policy with respect to this objective is to eliminate the conditions which give rise to the truth of the theory. In other words, we wish the von Thünen theory of the uban land market to become *not* true.' Harvey believes that this can only be done if the market economy is eliminated, so the task is the self-conscious construction of a new paradigm for social geographic thought, which may stimulate a political awakening and start a social movement with the ultimate goal of bringing about a social revolution. Geographical science would then become a tool in a Marxist revolution.

To this Berry (1974) commented that Harvey relied too much on economic explanations; in our post-industrial society the control is no longer economic but political, making a Marxist analysis more or less passé. Morrill (1974), however, in reviewing Harvey's *Social Justice and the City* (1973) confesses that he is pulled most of the way by the revolutionary analysis, but that he could not make the final leap that our task is no longer to find truth, but to create and accept a particular truth.

Revolution or evolution?

Just as Harvey favours revolution in society, so he supports the paradigm concept and the simplified Kuhnian model of the development of science through revolutions. 'A quick survey of the history of thought in social science shows that revolutions do indeed occur' (Harvey, 1973, p. 122). Harvey assumes that the *motivation* for the construction of a paradigm in social science is the desire to manipulate and control human activity and social phenomena. The quantitative paradigm, according to this view, came into existence as a response to pressures from the material, or economic, base of society, which indicated the desirability of discovering ways of manipulation and control, particularly within the planning sector (Quaini, 1982, p. 155).

Harvey (1973, p. 121) does not regard Kuhn as a revolutionary, because of 'his abstraction of scientific knowledge from its materialistic base'. Kuhn provides a dialectic–idealistic interpretation of scientific advancement according to Jan Widberg (1978, p. 9), who maintains that it is possible to describe the history of scientific thought within a discipline on the basis of four fundamentally different views. These are categorized through two sets of dichotomies:

	Mechanical	Dialectical
Idealistic	I	II
Materialistic	III	IV

A *mechanical* view implies that the development of science is linear, with each new generation continuing from where the old generation stopped. There are no revolutions, only growing specialization, professionalization, and the advancement of better methods and understanding. The *dialectical* view is expressed by Kuhn when he maintains that a science develops through contradictions and revolutions with changes of paradigms.

An *idealistic* viewpoint implies that ideas are the driving force behind the development and change in science. Each individual makes his own choice, the genius of scientists is what counts. A *materialistic* viewpoint implies that the material base governs the advancement of scientific knowledge. Scientific activity reflects the special interests of those who are in control of the means of production (Widberg, 1978, pp. 2–3). Both Harvey and Widberg are in favour of a dialectic materialistic view.

But it is also possible to argue that in geography paradigms, or rather schools of thought, have not succeeded each other, but to a large extent, continue to exist in parallel, whilst the new schools slowly absorb the older ones, leaving some former contradictions to linger on within the new structure. Figure 3.3 suggests that some concepts survive after basic shifts have taken place in the discipline.

Anne Buttimer (1981, p. 82) maintains that the idea of a 'paradigm' has proved appropriate for describing developments within the physical sciences; it fits less comfortably in the story of biological sciences and finds itself on rough ground when applied to any field that aims at a comprehensive understanding of humanity and environment. Everyone who has studied in some depth the life, work and experiences of those individuals who have taken a leading role in the shaping of our science, will appreciate that the paradigm model gives a distorted picture of actual developments.

Figure 3.8, like Johnston (1987), illustrates the existence of parallel schools of thought within geography since the Second World War. Johnston concludes that 'there is little evidence of either large-scale disciplinary consensus for any length of time about the merits of a particular approach or of any revolutions that have been entirely consummated. Certainly the quantitative and theoretical developments have had a major impact, but there are many residuals of the earlier regionalism... The failure to fit Kuhn's model to recent events in human geography leads to the conclusion that the model is irrelevant to this social science, and perhaps to social science in general' (Johnston, 1978, pp. 199–201).

From this we may draw the conclusion that the dichotomy between a dialectical and mechanical understanding of the history of our subject is an interesting academic study, but the truth as we see it lies somewhere between the contradictions. Shifts of major importance do occur, but they seldom encompass the whole scientific community – old ideas and concepts remain with us to a large extent; new discoveries may sometimes have the character of mutations – but usually look more like rephrasings of old truths.

To analyse the dichotomy between an idealistic and a materialisic view we have to discuss social research and values a little more closely and, in particular, try to get a better understanding of the debate on positivism and critical philosophy.

4 Positivism and Its Critics

The prestige and support which aids research stems from the general belief that research is an almost objective, value-free activity. Most people define research as an uncompromising search for truth, an activity unaffected by the emotions, beliefs, attitudes and desires of either the practitioner or of the society in which the research takes place. When research workers pursue their results as if they were political questions, many people will conclude that there must be something wrong with the research and its prestige sinks. Social scientists who work with less exact or less clearly definable data become special targets for such attitudes.

Natural scientists, as a rule, work with discrete materials which lend themselves to experiment and objective analysis. Social scientists have a weaker data base, are personally involved in their problems, and can seldom experiment with their material. The question of objectivity is therefore most acute for social scientists. The results of social science research are often regarded by the community as qualified viewpoints, whereas the conclusions of natural scientists are received to a much greater extent as truths. The discussion on the role of values in the social sciences is therefore important not only for research activity as such, but also for relationships between scientists and the general population and for the community's regard for its scientists.

Positivism

Scientific and philosophical discussion has produced two chief categories of *metatheory* (superior theories or theories about theories) for scientific research: positivism and critical theory. 'Both trends are in a sense more "climates of opinion" than definite schools of thought. There is far more discussion within the trends than between them' says Skjervheim (1974, p. 213). There are a number of different versions and definitions for each of these metatheories.

Critical theory is associated with a group of scholars frequently known as the *Frankfurt School*, represented particularly since 1950 by Jügen Habermas. Since we will not restrict discussion below to the work of the Frankfurt School, we will henceforth use the expression 'critics of positivism' rather than 'critical theory'. Critical philosophy is here taken to include both *humanistic* and *structuralist* approaches. Positivism is identified with the school of *logical positivism* as it was elaborated by the so-called Vienna Circle in the 1920s. Here, positivism will be placed in a wider context than logical positivism and will include *empiricist* and well as *logical positivist* approaches. This seems to be in line with logical positivism, which was intended to be a renewal of two closely related traditions in the philosophy of science: the British empiricism of John Locke (1632–1704) and David Hume (1711–76), and the continental positivism of Auguste Comte (1798–1857). There are however, other philosophers and scientists who belong in the empiricist and positivist traditions but do not accept the particular developments of these ideas adopted by the logical positivists of Vienna. There have been further developments of positivism since the 1920s. Karl Popper (1902–   ) was associated with the Vienna Circle but regarded as 'our official opponent' by them because he criticized their use of the *verification* principle as a central focus of positivist methodology and developed the alternative *falsification* principle (see p. 54). For this reason, Popper has been recognized as the founder of a new methodology of science called *critical rationalism* which is seen as an alternative to logical positivism. Following Johnston (1986a) we will include critical rationalism in our discussion of positivism. Leaving the thorny semantics of scientific philosphy, we will now try to clarify the leading principles and scientific impact of positivism.

From *empiricism* positivism derived the central thesis that science can only concern itself with *empirical questions* (those with a factual content), and not with *normative questions* (questions about values and intentions). Empirical questions are questions about how things are in reality. In this context 'reality' is defined as the world which can be sensed. This means that science is concerned with *objects* in the world. The *subject*, or subjects for which there is a world, or worlds, are excluded from the field of interest.

Disregarding the question as to whether what we can sense as objects comprises the whole of reality, it could be said that empirical questions are about what a thing is, but normative questions are about what a thing should be. 'How *are* the available food resources distributed between the inhabitants of the world?' is an empirical question. The corresponding normative question would be: 'How *should* the available food resources be distributed between the inhabitants of the world?'

Positivism holds that, since we cannot investigate such things as moral norms with our senses, we should keep away from normative questions; we cannot justify our tastes scientifically. Science can describe how things are, and experimentally or by some other measurement, discover the association of causes that explain why things are as they are. The research worker can, given his knowledge of contemporary associations of causes, forecast possible developments in the future from given propositions. But science cannot from 'is' statements draw conclusions about 'should' statements. Ideally, science is value-free, neutral, impartial and objective. When the scientist gives valuations, expressing 'should' statements he is no longer a scientist but possibly a politician.

The concept of positivism was established by Auguste Comte during the 1830s in France. The concept began as a polemical weapon against the 'negative philosophy' prevalent before the French Revolution. This was a romantic and speculative tradition more concerned with emotional than with practical questions and that sought to change society by considering utopian alternatives to existing situations. The positivists regarded such speculation as 'negative' since it was neither constructive nor practical, it showed that philosophy was an 'immature' science. Philosophers, like other scientists, should not concern themselves with such speculative matter, but should study things they could get to grips with: material objects and given circumstances. This approach was to be recommended as 'the positive approach'. Comte himself wanted to direct the development of society, but stated that the nature of positivism is not to destroy but to organize. An organized development should replace the disorder created by the Revolution. Free speculation, or systematic doubt, as defined by René Descartes (1596–1650), was identified by Comte as the *metaphysical principle*. The word metaphysics derives from the works of Aristotle as an expression for the chapters which followed the physical (or empirical) parts of his work. Metaphysics was later redefined as that which lies outside our sense perceptions or is independent of them. Positivists regarded metaphysical questions as unscientific. Comte held the metaphysical principle (systematic doubt) responsible for the French Revolution, which had started in emotional enthusiasm, to tear down the feudal structure of society, but had ended in despotism. In a positive society scientific knowledge would replace free speculation or make it unnecessary.

Many would argue today that this combination of conservative political ideas with a rigid definition of what is, or should be, a scientific approach is typical of positivism, but it would be wrong to use Comte as the only example of positivist thinking. Politically, the most prominent followers of positivism have been socialists and liberals. There are many examples of how positivism as a scientific ideal has had a liberating effect on science and society, and it has almost always worked towards democracy.

Positivism played a progressive role in the sense that it strongly opposed the belief that the Bible was authoritative in scientific inquiry. After a range of taboos against empirical research had been broken down during the

Renaissance, science developed as an independent school of thought, separate from religion, notably in seventeenth-century England. John Locke formulated the empiricist principle that all knowledge is derived from the evidence of the senses: what is not derived from the evidence of the senses is not knowledge. Reliable knowledge can only come from basic observations of actual conditions. To be scientific is to be objective, truthful and neutral.

Comte, who later defined positivism as a scientific ideal in line with Locke's principles, believed that alongside the natural sciences there should also be a science of social relationships (which he called *sociology*) to be developed on the same principles. As natural sciences discovered the laws of nature, so scientific investigation of communities would discover the laws of society. He admitted that social phenomena are more complex than natural phenomena but believed strongly that the laws governing society would eventually be discovered and that subjective elements in research would be eradicated. This belief is central to Comte's proposition that social development takes place in three stages: (1) theological when men explain everything as God's will; (2) metaphysical, and (3) positive when causal connections are discovered between empirically observed phenomena.

As was shown in Chapter 2 the publication of Darwin's *Origin of Species* was a major boost for positivism as a scientific ideal. The great stress laid by positivism on empirical data and replicable research methods enabled a marked development of science during the nineteenth century. Because metaphysical questions came to be regarded as unscientific, science developed its own objectives that were apparently free of belief and value postulates. Positivism tends to be anti-authoritarian in so far as it requires us not to believe in anything until there is empirical evidence for it and it can be investigated by controlled methods. We should not therefore accept authority because it is authority, but only give credence to things for which there is scientific evidence. This sceptical attitude, and the consequential search for certainty, has naturally enough brought conflict for positivists and led them into confrontation with dictatorial regimes.

This was particularly the case with the Vienna Circle of logical positivists founded in the 1920s. Its members were opposed to everything that smacked of metaphysics and unverifiable phenomena. They therefore became bitter opponents of Nazism, which they saw as a mixture of irrational prejudice and ideological dogma. 'Positivist' became a term of abuse in Nazi Germany and was applied to Alfred Hettner, among others (van Valkenburg, 1952, p. 110). The Nazis wanted research to be based on their own ideology. Moritz Schlick, the leader of the Vienna Circle, was murdered and its other members were driven abroad. As long as science is uncompromising in its search for the truth it will threaten regimes based on systematic lies and ideological postulates.

Nevertheless logical positivism also shows the characteristics of an ideology in so far as it claims that its particular mode of inquiry is the sole valid approach to scientific knowledge and that other modes are metaphysical and non-scientific (Johnston, 1986a, p. 18). In defining the rigorous principles that science must follow in order to be called science, the adjective 'logical' was added to positivism because it became necessary to use newly developed methods of *formal logic* in order to define the elementary statements or *axioms* which would constitute fundamental knowledge and to derive further statements of knowledge from those axioms. Euclidian geometry provides a classical example of this process, using a series of axioms to derive a system of geometrical knowledge by a formal scientific verification procedure. From fundamental propositions and formally proved statements or laws, new testable statements or *hypotheses* can be formulated and in turn must be tested against reality in order to establish their veracity (Johannessen, 1985, p. 59).

A major aspect of logical positivism is its emphasis on the *unity of science*. Scientific status is guaranteed by a common experience of reality. A common scientific language and method ensures that observations can be repeated. Since science has a unified method, there can only be one comprehensive science. The common method is the hypothetic-deductive method and the model discipline is physics. The language that will make a unification of science possible is the physical language or *thing language*. The ultimate aim is, in the words of Rudolf Carnap, to construct 'all of science, including psychology, on the basis of physics, so that all theoretical terms are definable by those of physics and all laws derivable from those of physics' (cited by Skjervheim, 1974, p. 222). The poles and the system of latitude and longitude are the only special definitions which must be made before pursuing geographical research. It follows from this that disciplines are to be distinguished from each other by their object of study, and not by their method (Gregory, 1978, p. 27).

Criticisms of positivism

It has been asserted that positivism is not so anti-authoritarian as it claims to be because it seeks authority from the methods of natural science. This may lead positivists into thinking that there are technical solutions to all problems – an essentially conservative standpoint. The wish to be free from value-judgements may lead scientists to build ivory towers for themselves wherein research is excluded from any discussion of objectives and decisions. Positivist research workers might restrict themselves to describing how things are and how they will develop if they continue on the same track as now. Critics maintain that the prestige of modern science creates an aura of inevitability around these 'are' statements and tendencies.

Others go further in arguing that value-free research is impossible. Subjective elements will intrude in many stages of the research process, especially at the stage when research workers choose a topic for study from the many available. We can, for example, guess that a research worker, starting from his/her own well-established and strong opinions as to what the distribution of the world's food supply *should* be, will choose to investigate the empirical question as to how the food supply is *actually* distributed. Even if the research worker does not deliberately consider what the distribution should be, it would be difficult for him/her wholly to exclude his/her own views at the stages of problem formation and the interpretation of the results. It is also obvious that once results are available, the description of the existing distribution will influence the views of many decision-makers as to what the distribution should be. In this process we can say that scientific activity is itself shaping reality. It is no longer a passive observer.

Other critics maintain that the belief of positivists in the unity of science is wholly unrealistic; positivism allows its view on the logic of science to influence its conception of the content of science. We should not oversimplify things by laying down rules as to how science should function without taking account of what actually happens within the livelier research traditions. The fact is that several main lines of scientific inquiry, including important schools in psychology and social science, do not show any sign of developing towards the ideal of a unified science. Ideas about unified systems of concepts belong on the drawing boards of the theoreticians of science; the inner drift in science itself is to give each area of investigation its own form of expression. It is even possible to argue that each and every scientific school of thought is a form of cognition, an agreed approach to the analysis of the world. Teaching a discipline consists in teaching its current forms of cognition. When, for example, one learns to see things geographically it is not reality itself one learns, but a perspective on reality. What the positivists are trying to do is to base all knowledge on methods carried over from the natural sciences into the human sciences. They have developed a specifically technical conception of science, and try to exclude scientific traditions that do not adapt to their recommended technical language and methods. A typical example is Schaefer's rebuttal of the chorological viewpoint and his efforts to make geography into a *spatial science,* see pp. 120-1. Wilhelm Dilthey (1833–1911) considered that while we *explain* nature, we *understand* social life and human intentions. This appreciation lies at the root of the *hermeneutic* (Greek *hermeneuin* = to interpret) tradition within social science which tries to reveal expressions of the inner life of man by *verstehen* (a German word which means something between understanding and empathy), by putting oneself in another man's shoes. The distinctive properties of social science which have developed out of the Diltheyan tradition necessitate a twofold division of the sciences into *natural* sciences and *cultural* sciences (Dilthey's term *Geisteswissenschaften* includes both intellectual and spiritual conceptualization). We should note here that English-speaking peoples generally use the term 'science' in the context of a positivist approach to research following the model of the natural sciences rather than those of the arts and humanities. The German expression *'Wissenschaft'*, on the other hand, corresponding to terms for science in most European languages, is much wider and comprises all forms of methodological study carried out in a systematic way and based on defined theoretical assumptions about the nature of research objects (Johannessen, 1985, p. 153). There are at least two main types of *Wissenschaft* which are separate from and not inferior to each other. Wilhelm Windelband (1848-1915) agreed with Dilthey in rejecting the positivist concept of a unified science, but preferred to distinguish between the empirical sciences, which he defined as *nomothetic* (law seeking) sciences, and the *idiographic* (descriptive) or historical sciences. The distinction has had a considerable impact on the debate on geographical methodology.

The Diltheyan tradition supports the use of empirical methods within the natural sciences but does not agree with Comte and Carnap that the social/cultural sciences should copy the methods of natural science. When social scientists borrow models of system building from natural sciences they must treat all their elements as objects. When the mind is treated in this way it is materialized either directly by being conceived of as the thing that thinks, or indirectly by being considered as a relation between objects in the world. The same applies to behaviour. 'What is lost to view is mind as correlate of the world of objects, as that for which there is a word constituted' (Skjervheim, 1974, p. 216).

At the extreme, we might talk about brain processes instead of ideas or images, but we cannot study human behaviour in the same way as we study animal behaviour. The difference is that men have *intentions*. Intentional expressions such as 'to imagine something', 'to believe something', 'to love somebody' cannot be translated into the 'thing' language of the natural sciences: they cannot be understood as objects as seen from the outside. If you study your fellow men as physical objects you will not get to grips with their intentions. It is better to build bridges to other people by breaking down the barriers between the observer and the observed and creating an intersubjective understanding. This is the principle of *subjectivity* in social science, which says that behaviour has to be studied and described in terms of the actor's orientation towards the situation.

This position is connected with Immanuel Kant's criticism of empiricism as a philosophy. As a man of deep religious belief, Kant worried about what he saw as 'nihilistic implications' of empiricism. Neither empiricism nor positivism leave room for a God, nothing is *a priori* certain. Kant's need to ordain certain main features of truth was satisfied by his doctrine of 'categories', in which he claimed that if there is no prime cause for the content of reality, the form of reality must be primarily given. What the well of consciousness is filled with is an empirical question, but regardless of what is put into it, the content is shaped by the form of the well. Humankind cannot know how things are in themselves, we only recognize things as they take shape through our senses and by conceptualizing them. The reason why pure chaos does not reign within the field of scientific activity is that human perception and reflection are built upon common categories within which impulses are classified (space, time, cause). Kant classified the branches of science, as we saw above, into three corresponding categories (p. 16).

Dialectics, Hegel and Marx

Georg Wilhelm Friederich Hegel (1770–1831) made scientific inquiry even more difficult by arguing that the categories we use for classification and thought (structure of concepts, speech) are not fixed for all time, but are historically and socially conditioned. Often we cannot gain a full understanding of a thing by merely studying it on its own. We must also consider its antithesis – its opposite. A geographer, for instance, is often in a far better position to describe his home area, however well he knows it, after he has had extensive experience of foreign parts. We might cite the comparative method of Ritter and Humboldt. Insight might be improved through a constant consideration of the antithesis which throws new light on the thesis. The development of knowledge on the Hegelian model is usually described as *dialectic*. As we increase our insight into the thesis by contrasting it with its antithesis so we heighten our understanding of the synthesis, which, in its turn, enables us to set up new theses and antitheses against each other, etc. This process does not achieve a permanent form of knowledge, correct for all time. Knowledge and science are not like a steadily growing anthill of pine needles, but are better defined as continually changing and deepening processes.

Gunnar Olsson (1975, p. 29) suggests that the crucial point about dialectics is that understanding and creation themselves are moved by dialectical transitions, truths are relative, statements can be designated as 'true' only at a given point in time and, in any case, can be contradicted by other 'true' statements.

> While conventional reasoning knows only the either-or distinction of the excluded middle, reality knows the both-this-and-that relation of dialectics and many-valued logics. Since contradiction is not external to reality but built into its structure, the language in which reality is discussed should itself have the same characteristics of internal negation. It is in this sense that reality is dialectical, for both reality and dialectics are governed by perpetual processes of internal tensions and not by stultifying juxtapositions of opposites. As a consequence, both the empirical and the logical bases of our theories should be open to conceptual change. But the aim is not to falsify for the sake of rejection. It is rather to falsify for the sake of creative understanding. This is possible, because dialectic movement is not inference but deepening of concepts.
>
> (Olsson, 1975, p. 28–9)

Hegel (1975, p. 153–4) discussed the dialectical method with special reference to geography. He differed from Kant, but agreed with his contemporary Ritter and with other German idealists in defining geography as a historical rather than as a naturalistic discipline, 'a study of the possible modes of living offered by the environment to people settled in various regions of the Earth' (Quaini, 1982, p. 19). There is a dialectic relationship between the geographical environment and the way of life of its population as the historical development of civilization gradually frees people from the constraints of the natural conditions under which they live.

It has been maintained that Karl Marx (1818–83), who developed the dialectical method further, was also influenced by Ritter – we know he attended Ritter's lectures – as he turned his thoughts from Hegelian idealism to historical materialism (Cornu, 1955). In so far as the most important methodological texts of Marx are primarily devoted to a critique of Hegel, idealism and the mysteries of speculative construction, they naturally include rather important elements of positivism. Marx believed that it was necessary to turn from the abstract to the empirical (Quaini, 1982, p. 29). The intellect was for him more a product of material conditions than their foundation. The material, empirical world and man's behaviour therein was the base upon which thoughts and ideologies formed a *superstructure*.

A positivist aspect of Marxism is the theory of realistic knowledge. Knowledge means cognizance of an objective truth: it regards the world as concrete. Marxism also proclaims the unity of science, but the basis for this unity is not so clear-cut as in positivism. Engels leaned to the natural sciences when he maintained that the gradually increasing similarity between theories of social science and those of natural science would lead to the accommodation of nature and society within a unified philosophical perspective; we may here trace the ideas of Darwinism. In his youth, Marx also wrote about a unified science which comprised nature, society and human psychology, but while positivists maintained that a unified science should be based upon the methods of the natural sciences, Marx considered the philosophy of the social sciences to be potentially far superior to that of the natural sciences. Therefore the eventual fusion of the two fields of study would come about through the socialization of the natural sciences (Harvey, 1973, p. 128).

Marx asserted that we know only one science, the science of history (Quaini, 1982, p. 35). It also follows from the grand Marxist theory that society develops in stages in accordance with developments in the factors of production. Marx refused to accept the scientific laws governing society as eternal. This view contrasts sharply with the claim of positivist science that scientific laws are universal in space and time. Engels pointed out that 'to us, so-called economic laws are not eternal laws of nature but historical laws which appear and disappear' (cited by Gregory, 1978, p. 73). Marx was particularly critical of the economists Adam Smith and David Ricardo; he considered their outlook on reality to be unhistoric and non-dialectic. Society has inbuilt conflicts which will resolve themselves by change both in practice and in theory.

Subjectivity and objectivity

Critics of positivism maintain that metaphysical assumptions cannot be excluded from science. Facts are not facts in themselves: they represent those parts of reality which can be appreciated with the concept apparatus available. Facts are facts only in relation to a given scientific aim which is itself structured by the values intrinsic in society. The scientific process is therefore restricted by the environment in which it takes place and is constrained within the limits of the perception of research workers. This view of science implies that theories are preconceived and therefore determine observations rather than providing explanatory structures after empirical observations have been made. Consequently, the proponents of different theories see the world in different ways and the comparison of different theories by submitting them to objective tests, which any qualified scientist could carry out, is impossible. We may have some difficulty in explaining the progress of science in this rather frustrating situation. Some offer a dialectical solution; scientific discourse is regarded as a structure in which theories and observations progressively transform one another (Gregory, 1978, pp. 57-8).

Although some regard these assumptions as valid throughout science, most critics of positivism would stress the difference between *natural* and *social* sciences. Immanuel Kant based his lectures on empirical research in physical geography and did not regard this as being in conflict with his rejection of empiricism as a general philosophy for all sciences. Natural scientists have not regarded the discussion of positivism as an urgent task, for the research that they do is independent of their philosophical stance. They have been able to construct a free-standing scientific language - the *'thing' language* - which satisfies their need for precision. This language has admittedly been established through the subjective appreciation of nature by scientists, but this creates few problems as long as there is a measure of agreement on the experience of the senses within the scientific world. Nature can only answer in the language in which the question is put - which is the language of science. Therefore mistranslations can only occur through the faulty use of accepted methods and language.

Many scientists would say that much of the criticism of positivism has litttle relevance to research procedures in natural sciences but has more relevance to the application of science. It may be possible to pursue more or less objective research within the natural sciences, but the results of science are applied by society in such a way that science becomes a tremendous force which transforms the community (Ackerman, 1963, p. 430). Value judgements are implicit in the application of scientific results, in nuclear physics, for example, and consequently the natural scientist cannot avoid making up his/her mind about them. Even the priorities given to different types of research are connected with values, it is not irrelevant whether we give priority to nuclear physics or to ecology.

In social science *subjectivity* or the problem of values is deeply involved in both theory and practice. Concepts in social science are related to human evaluation; a typical example is the concept of *natural resources*. A natural scientist might study coal as a thing in nature, but in social relationships coal is a resource which must be translated as 'something of value to man'. Coal is only interesting to social scientists because it is a resource and forms the basis for coal-mining districts. But coal has not always been a resource, and not all coals found in nature are resources. The market situation and the cost of extraction may lead to closure of a coal-mine even if there is a lot of coal remaining. The human evaluation which creeps in makes the use of the 'thing' language difficult in social science.

Another problem is that ordinary language must be used widely in the social sciences because it is spoken by the objectives of the research and also because there is a close affinity between daily speech and technical language. When for example, we ask a commuter for his opinions about his own pattern of life we must take account of the concepts of the interviewee. A problem arises when we define our concepts 'scientificially' before embarking on a research project and later use these definitions to interpret our results without critically evaluating what happened during the investigation. The person who has been inverviewed may have placed a wholly different construction on the concepts. A dialectic between subject and object takes place in the social sciences. It is impossible for the research worker who is investigating social phenomena to regard them as objects wholly external to himself. The subject is himself part of the object: the social scientist acts as a part of the society he/she studies.

The dialectic between the subject and the object leads on to what has been termed *double hermeneutics*. The social scientist explains whatever he has understood about the beliefs and attitudes of his fellow citizens in his/her writings, but the people he/she writes for are more or less identical with the people he/she is writing about. If the reader understands what the writer has understood, he/she may be led to change his/her attitudes or actions. The new attitudes can then be investigated again by the social scientist, explained and understood *ad infinitum*. The meaning ascribed to the one constantly mediate the meaning ascribed to the other through double hermeneutics (Skjervheim 1974, pp. 298-9; Gregory, 1978, p. 61).

Since our knowledge of the world is established through the concepts of science, reality and knowledge can be changed through human reflections and practice. Reality, as it is constituted by scientists, can therefore be transformed into something else. *Critical theory*, as developed by the *Frankfurt school* and by Habermas, suggested that science should take an interest in these possibilities of change. Habermas asserted that the relationship of the social sciences to the community is similar to that of the psychoanalyst to his patient. The psychoanalyst treats his patient by using his own intimate *verstehen* or understanding of the patient. He tries to make the patient understand the underlying causes of his problems and encourages him to believe that these auses can be altered. The task is to convert what the patient believes to be permanent constraints into *pseudo-constraints*. The patient who becomes onscious of these constraining conditions may be restored to health if he eally wants to be healthy. Social scientists, who claim to be professionally stablished reflections of society, must also reveal pseudo-constraints so that potential opportunities for change in society are clarified.

For this purpose the Frankfurt school developed *Ideologiekritik* which aims o enlighten agents about their true interests. A distinction is made between deology in the pejorative sense and ideology in the positive sense. *Ideology in he pejorative sense* is a system of pseudo-constraints or 'systems of beliefs and ttitudes accepted by the agents for reasons or motives which those agents ould not acknowledge' (Guess, 1981, p. 20). In general such an ideology nakes it possible for a minority group to impose *surplus repression* on their ociety, that is, more repression than is needed to maintain that society. The other members of society accept the minority ideology, unaware that the nderlying motive of the minority is 'surplus repression'. *Positive ideology,* on he other hand, represents the desiderata for a particular society which reflect he true interests of its members. This is something to be constructed, created r invented through discussion and reflection within the social sciences. 'A ritical theory, then, is a reflective theory which gives agents a kind of nowledge inherently productive of enlightenment and emancipation' (Guess, 981, p. 2).

The parallel between psychoanalysis and social science could be developed urther if we accept *a priori* that society is sick. Social scientists are then naking a conscious value judgement that it is their obligation to cure a sick ociety. Some social scientists would extend this analysis further, believing that heir research should join the battle for definite political values or ideologies. lthough there are certain rules for *ideologiekritik*, it is quite difficult to efine an ideology objectively in the positive sense in so far as the 'agents' do ot understand their 'true interests'. This is the point made by Lenin when he rgued that 'the correct proletarian world-view must be introduced into the roletariat from the outside by members of the vanguard party' (Guess, 1981, . 23). We will return to these problems in our discussion of *structuralist pproaches*, which, to a large extent, have been inspired by the Frankfurt chool.

Positivists, on the other hand, argue that adherents of critical theory onfuse scientific problems with others of major human interest. It is possible o describe ideologies and their *raison d'être* scientifically: it may well be ossible to unmask the real motives behind an ideology in the pejorative sense. 3ut it is not possible to construct positive ideologies scientifically: this is a task or political resolution. Science should only study things that can be treated bjectively; if human intentions are not susceptible to such scientific inquiry, cientists should refrain from analysing them.

Most positivists will agree that value judgements play a major role in the research process and that science ultimately takes part in the shaping of society. Positivism is, however, not a description of how research is actually carried out; it represents an ideal of how it should be done.

Practical consequences for research

The chief effect of the positivism debate on practical social research has been to enliven discussion about influence of value judgements on research activity. The thoroughgoing positivist standpoint stresses the importance of reducing the value element as far as possible. Research workers would be wise to refrain from problems on which they hold strong opinions which might influence the research process or cause faults which would reduce the value of the findings. Ultimately, we should totally avoid subjects where strongly divergent views are held so as to escape being implicated in political conflicts.

Others consider that we should not avoid contentious questions or even questions in which we have strong interest ourselves; in these circumstances we should be on the alert for outbreaks of subjectivity. This can be achieved by maintaining careful accuracy in description and by carefully describing our methods so that other research workers can confirm our results.

Some scientists would not regard this as sufficient. As well as taking care to avoid subjectivity, research workers should express their personal viewpoints clearly so that their significance can be evaluated and accounted for in the overall consideration of the results of the research.

A contrary view is that research workers should take up exactly those questions in which they feel deeply involved. The influence of value judgements can be positive when it motivates us to greater efforts. Research workers should express rather than try to eliminate the influence of values on their work so that these influences, being observed, will enable different views within the research environment to correct each other.

Some would go as far as to say that research workers should use science to fight for their values. If the 'value' is a political viewpoint of the research worker, he/she may set the problem and publish the results of research in order to support his/her political viewpoint. This attitude is supported by the argument that research, according to the ideals of the positivist, does not consider what the community could have been, only what it is. Such research supports the existence of, and consequently provides unconscious evidence for the values of the surrounding society. The research worker who does not share these values must therefore be free to pursue research with the intention of changing basic values and therefore the nature of society (cf. Harvey and Peet's views, pp. 83, 114).

There will undoubtedly be different views as to how we should tackle the practical research problems created by value elements. We may agree that neither research ethics nor objectivism demand freedom from values; the influence of values must be accepted as an inescapable element in research

Research ethics therefore become closely associated with the degree to which value judgements are clarified: 'We need viewpoints and they presume valuations. A "disinterested" social science is from this viewpoint pure nonsense. It never existed and it never will exist,' says Gunnar Myrdal (1953, p. 242).

The practical consequence of such an appreciation is that the research worker must be free to choose research projects he or she regards as critical. This implies that scientists themselves, by and large, should have the power to decide how the funds for research should be distributed. Certainly each community will have a research policy but this should not be carried so far that politicians and those assigning tasks at the administrative level outside the scientific environment, actually determine research tasks in detail. This approach to the freedom of research is widely shared among scientists, although in many countries the reality does not confirm to this ideal. Positivists have always held this view, and Marxist theory stresses the importance of the relative autonomy of science, although in this respect the practice of communist countries often deviates from theory. If the description of scientific activity contained in critical theory should become widely accepted, however, it might be difficult for science to retain a degree of autonomy even in democracies, for it is much easier to justify the demand for free inquiry when it is held to be value-free than when it is admitted to be guided by the aim of revealing surplus repression in society.

Politicians and the people in general are just as qualified to make value judgements as are scientists. If science is admitted to be a force that transforms society, and the ivory tower of science becomes a governing structure of society, it must clearly be brought under democratic control. It is impossible for science to maintain both privileged autonomy and a commanding position. Up to now scientists have generally regarded their autonomy as more important than their power, and have consequently tried to separate their political from their scientific activities. As both a scientist and a politician, the author appreciates that he has been in a privileged position in his political activity, since scientists are generally better trained to formulate problems and to sift out the essential elements from voluminous official documents than is the ordinary citizen. For this reason the influence of science and scientists may be much more of a problem for democracy than the influence of society is for science.

Value elements are most significant in the first phases of the research process when research problems are chosen, set and defined, and also in the concluding phases of research when the results are interpreted and presented. In the intervening data-handling phase, value elements do not play such a large role; they primarily concern the classification of data.

When interpreting and presenting research the problem arises as to how far to carry the conclusions and where to cut short. Is the assignment completed when the relationships shown by the data have been described, or should we also use our imagination and theoretical insight to add something about the circumstances under which these relationships will change or disappear? This problem is particularly acute for social scientists, where the possibility of changing direction depends on human decisions.

In fact, everyone agrees that research workers should give a clear explanation of the conditions for and the circumstances leading up to their results; this is essential to scientific integrity. The majority will also agree that, within the social sciences, the relevant environmental conditions may include the existing political and social system. It would also be reasonable to consider those aspects of the social system under investigation which, if they were changed, could change the situation under investigation. There is, however, disagreement as to how far one should question the normally accepted environmental conditions. The majority view is that scientists overreach themselves if they try to demonstrate the correctness of a particular political viewpoint and thus erect a new kind of teleological philosophy of science (cf. Ritter's teleology). The boundary between science and politics is, however, often difficult to trace. Scientists who feel strongly that their society is governed by an élite group may feel justified in acting as 'counter-experts' on behalf of the less articulate ordinary people. They must then decide whether they are justified in using their status and employment as professional scientists on such an assignment or whether to do it in their spare time as well-informed ordinary citizens.

It is also generally agreed that it would be an untenable situation in universities if a piece of research work, or an examination question, could only be assessed by examiners who shared the political outlook of the candidate. We all recognize, however, the difficulties in giving a full and objective judgement of a piece of work in the social sciences.

Idiographic traditions in geography

The question of the role of values in research has only been debated by geographers relatively recently. One of the reasons for the lack of discussion has been that geography has had a stronger association with the natural sciences and is more 'concrete' than the other social sciences.

The traditional view is that the natural sciences are more objective than the social sciences, but there are, however, considerable differences between an 'abstract' and quantitative science like nuclear physics and a 'concrete' and less quantitative science like geology. The smallest objects in physics, such as the electron, are not capable of observation, so we may say that they are 'abstract' because they only exist in theory – a theory nevertheless based on numerous and exact quantitative measurements. The problem of empirical observation at this level may be more acute in physics than in geology, but any research worker who is studying the influence of one variable factor on a single research object, who can measure this influence exactly and present his/her results numerically, will have very few problems concerning objectivity.

The fact that geography in its intermediate position within the sciences includes elements of natural science is *one* reason for the lack of positivist debate in the subject. Another reason is the idiographic tradition in geography which has been supported by geography's strong links with other idiographic disciplines like geology, biology and history. Physics – regarded as the positivist model science – is characterized by the hypothetic–deductive method, well developed quantitative techniques, and the establishment of laws. Physics is the model for scientific activity in chemistry, geophysics, medicine and, to some extent, in the physiological sections of zoology and botany. The systematic branches of botany and zoology have traditionally been confined to a classification and description of species. Only during the last three decades has an increased interest in ecological relationships led to discussion about the formulation of laws and methodological issues in these branches of the biological sciences. This development runs parallel to the 'quantitative revolution' in geography. We may note that geography has its strongest contacts with the systematic parts of biology through plant and animal geography.

Geology is the natural science that has traditionally been closest to geography. The research methods of geology are described *inter alia* by Simpson (1963, p. 46) as different in nature from those of physics. He associates geology with what he calls historical sciences. Geology refrains from the formulation, verification or rejection of hypotheses through experiments and the establishment of universal scientific laws. Its approach is empiricist, but does not follow the strict scientific rules of logical positivism. It describes and clarifies 'concrete' simple phenomena and puts them into a geological chronology and classification.

Similar comments may be made concerning traditional views on history as a discipline. W. H. Dray, for instance, argues that 'History . . . seeks to describe and explain what actually happened in all its concrete detail . . . Since . . . historical events are unique, it is not possible for the historian to explain his subject matter my means of covering laws' (Dray, 1966, p. 45). Whilst, in physics, individual phenomena and their combinations cannot be presented as really new objects, historical phenomena, singly or in combination, can hardly ever be subjected to a uniform form of measurement; they exist as truly new phenomena. The laws of the natural sciences may be regarded as having unrestricted universal validity but historical generalizations are not valid for all times and places.

The views expressed above would be supported by the majority of historians although there are some who disagree. O. F. Anderle, for instance, expresses a positivist view:

Though the canonisation of the idiographic method is supposed to establish the independence of the historical from the natural sciences, it really just commits the former to an earlier stage of the latter. Descriptive historiography is not a new science with an independent method but just an antiquated form of natural science.
(Anderle, 1960, pp. 40–1)

Oswald Spengler and Arnold Toynbee searched for generalizations or historical laws as part of their attempt to write 'large-scale' history. The ideas of Marx have been fruitful in economic history for, although only a few research workers have followed them slavishly, they have had a major impact as law-formulating elements in that subject.

The majority view on the significance of individual occurrences which has dominated these neighbouring sciences has, as we have seen above, also been important in geography. The determinism of the nineteenth century proved to be rather an unfortunate attempt to establish laws and to use hypothetic–deductive methods. Its lack of success led to scepticism towards nomothetic approaches in geography. Geographers therefore turned their backs on that major element of positivism – the unity of science with one methodology whose results are not modified by time and space.

Even during its most idiographic phases geography has been prepared to accept certain 'laws' or generalizations. These generalizations have not been regarded as truths in themselves but rather as tools with which to measure truth. We may for instance suggest a law which gives an ideal model for the distribution of towns in a region. This 'law' may then be used as a tool to evaluate the many discrepancies and to compare the distribution of towns in one region to that in another (cf. Chisholm's arguments on geographic laws, p. 76). This seems to be identical with Max Weber's (1949, p. 80) views on social science methods and law formulations. Weber was one of the founders of the hermeneutic tradition. He is regarded by some as a forerunner of the school of critical theory represented by Karl Mannheim, Herbert Marcuse and Jürgen Habermas, all of whom emphasized the need for distinctive methods and theories in social science. There is accordingly a considerable degree of consensus between the traditional geographical viewpoint and critics of positivism with regard to the universality of scientific methods and laws.

After the 'quantitative revolution' this situation changed. Schaefer (1953, p. 238), for instance, attached the 'old Kantian parallelism between history and geography', refused to accept the hermeneutic method of *verstehen* (empathy/understanding) as scientific, and insisted that 'science begins only when the historian is no longer a historian in the narrow sense and tries to fit his facts into a pattern' (p. 236). He wanted geography to establish itself as a law-seeking discipline and use the 'scientific' method. Since Schaefer had had his training in the Vienna circle of logical positivists, his arguments are more clear-cut than those expressed by most advocates of the quantitative school.

As a consequence of the 'quantitative revolution', however, many geographers came to consider that science really provides a unity, that geography ought to become a law-seeking science and should use the hypothetic–deductive method. In this way they accepted a major element of positivism.

Geography as an empirical science

There are other elements in positivism that have been found in geography since Darwin's time. Geography has clearly been defined as an empirical science. Its data are concrete, it studies what really exists (especially what exists at the present time). The question as to what reality could or should consist of is regarded as unscientific, being instead political or metaphysical in nature. This view may well represent fewer problems for geography than for sociology and other social sciences. That part of the data base of geography which concerns natural conditions is concrete and can be unambiguously defined by natural science terminology and methods of measurement.

Much data in human geography are similar to data in physical geography in that objects which appear on a map or aerial photograph including patterns of settlement, lines of communication and elements of land-use are as concrete as the data used by agronomists, geologists and biologists.

Although some other material in human geography is not so clearly manifest in the cultural landscape, most of it is concrete and *measurable*. We may consider, for example, the numbers settled or employed at a place, transport as measured in quantities of goods carried, or numbers of vehicles or persons, the use of raw materials and energy in production and the amount of material available. These are data which are in principle as easy to handle as those which the 'concrete' natural scientists study. There is a difference, however, in so far as geographers are often interested in the general view; they look at things in a reducing glass (equivalent to the scale of the map), while natural scientists often use a magnifying glass. Consequently, it is normally rather difficult for geographers to measure their data directly with scientific precision and instruments.

We must often be content with data we have collected through interviews, which may be affected by the perceptions of both interviewers and interviewees. We may use data drawn from statistical publications which may have been collated from a number of sources. In both cases subjective elements can introduce flaws. The definitions of science may be different from those of daily speech. Another problem may arise when officials who prepare the statistical material for publication do not understand or do not use definitions in a proper manner. A third problem is that the definitions change from one census to another; for example, the concept 'household' had quite a different meaning in 1970 than in 1900. A fourth problem, which is also important for students who follow a development through time, relates to changes in the geographical units used. Data on present-day English counties are not comparable with data from the 1971 census because of the major boundary changes in 1974. 'Urban area' is a reasonably precise, scientific concept, but its very definition determines that the size of the urban area normally increases from one census to another as settlements formerly beyond its fringes are swallowed in the expanding town. The population growth in urban areas is due not only to the growing concentration of settlements but also partially to the increased outward movement of the towns' inhabitants. The examples show that a satisfactory definition and understanding of the data is very important. They show also that geographical data lie in a transition zone between the precise data obtained through measurement in a subject like physics and the imprecise data sociology needs to use.

Geography is similar to social anthropology and sociology in its concentration on contemporary data. Geographers, however, usually work with concrete or quantitative data, whilst sociologists and social anthropologists use 'interpreted' data – data about people's values – to a great extent. Sociologists are often concerned with the interviewee's subjective understanding of a value-loaded question. They must make certain that the interviewee understands the question exactly so that there are no misconceptions. Geographers have this problem too, but many geographical questions are easier to define precisely. Sociologists must decide whether the answer of the interviewee objectively expresses his/her subjective meaning. This is a problem recognized by geographers who have worked with 'soft' interview data. We often interview someone who has not thought about our question before, and either gives the answer he/she believes will be most acceptable to us or the answer that is in accordance with what he/she believes to be the general understanding of the question, even if this does not coincide with his/her own point of view. A young lad who was asked why he had moved from mid-Wales to Birmingham answered the question the easy way by saying there were no jobs in mid-Wales, which was an acceptable answer. He concealed his personal reasons for moving: 'Things are more exciting in Birmingham and there are more girls around.' Since the data on which sociologist's work are 'soft' and the problems they decide to study are often value-loaded, it might have been expected that the traditional views of scientific theory and methodology that have dominated history and geography would have been held in sociology also. In fact positivism has had considerable significance in sociology. Important schools of sociologists and psychologists have sought laws and have used the hypothetic–deductive method to a much greater extent than geographers and historians. The discussion of positivism has consequently been much more thorough in sociology.

The quantitative revolution and positivism

Quantitative methods may be employed by both critical and positivist schools of thought. However, when geography began to draw on economics in order to articulate more formal location theories, its own somewhat fuzzy empiricism was considerably strengthened and sharpened, observes Derek Gregory (1978, p. 40). The quantitative revolution involved the acceptance of elements in positivism which had previously been disregarded, namely the concept that there is *one* science and *one* methodology which extends from the natural into the human sciences. By rejecting the notion that geographical phenomena are singular, the quantitative school discarded the idiographic traditions of the discipline and set out to discover universals; to build models and establish theoretical structures into which geographical reality might be fitted.

The more distinguished proponents of the quantitative revolution, however, make the essential reservation that their models and laws cannot be understood as if they were laws in natural science. They are measuring rods, tools used to test departures from geographical reality. Critics like Gregory (1978, p. 40), however, argue that even if it has not been possible to show that geographical phenomena are subject to universal laws, there has still been some value in regarding them *as if* they were. Some of the quantitative models and laws, he maintains, have been used as devices whose utility is measured by the success of their predictions and not by their implicit validity or truth. This approach to laws, which may be termed *instrumentalism*, was borrowed by geographers from neoclassical economics in which (according to Gregory, 1978, p. 41) it has played an important supporting role. Instrumentalism refers to the extent to which models and laws are seen as instruments of manipulation rather than explanatory devices. Chisholm (1975, p. 125) refers to the same usage as *normative theory* (see p. 76) above

Johnston (1986a, p. 33) maintains that Harvey's book *Explanation in Geography* (1969), which gave the most thorough representation of the philosophy and methodology of the quantitative school, also presented a basically positivist methodology with strong overtones of logical positivism. Johnston (1986a) further associates the more important theories within the quantitative school, including central place theory, land-use theories derived from von Thünen, industrial location theory and spatial interaction theory, with positivism. He agrees that 'empiricism, positivism and empirical research are not the same thing, and that quantification is not exclusive to any single philosophy. But much research using quantitative methods in human geography has been closer to the positivist than any other approach' (Johnston, 1986a, p. 52). Bennett (1985, p. 220) however considers that much of the critique of the quantitative school as positivist

has been directed at an abstract and misinterpreted view of much of quantitative geography, one which attributes methods, views and conclusions to quantitative geographers which most of them never held, or if they ever did hold them, have since abandoned, or, if they still hold them in some form, do so only in part alongside wider views.

Bennett (1985) also makes the point that the critique of geography as positivist relates almost exclusively to human geography, and is generally irrelevant to the important body of geographical work concerned with physical-human relations. To a large extent, the critics who seek to demolish the quantitative school by labelling it positivist also accept uncritically that geography is exclusively a social science. This often leads them on to Hurst's conclusion (1985) that

> geography has neither existence nor future as an independent research discipline. This is to underline the existence of only one [historical materialist] science of society which entails both the theoretical/scientific practice needed to unravel socio-economic relationships and their explanation in a historically specific concrete situation. This science of society submerges the extant problematics of history, anthropology, political economy, psychology, etc.
>
> (Hurst, 1985, p. 80)

We might agree with Bennett (1985) that it is a fallacy to equate the quantitative school to positivism, even if it has tended to be more positivist than previous schools of thought within geography. The quantitative school laid greater emphasis on the unity of science, on hypothetic-deductive methods and on the use of 'hard' data. Few of its members, however, have been willing to accept the strict methods prescribed by the logical positivists as the only road to scientific knowledge. As the theoretical work of the quantitative school encouraged geographers to become more involved in planning, it became clear to most of us that geography as a science is involved in shaping reality by explaining how situations are and what they could be like. Most research workers were perfectly aware of the political implications of this. Additionally, there was no agreement amongst quantitative geographers as to the degree of universality of laws and models. Among the most quantitatively inclined geographers, few are ready to argue that the laws and models of human geography and of the social sciences in general are unchanging and universal. Societies change and so do the laws of society. We can divide the world into different universes: capitalist, socialist, etc. with laws that differ.

There is no common agreement either on the role of science in advocating change. The traditional viewpoint has been positivist, in line with the views of Rudolf Carnap, one of the central figures of the Vienna Circle of logical positivists, who said in his autobiography:

> All of us in the Circle were strongly interested in social and political progress. Most of us, myself included, were socialists. But we liked to keep our philosophical work separated from our political aims. In our view, logic, including applied logic and the theory of knowledge, the analysis of language and the methodology of science, are, like science itself, neutral with respect to practical aims, whether they are moral aims for the individual or political aims for a society.
>
> (Schilpp, 1963, p. 23)

This view of science is widely held amongst geographers involved in research partly because geographical data are generally 'concrete'. In recent decades, the discipline has become more and more involved in applied research. The quantitative methods and models have, to a large extent, been developed because they are thought to have considerable predictive value. This raises the immediate problem as to whether in forecasting we should rely on the projection of current trends or try to envisage alternative scenarios. The political outlook of the research worker is very likely to affect his answer to that question. The author thinks that the important requirement of objectivity demands that we should analyse and state clearly those assumptions (or pseudo-laws) which can change or may be changed, and also the consequences such changes may have on social development. It would be dishonest for research workers interested in the prediction of future changes not to do this.

Not all scientists will be able to attain such an ideal of objectivity. Those who support, even subconsciously, the maintenance of existing social structure soon come to believe that the overturning of certain assumptions or pseudo-laws is unrealistic or wrong. Those who favour the overthrow of the social order, on the other hand, will easily overestimate the possibility of converting the collection of empirical laws into pseudo-laws. This position appears to be held by Gregory when he states (1978, p. 77) that 'the function of social science is to problematize what we conventionally regard as self-evident'. Gregory's argument leads on to *structuralist approaches* to human geography, whereas other critics of positivist tendencies within human geography have been encouraged to adopt *humanistic approaches*.

Humanistic approaches

The discussion above led to a division between the *empirical-analytical* and the *historical-hermeneutic* sciences (see p. 91–2). These operate through different methodological frameworks: 'the former produces predictive knowledge for technical control, the latter interprets meanings to understand actors and promote consensus' (Taylor, 1985, p. 95). Developments within society at large have favoured the progress of the empirical-analytical sciences. In geography, the 'quantitative revolution' ensured the dominance of this approach, which had previously been held in check by the retention of a holistic philosophy. After the empirical-analytical 'take-over', the concepts of 'space' and 'location' were found to be insufficient to make a coherent core for geography and the subject splintered apart into a collection of 'diverse and only loosely related groups of researchers travelling in no particular direction' (Taylor, 1985, p. 103). Taylor maintains that the attraction of specialization will diminish in the years to come. More general training will be acceptable as no one can be guaranteed that a special set of skills will continue to be useful over a whole lifetime. Geography should do well out of this, claiming to offer an intellectually respectable alternative to *ad hoc* interdisciplinary arrangements. We can, as Taylor (1985) suggests, expect the emergence of a third 'pure' geography, supplanting the former spatial science and regional synthesis but coming closer to the holistic approach of regional geography and including elements of both humanistic and structuralist approaches.

One important observation is that geography, more than any other natural or social science, is a *visual science* with similarities in this respect to architecture and the history of art. We analyse landscapes and methods of visual presentation in our teaching of geography. The visual models and thematic maps that explain geographical patterns increase our knowledge and understanding of the world, partly because they activate modes of thought words and numbers cannot reach.

Neurosurgeons have shown that analytic, objective and so-called scientific modes of thought are associated with the left half of the brain (Figure 4.1).

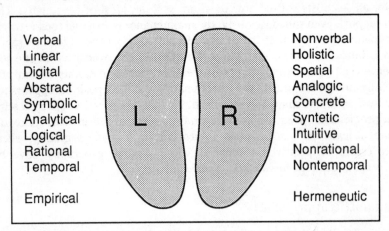

Verbal	Nonverbal
Linear	Holistic
Digital	Spatial
Abstract	Analogic
Symbolic	Concrete
Analytical	Syntetic
Logical	Intuitive
Rational	Nonrational
Temporal	Nontemporal
Empirical	Hermeneutic

Figure 4.1 Comparison of left-hemisphere (L) and right-hemisphere (R) functional characteristics of the brain

These thought processes, however, will only function when they have been stimulated by impulses from the artistic, holistic, visual, intuitive and irrational thoughts based in the right half of the brain. Visualization helps us to exploit the full capacity of the brain but also implies that we must take into account those intuitive and less rational elements which contribute so much to our intellectual life. This goes to the core of *humanistic approaches* to geography in which research involves a personal approach, to a very large degree, employing both intuition and imaginative interpretation.

Granö suggests that the focal point of geography as a holistic science is not the relation between humanity and nature as the object of study nor the explanation of humanity's activity in terms of nature nor the integration of humanity and nature in regions or landscapes.

Rather it is the question of the reciprocity between man's mind, which is the *subject* and his environment - an attempt to explain land and nature in terms of man. Man's perceptions, experience, knowledge and action form, together with his environment, a totality, a unity which constitutes the basic premise of geographical enquiry.

(Granö, 1981, p. 23)

We cannot appreciate how the world, the 'real' environment actually is: we can only know how we interpret it on the basis of our experience and knowledge. In Figure 4.2 experience is isolated from knowledge. The immanent sensation of the environment, or *perceived environment*, is the same for everyone who is exposed to the sensation, but each person will have a different 'after-image', or *cognized environment* based on his or her own experience, knowledge, memory, etc. Our individually cognized environment constitutes the total of our knowledge of the environment together with our imagination of it and thoughts about it. These form the foundations of our actions, which, in turn, transform the *real environment*.

> As knowledge has developed, so the cognised environment created by mystical, speculative and subsequently rational thinking has been subjected to an increasing number of influences from perception. The development of empirical science meant that attempts were made to identify the cognised environment as nearly as possible with the real environment.
>
> (Granö, 1981, p. 25)

Humanists believe that this is impossible.

Humanistic approaches focus on the actor: the aim is to achieve an understanding of events, the thoughts underlying the actions that produced the world of experience. 'The role of the researcher is not that of a technician, one who promotes a certain solution, but rather that of a *provocateur*, one who promotes thought and reflection.' The only goal is 'to increase *self-awareness* and *mutual awareness*' (Johnston, 1986b, p. 103). Olsson (1978, p. 110) regards the spatial science and humanistic schools of geography as being essentially opposites. The first aspires to formalized construction of knowledge, the latter to creative presentation. The humanistic approach cultivates the subjective interpretation of the world. Each one of us has his own subjective cognition of the 'landscapes of fear'. Tuan's book *Landscapes of Fear* (1980) represents his personal creative presentation of the phenomena. Reports of such personal cognitions give us a certain understanding of the relations between the actor and the environment, but if we follow a *phenomenological* or an *existentialist* philosophy (see p. 80–81, we cannot claim to be undertaking objective research. It is not possible, says Guelke (1981, p. 135) for a scientist who tries to understand a particular action to include the emotional life of the actor, he cannot replicate emotions and irrationality. This is especially the case when we try to interpret actions that happened in history: it is then rather difficult to make psychological assessments of the actors. Working within the humanistic tradition (see p. 80), Guelke (1981, 1982) advocates *idealism* as an alternative to phenomenology and existentialism. The idealist uses the method of sympathetic understanding *(verstehen)*, and restricts him/herself to thoughts that are in some ways rational in order to

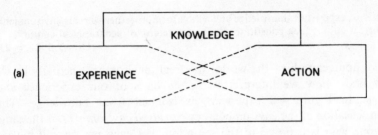

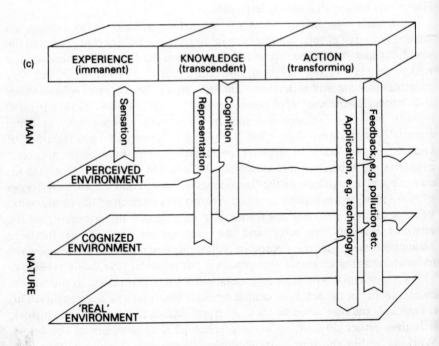

Figure 4.2 The cognized environment, which is the basis of our knowledge is not identical to the 'real' environment in which our actions take place. (Granö, 1981, p. 24)

lucidate the reasons behind particular actions. The focus is on the actors, their intentions and meanings. This may be seen as an approach which supplements empirical research. Pickles (1985, p. 52–3) points out that phenomenology is not a type of irrational anti-science. Phenomenology provides the "essential" basis for science, but does not replace it. In geography, humanistic aspects of the traditional schools, like the French regional school, have been clarified and developed further. There have also been some thought-provoking representations of, for instance, the feeling of home, identification with a place (Buttimer and Seamon, 1980), different conceptions of space (Sack, 1980) and human territoriality (Sack, 1986, Malmberg, 1980).

There are two main lines of criticism of humanistic approaches. The first, positivist criticism, has however, lost ground as the number of geographers who remain convinced and clear-cut positivists diminishes rapidly. The second, largely structuralist critique 'presents the atomistic focus on the individual in humanistic work as a distortion of reality: it gives individuals freedom to act when in fact they are very much constrained, if not constricted, by external circumstances over which they have little control' (Johnston, 1986a, p. 95).

Structuralist approaches

Positivism implies that if 'we are to explain processes we must discover the regularities or universal laws governing their behaviour. Hence the thrust of research must be towards the discovery of order' (Sayer, 1985, p. 161). This strategy might work within the natural sciences, particularly in physics, but in human geography regularities tend to be approximate, temporally and spatially specific and unique rather than repetitive. It is even possible to maintain that most models and theories put forward by the spatial science school are descriptive rather than explanatory. *Descriptive models*, like the *gravity model*, are valuable and scientifically respectable in so far as they provide new knowledge as to how things are. A presentation of cases which either follows the model or deviates from it does not explain the factors that produce the present situation. Even if we succeed, for example, in fitting the gravity model to some migration data and so establish some correlations between data sets, we have not shown what actually produces this correlation. Note that this does not mean that regularities can never be causal but rather that whether they are can only be determined by a different kind of analysis' (Sayer, 1985, p. 162). Causes are not associated with correlations and regularities, these are *surface appearances*. We need to look for the *mechanisms* within *deep structures*.

The form of the pieces in a jigsaw puzzle, or in a cultural landscape, does not tell us much about the machine or mechanism that cuts the pieces. So we need a *structuralist approach* to obtain an understanding of how the

mechanisms or driving forces within the structures, often called the *real lev*
form the outcomes at the *empirical level*.

In most forms of structuralism there are no deterministic relationshi
between the real and the empirical level. The French anthropologist Lév
Strauss offered the analogy of a camshaft machine cutting jigsaw puzzles. Tl
machine is designed to make only a certain number of movements but the
can cut a large variety of pieces. So we cannot understand the nature of tl
mechanism (the machine) if we only study the outcomes (the puzzles). V
must study the mechanism itself but we cannot do this by direct observatio
We must try to establish a theory of the mechanisms and find out whether tl
theory is consistent with appearances at the empirical level (Johnston, 198
p. 195).

A variety of structural approaches have been identified within t
humanities and social sciences. Linguists have established a school
structural linguistics that teaches there are biologically imprinte
fundamental characteristics of language systems. Structural principles
language are so readily absorbed by children that they must be transmitt
genetically. Structural linguistics analyses speech in order to identify the
deep structures, which may be common to all languages.

Social anthropologists, in particular, Claude Lévi-Strauss, have transferr
the ideas of structural linguistics to the study of social life and maintain th
human behaviour is preordained by unconscious forces beyond human contr
(Johnston, 1986a, p. 99). The myths and rites of a particular society may
studied as transformations of deep structures at the real level. Lévi-Strau
believes, for example, that it is possible to identify certain basic elemer
within myths that may then be projected into a theory concerning the nature
these deep structures. Using the camshaft analogy given above, Lévi-Strau
believes that we can understand the nature of its gear-box even if the on
things we can actually observe are the characteristics of the jigsaw puzzl
Those types of structuralism (Figure 4.3a) which seek the universal, ba:
structures of the human mind have been called *structure as construct* typ
(Johnston, 1986a, p. 97). Johnston notes that they have had little impact (
geography. The only interesting examples are concerned with childrer
perceptions of space and acquisition of geographical knowledge (Sack, 198(

What Johnston (1986a, p. 101) calls *structure as process* types
structuralism have had more impact in geography. They are not concern
with permanent mechanisms in deep structures or in the human mind, b
investigate structures at the societal level. As societies change throu
dialectical processes, such structures are gradually transformed a
geographers are interested in the empirical effects of this process of structu.
change.

Most literature in this field may be recognized as *Marxist structuralis.*
Figure 4.3 identifies three levels in such a structural model: (1) the *real* whi

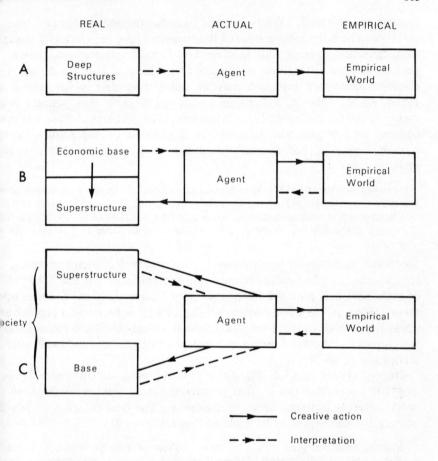

REAL ACTUAL EMPIRICAL

A

Deep Structures Agent Empirical World

B

Economic base

Superstructure Agent Empirical World

C

ciety {

Superstructure

Base Agent Empirical World

⟶ Creative action

⟶--- Interpretation

gure 4.3 Different models of the relationships between mechanisms (the real level), decisions (the actual level), and outcomes (the empirical level)

a. Structure as construct – the camshaft analogy of Lévi-Strauss
b. The individual agent is determined in his/her actions by the mechanisms of a dialetical process between the empirical and the real – as in a structural Marxism which denies human agents a decisive role. The superstructure, in this case, is moulded by the economic base
c. Base, superstructure and agent in the realist model. The agent plays a decisive role as interpreter and creator of transforming actions (after Johnston, 1986b, p. 60)

mprises the driving forces *(mechanisms)* within the structures; (2) the *actual* which the agents (people) make the *decisions* to act on the basis of peratives or interpretations of the mechanisms; and (3) the *empirical*, in iich the *outcomes* of the actions may be studied. In the 'structuralism as ocess' type of study the real level is also the *societal level*, within which an onomic base and an *ideological base* (or *superstructure*) may both be

recognized. Marxism, as a theoretical base for the social sciences, tries
understand how the mechanisms of the economic base are gradually chang
in a dialectical process that involves both actual and empirical levels.
general, it is the mechanisms of the economic base that form the determini
element; hence this approach may be called *quasi-determinist* (Johnsto
1986b, p. 56). The individuals or agents are more or less puppets bei
manipulated by the economic mechanisms. The ideological base (religio
culture, etc.) is generally relegated to a position of dependence on t
economic base, if not directly determined by it. Duncan (1985, p. 1ĩ
maintains that

> the rhetoric of structural Marxism may sound radical, but the moral of human acti
> is ultra-conservative, portraying actors as prisoners of fate caught in slowly grindi
> structures not of their own making, waiting for the evolution of the social structu
> through contradictions to move them on to a higher stage in the evolution:
> process.

Moreover, as *historical materialism* is concerned with hidden structures, t
theories can never be finally demonstrated or empirically verified. 'The "tes
of such theories is provided by the success or failure of actions founded up
them' (1986a, p. 109). So Marxism is as much a guide to political practice a
scientific method. In this connection there is a close relation between Marx
structuralism and *critical theory*, as developed by Habermas and the Frankf
school (see p. 96-7).

Harvey (1973, pp. 129-30) states that the essential difference betw
positivism and Marxism is 'that positivism simply seeks to understand t
world whereas Marxism seeks to change it'. The political aims of Marx
science are also expressed by Richard Peet (1977, p. 21):

> Marxist science begins with a material analysis of society, proceeds throug
> critique of capitalist control of the material base of society, and proposes soluti
> in terms of social ownership of that material (economic) base . . . the political a
> of Marxism provide a common scientific purpose. As a holistic, revolution
> science, Marxism provides a firm theoretical base for the radical movement
> geography.

Geographical studies inspired by Marxist structuralism are mainly fou
within economic geography (see e.g. Massey, 1984; Thrift, 1986) and soc
geography (Harvey, 1973, 1985a, 1985b). Although Quaini (1982) points o
some interesting relationships between Marxism and ecological questions, v
little Marxist-inspired work on humanity–environment relations has been do
by geographers. Bennett (1985, p. 221) criticizes Harvey for regarding t
effects of the physical environment as merely a product of the social syst
with society as a result of social control. Resource problems are seen only
distributive problems deriving from the class structure.

> This ignoring of physical questions is sometimes justified by the view that
> concept of "human agency" can be applied only to "human matters"; if this is
> then this justification accepts social theory as at best a partial theory and hence

limited relevance to geography which has physical–human relations at its core.

(Bennett, 1985, p. 221)

Quaini (1982) however, still finds physical–human relations important, but argues that the traditional subordination of human geography to physical geography should be either broken or, preferably, reversed.

Johnston (1986a) finds it philosophically indefensible to merge human and physical geography. He advocates human geography as a social science that studies aspects of society relating to place and space (including the physical environment). For the study of human geography, Johnston (1986b) develops a transcendental *(realist)* approach to structuralism, based on the structuration theories of Anthony Giddens (1979) (see Figure 4.3c). Giddens argues that most structuralist models pay too little attention to the role of the human agent. In his model the *agent* has a central position. The agent will have incomplete knowledge of both the empirical world and the 'mechanisms' or social rules of society that structure his actions. If we are to make a scientific analysis, however, we must assume the agent's actions to be rational within the context of his/her incomplete knowledge. In Gidden's model, the agents, or actors, are not puppets, they are always interpreters between the real and the empirical level. They interpret and transform the empirical world, but these interpretations and transformations are constrained and enabled by the structures at the real level. Even the structures of the economic and ideological base are interpreted and transformed by the agents.

Individuals are born into societies that trap them in social structures that constrain and enable. But as we live under the rules made by society, we are also reproducing them, not necessarily in the same form. Rules are gradually changed, since every individual is an interpreter. The gradual transformation of a language is an example. Religions and political ideologies are also gradually transformed through continual individual interpretations.

Giddens (1984) argues that social actions always take place within a framework, an empirical connection. The most important framework for humanity is place (Giddens, not himself a geographer, uses the term 'locale' for place). Actions are imprinted by socialization in places. Places are created and recreated by people who use their intellectual capacities within the frames set by social rules and mechanisms. While empirical research may show us how this happens and describe what constitutes the mosaic of a geographical pattern, only theoretical research can answer the more fundamental 'why' questions about the relations between agents and what they regard as constraining mechanisms.

When geographers observe the geographical mosaic, they can, says Johnston (1985, p. 335), regard every place as *unique* but not as *singular*. General rules and societal structures exist, but they are adapted at each place in a unique combination of individual interpretations made by the actors at the specific 'locale'. The structural rules of society, like the capitalist mode of production, are indeed given. Capitalism is not however a deterministic mechanism; its imperatives have been interpreted in a large variety of forms. Former interpretations are imprinted as a part of culture and create frames for new interpretations. Actions based upon these interpretations also result in distinct physical landscapes, which in turn constrain and enable new interpretations and actions.

Giddens's realistic model is a social science model that is used by Johnston (1986b) to give a coherence to research in human geography. Johnston (1986a, p. 156) maintains that we cannot avoid choosing between different approaches, but this variant of the structuralist approach integrates the empirical research methods of the spatial science school with humanist approaches that stress an understanding of the roles of individual actors. We might even argue that the traditional bridge-building role of geography between the natural and social sciences could be incorporated into an extended structuralist model (see Figure 5.4, p. 137).

While social scientists are only interested in outcomes brought about by human beings, geographers are additionally concerned with the environment brought about by nature and with the constraints and relations between this environment and the activities of humanity. In this connection, the empirical level involves not only outcomes but also structures or mechanisms that enable or constrain. The limitations, possibilities and mechanisms of the physical environment are interpreted by agents in just the same way as the limits and possibilities set by society. How and why environmental constraints are interpreted so variously by different actors at the same place, and how interpretations can also differ from place to place, should be of crucial interest to society. Places matter and so does geography as a mediator and bridge builder between different approaches. Such a position is, however, difficult and frustrating: it fails to provide us with any blueprints for our research.

Are dichotomies overemphasized?

In conclusion, we might point out that it would be foolish to force the dichotomy between the positivist and critical approaches to the extent that geography or even individual geographers are characterized either as wholly positivist or as entirely committed to critical approaches. The majority of geographers belong neither to one camp nor the other, for both sets of ideas concern us. The changing balance between them represents variations in the emphasis put on different elements of metatheory. As for 'scientific revolutions' in the sense that Kuhn described them, in geography they have been more like changes in intonation. The basic elements of the old paradigm are not rejected but carried along in some other form. Geography and disciplines like it have not totally rejected old theories in the same way as has happened in theoretical physics (Kuhn's original specialism).

Dichotomies like the one between positivism and critical science fascinate us because they provide us with simplistic illusions of having understood something significant. When it comes to the point, truth is not simple. James 1972, pp. 506-7) considered that acceptance of the many dichotomies is a semantic trap and that the attribution of fixed meanings or interpretations to word symbols may result in unreal conflicts between them. He suggested that the following dichotomies have done particular damage to geographical thinking:

1) that geography must be either idiographic or nomothetic, but not both;
2) that physical and human geography are clearly differentiated branches of the discipline with separate concepts and methods;
3) that geography must be either systematic or regional;
4) that geographical methods must either be inductive or deductive; and
5) that geography must be classified as either a science or an art (the positivist-humanist discussion).

In fact geography straddles all these dichotomies.

Geography, like many other disciplines, must be both idiographic and nomothetic. There is a continuous transfusion from one to the other: most research contains something of both. An integration of physical and human geography is one of the tasks that justify the existence of the subject. The division between systematic and regional geography is only expedient on strictly practical grounds, one merges into the other. Both induction and deduction should generally be used in the same scientific analysis.

In this sense James argues that much of the antagonism within geography is more of a battle of words than of realities. Since the subject began, every new generation of geographers has asserted that they have founded a new geography, and they have argued for it by overstressing the differences between the 'new' and the 'old'. This is a reason for asking coldly and plainly, 'What is really new?' A study of the development of the discipline shows that it has not experienced any real paradigm shifts. It can turn on a change in intonation, for example, in the direction of more interest than before in the nomothetic aspects, or it can turn towards innovations in technique, method or conceptual thinking. Sometimes a change occurs when a whole new world of information makes it necessary to alter our perceptions, but 'new' concepts are seldom as wholly new as their discoverers believe, although they can contribute useful additions that increase our understanding of the phenomena we observe in geographical reality. This view of geography is directly opposed to Kuhn's theories, arguing that new knowledge builds up and extends the old. When a new generation maintains that there has been a scientific revolution this is often due to an overemphasized enthusiasm for the excellence of the new material and partially because they have forgotten – or chosen not to notice – what the old tradition stood for.

When we analyse the new 'critical' revolution, it seems to show some of the same characteristics, noted by Taylor (1976) as typical of scientific 'revolutions' in general and the quantitative revolution in particular. The nev generation uses the strategy of making the new geography seem so difficult t understand that it is unlikely that the 'old guard' will master it. It is quite clea that Gregory's *Ideology, Science and Human Geography* (1978), Entrikin' paper on 'Contemporary humanism in geography' (1976) and Gunna Olsson's *Birds in Egg* (1975) repel those who are not familiar with the methods of argument and concepts of philosophy in the same way as Haggett' *Locational Analysis in Human Geography* (1965) put off those who were no familiar with mathematics and statistics.

We ought not to avoid real logical and philosophical difficulties, but neithe should we express ourselves in unnecessarily complicated language or symbo so that our message only reaches a part of our potential audience. One of th traditional ideals we have in common with history and other 'arts' subjects to express ourselves as clearly and simply as possible.

'Let one hundred flowers bloom'

Another tradition, derived from history and other 'arts' subjects, is th *hermeneutic approach* (see p. 91). History, the analysis of literature, and tho parts of geography concerned with past events and distant cultures, have n problem of 'double hermeneutics' because what is being studied cannot b changed. Either it is completed, like a work of art, or the people who a involved cannot be influenced (Papuan head-hunters do not read Dr X's thes on their habits). Many objects of study not liable to change, such as the stud of the historical geography of Britain, are of importance to geography. Th *verstehen* method may be invaluable in the right context, in just the same wa as the *scientific methods* derived from the 'geometrical sciences' a appropriate to other investigations. Models and theories developed diffusion and location studies, for example, provide important measuring ro for an improved understanding of geographical reality. We should also realiz when studying contemporary situations subject to change, that the results our research may influence the development of society. Such cases involve t problems of *double hermeneutics*: what we reveal is only what we ha understood or modelled. Those concerned, however, may act upon a ve limited and crude understanding of our explanations and thus change t situation being explained, making new scientific explanations possible. Th process can continue in a never-ending hermeneutic spiral. As researc workers, geographers also belong to the society under research and a incorporated within its general understanding, beliefs and way of life. *structuralist* approach involving a search for the structures that enable a constrain is thus of crucial importance.

Each of these approaches and kinds of knowledge: the empirical-analyt derived from the natural sciences; the historical-hermeneutic derived from ar and history; the double hermeneutics derived from critical theory as explain by Jürgen Habermas and his colleagues; the structuralist approach of *realism* as developed by Anthony Giddens and others, are relevant to geography. The extent to which we rely on each of them should be related to the nature of our research problem rather than to strong dogmatic prejudices of our own.

We should approach the problem as to whether the history of geography has been influenced by idealistic or materialistic considerations (see p. 84) in the same way. It must be obvious from the comments above that, in the author's view, materialist considerations, and also the nature of contemporary society or 'spirit of the age' *(Zeitgeist)*, influence science to a very large degree. These influences are easiest to demonstrate, however, during the earliest phases of scientific development, from antiquity through the middle ages to the nineteenth century. The break-through of the positivist ideal changed this situation: science attained a relative independence that made it much easier for individual scholars to influence research ideas and learning. The contributions of Vidal de la Blache in France, of Schlüter in Germany, of Hägerstrand in Sweden, of Haggett in Britain cannot be regarded as having been conditioned by the material base. The work of Marxist-inspired geographers living in capitalist countries demonstrates the limited constraints provided by the structural mechanisms of the economic base. The relative freedom of science has never been greater, nor have the opportunities for the individual scientist to contribute to the development of his discipline, although other conditions, including the quantity of publications and the degree of specialization within science, make it difficult for him to reach the whole of his potential audience. Like all other citizens, however, scientists live in a society that will try to control their activities to some extent, especially in so far as the taxpayers generally supply the research funds. In North America especially, where funds are derived from business sources to a great extent, the research worker may experience a conflict of loyalties if he/she feels that the big firm (or the government agency) has interests incompatible with those of the population as a whole. So, while the individual scientist eventually becomes involved in politics like any other citizen, the development of science itself is conditioned both by the genius of individual research workers and by the development of society at large.

5 Geography, a Discipline of Synthesis

Explanation and description

Adherents of the spatial science school criticized geography for being short on theory and long on facts. Harvey (1969, p. 79) maintained that the commitment of geography to inductive methods 'has not only relegated most geographic thinking and activity simply to the task of ordering and classifying data, but it has restricted our ability to order and classify in a meaningful way. Where explanations have been attempted, they have tended to be *ad hoc* and unsystematic in form.'

Chapter 4 (p. 111) has shown how the spatial science school may also be criticized for developing greater refinements of description rather than explanations. It has been alleged that some spatial scientists even try to equate explanation with description. King and Golledge (1978), argue, says Johnston (1980, p. 404)

> that a series of *descriptions* should identify common features which can be incorporated into *generalisations*, and these in turn are elevated into *theories* (or laws) which are valid for *prediction* ... One of the descriptions generalisations/explanations with which King and Golledge deal is the rank-size rule and yet on inspection this rule contains no explanatory power whatsoever.

The aim of geographical research is to describe and explain the world we perceive. This world consists of *unique* but not *singular* places: each is formed through a unique interpretation of and adaptation to *general structures*. The rank-size rule, for example, makes the empirical generalization that the population of a nation's second largest city will have half of the population of its largest city, the third largest city will have one-third of the largest city's population and so on. The underlying reasons for this distribution are not explained. Since some countries show important deviations from the rank-size rule, it can only be applied as a general measuring rod, but, as such, it is a useful aid to description. More refined spatial science models, like Christaller's central place theory and Hägerstrand's diffusion theory have greater explanatory power. Even these, however, refer to particular situations or societies. The diffusion of agricultural innovations among freeholding farmers in central Sweden involved different explanatory factors to those affecting the spread of the same innovations within the Soviet Union with its collective farming system. So geographical explanation is not as simple as the spatial scientists originally suggested.

Spatial scientists of a positivist tendency have been content to study surface appearances and have refrained from structural analysis, which many social scientists regard as the real way to explanation. On the micro scale, humanistic approaches such as *idealism*, appear to offer a possible route to explanation. Such approaches are, however, only feasible in explaining empirical situations in which only a small number of decision-makers are involved. They may add to our understanding of unique situations, but are of little use in those studies of very large populations that make up much of the subject matter of geography.

On the macro scale, *Marxist structuralism* might offer a solution. Gray (1975, p. 231) claims that structures identified by Marxist analysis, such as capitalist economic development and its relationships, 'is the underlying and missing variable causing the surface of reality which geographers examine'. But, points out Johnston (1980) the process of capitalist development is such a general trend with so many other independent variables that it cannot explain any particular 'real' spatial pattern. 'Thus, if one accepts the existence of the process one must accept any pattern as a realisation of that process: the existence of the process is not falsifiable' (Johnston, 1980, p. 408). Marxist structuralists may maintain that they are interested in macro socio-economic processes that have spatial impacts but they seldom show much interest in the variations of those impacts. On the other hand Marxists criticize the spatial science school for presenting as universal, theories that are historically specific. In conclusion, it might be suggested that general theories, being either spatial or historical, do not offer ultimate solutions to the problems of geographical explanation. One ignores the underlying processes of change, the other neglects the visible geographical variations. We might agree with Johnston (1980, p. 410) that geography must 'explain not only the general processes but also the particular geographical realisations'.

It might even be maintained that in a frenetic search for grand explanations we have forgotten the value of descriptions that enlighten us. During the last decades, geographers have been so strongly socialized into the theoretical social sciences they have lost many of their former contacts with the other idiographic sciences such as biology, geology and history. Description is a legitimate scientific endeavour as long as it creates new knowledge.

Bernal (1969) distinguishes two groups of social sciences. *Descriptive social sciences* are associated with idiographic traditions and include anthropology, archaeology, geography, history and some branches of sociology. They describe the structures, operation and development of former and existing societies. *Analytical social sciences* are oriented towards nomothetic approaches and include economics, political science and psychology. Within these analytical social sciences the accumulation of knowledge through description is not as important as the search for structural explanations for different aspects of social life. Most scientists would have reservations about this strict bisection of the social sciences. In every science there is interplay between description and explanation, between the study of unique occurrences and general theory. We have seen that this is particularly true in the case of geography. During the quantitative 'revolution' most research workers however, felt an urgent need to develop theoretical explanations. Since the spatial science school has been criticized for not having found real explanations and other routes to explanation have been explored and found to be too simplistic, a general frustration has set in. The tendency for these debates to create distinctive camps fighting each other over the heads of their students (or trying to recruit them as adherents) has threatened to splinter geography. So let us now forget the strife between different schools of thought and try to find out what unites geographers. Let us begin to look at geography as a discipline of synthesis. We do so by analysing the different routes to explanation and description that have a tradition within the discipline.

Scientific analysis

Harvey (1969) claimed to identify six recognizable forms of scientific explanation in geography: cognitive description; morphometric analysis; cause and effect analysis; temporal modes of explanation; functional and ecological analysis; and systems analysis.

   Cognitive description is the simple description of what is known, resulting from a more or less successful ordering and classification of the data which have been collected. No theory is involved explicitly but, because the classification usually follows some predetermined ideas about its structure, this involves an element of theory. As an advocate of the 'quantitative revolution', in 1969 Harvey relegated cognitive description to the lowest order of explanation, although he observed that sophisticated presentations have been made in this way. The advocates of hermeneutic methods in the humanistic schools of thought, on the other hand, often stress cognitive description, maintaining that the quality of an explanation may owe more to the depth of cognition *(verstehen)* to the clarity of expression and perhaps also to the personal commitment of the investigator than to 'technical' methodological procedures.

   Morphometric analysis is a special form of cognitive description where systematization and classification develop from a geometric, spatial, coordinate system. This makes it feasible to undertake network analyses and to study the shape and pattern of the location of towns. Morphometric analysis can lead to certain types of predictive and simulation models. With a knowledge of the geometrical laws of central place theory, the population density and the size and location of two given central places, it is possible to predict the rest of a central place system. Geometrical predictions of this sort have had increasing significance in geography.

Cause and effect analysis develops from the assumption that previous causes can explain observed phenomena. We look for causal relationships which are, in their simplest form, of the type 'cause A leads to effect B'. This implies that 'cause B cannot lead to result A'. Causal laws may be discovered by the hypothetic–deductive method, or more simply, by comparing data from different phenomena in a region.

After comparing a map showing precipitation on the North American prairies with a map of wheat yields there, we might decide that there is a close relationship between the amount of precipitation and the size of the crop. We know that precipitation affects the wheat yield but that a high yield of wheat will not bring about a heavy precipitation.

The causal relationship is obviously oversimplified when we only formulate it as one link – we would do better to express the relationship as a chain of causes: the precipitation brings about certain humidity conditions in the soil that will ultimately influence yields of wheat in that area. We cannot even be satisfied with a single chain of causation; the precipitation is not the only significant factor. The nature of the soil, whether sand or clay, for instance, determines the extent to which the precipitation can be stored in those soil horizons where it is accessible to the plants. Other factors include the availability of nourishing salts in the soil, the development and use of improved plant varieties by humanity, and also fertilization. We can therefore build up rather complex cause and effect analyses using multiple regression or factor analysis (see Haggett, 1965, pp. 297–303) as tests of the relative weights which should be ascribed to individual factors in the system we are studying.

The general conclusion has been that causality laws are deterministic – that the cause is present, the effects will follow. If the effect does not follow the cause, the causal law must be rejected, according to this view. The association in geography, during the late nineteenth century after Darwin, between deterministic approaches and causal analyses, brought causal analysis into discredit later on.

Since the Second World War many students have come to realize that a causal analysis does not necessarily involve deterministic causal explanations. This point is made by Montefiore and Williams (1955) in asserting that determinism is really an act of faith, that causal laws are never absolutely true, and that they cannot be verified. In so far as 'exceptions prove the rule' we try to recognize the 'law' that has the fewest possible exceptions. In this connection 'determinism' is only a sightline for scientific work. The objective is to perfect each causal law as far as possible in order to maximize the *probability* that a given cause will lead to given effects. Calculations of probability have been included included in causal analyses to an increasing extent.

Temporal (or *historical*) *analyses* provide scientific procedures for describing or explaining phenomena in relation to their development over time. From one point of view, temporal analyses may be regarded as forms of causal analysis. History can be seen as a causal series which started at the vaguely defined 'dawn of history' and ends today. There have certainly been studies which sought to analyse a long process of historical development, but such explanations cannot be so precise as one would normally wish from cause-effect analysis.

Temporal analyses may be classified according to the assumptions of the research workers in the following ways.

(1) The investigator may assume that there is no provable mechanism which governs development. This has been the most common approach among historians and geographers whereby historical and geographical phenomena are regarded as unique. From such a viewpoint, the analysis becomes a description which does not try to formulate laws for development, but may however, provide a degree of explanation. Some situations are seen a particularly important and are discussed; others are excluded because they ar regarded as insignificant. There are special but not general explanations fo individual phenomena.

(2) The investigator may hypothesize that the observed development i governed by some mechanism. This hypothesis may be that time itself combined with certain natural laws, is a governing factor. Such approaches ar found in Davis's cyclical system for the development of land forms throug stages of youth, maturity and old age, and in Rostow's stages of economi development. The problem with these theories has been to relate the situatio in an individual region to the relevant stages of development unambiguously Rostow (1960) points out that some countries may find themselves in tw different stages of economic development at the same time. The Marxi theory of the economic development of society is another example of th approach, often associated with the view that the nature of development predetermined. We can, however, have temporal theories that are n deterministic. The problem is that a satisfactory calculation of probabili depends on the availability of quantitative data and a large number of simil individual occurrences. This is a general problem for temporal theories in t social sciences which can seldom be verified or subjected to statistical significant probability tests. In a theoretical social science like economics, it generally agreed that while theories cannot be verified, they may be regard as *valid* if they have predictive value. Even this weaker test of validity ca seldom be done under the ideal circumstances that are prerequisite for t theory. The testing of an economic theory in a given society will almost alwa be hampered by political modifications of the prerequisites. This is also true

many theories in geography, including economic location theories.

(3) Research workers may believe they have sufficient empirical data to state the existence of a form for the mechanism that governs development. In this way, single phenomena can be explained by a satisfactorily recognized process. We may describe a situation in terms of a law which states that an event is probably due to certain previous causes. The natural sciences have been able to establish such probability laws. Our knowledge of biological evolution, for example, is no longer just hypothesis but is founded, to a considerable extent, on the empirical results of research in genetics and the study of fossil remains of earlier life forms.

Although in-depth studies by geomorphologists in recent years have brought about a fairly comprehensive understanding of the processes which govern the formation of landscapes, human geographers have made little progress in the formulation of laws which govern processes: we would be wise to think in terms of hypothesis and theories in this area of the subject.

Both causal and temporal research approaches have and will be used in geography but changes in the philosophy of the subject during its long history have, to a large extent, regulated their employment. Some schools of thought have wholly rejected one, the other or both of these explanatory forms; other schools have devoted themselves to causal or to temporal analyses. Functional–ecological analyses and systems analyses have been more closely associated with the development of geography and will therefore be treated in more detail.

The geographical synthesis

In any discussion of methods, we are concerned with the logic of explanatory models, considering whether they are really tenable scientifically and if there is an in-built logical cohesion in our methods. When discussing the philosophy of the discipline, we are concerned with value judgements, including the metaphysical values upon which we may build a paradigm for the subject. We have seen in practice, however, that fundamental methods have been developed on the basis of metaphysical comprehension. Considerations of method, world outlook and the philosophy of the subject are so involved with each other that it is almost impossible to separate them.

The view that geography is a synthesizing subject has always been basic to the philosophy of the discipline. A belief in synthesis has been the teleology of geography, the purpose that justified the activities of geographers. However, criticism of the traditional regional synthesis developed alongside the quantitative revolution using the argument that methods developed in French regional geography cannot be applied to modern industrial communities (Wrigley, 1965). Harvey (1969, p. 71) maintained that the regional synthesis had been saddled with an unobtainable goal, whilst geographers were in fact working on systematic aspects of problems. Nevertheless, Dickinson (1970, p. 49) surely exaggerates when he maintains that quantitative geography 'does not concern itself with, and in America directly opposes, integrated studies of chorological phenomena in special regions'.

Modern quantitative or critical geography has not abandoned the idea of synthesis. Many of its leading research workers have been specifically concerned in a search for synthesis through new forms of analyses. Haggett called his general textbook *Geography — A Modern Synthesis* (1983). Bunge, one of the more prominent American 'critical' geographers, said (1973, p. 329) that geography is 'the integrating science, so we call upon co-workers in geology, sociology and so forth to discuss planning for a region or even the lesser labour of just understanding a region with no ambitions humanly to improve it'. Asbjörn Aase (1970, p. 13) questions whether geographers will not soon be required to resume discussion of the development of a new regional geography with new methods of attack. He points out that the planning of a modern society requires a good deal of research on the development of synthesis, but that this work at the moment is almost wholly in the hands of economists and architects, leaving geographers on the sidelines in their exclusive concern for systematic geography. Modern geography can, however, develop methods which can be used in the formation of regional synthesis. In Johnston's *The Future of Geography* (1985), many of the contributors, particularly Taylor, Bennett, Orme, Simmons and Cox, envisage a future for a holistic geography with physical-human relations at its core.

In modern geography the argument for the further development of a geographical synthesis is practical in character and goes along the following lines: society requires syntheses at different geographical levels. Geography has worked with practically all the relevant phenomena during its historical development and has devised methods central to the formation of syntheses The syntheses needed, especially in planning, will provide a basis for the development of the discipline and possibilities for new jobs for geographers.

Traditionally, however, the concept of synthesis has been associated with basic philosophical beliefs within the discipline. This is shown in Figure 3.3, which relates modern systems analysis back to the idea of regional syntheses and Ritter's concept of *Ganzheit* (wholeness). The vision of the great overarching unity of nature, held by both Ritter and Humboldt, was characteristic of the idealistic philosophical ideas of their time. All phenomena are related and have a role to play in this unity. Also, the 'wholeness', in addition to its linking functions, is something more than the sum of the parts - it is seen as an organism. Other subjects study single phenomena but geographers should try to understand the synthesis that reveals the 'wholeness'.

Functionalism and functional explanation

It is basic to this view that scientific analysis and understanding must be teleological - must analyse and explain individual phenomena in relation to their assumed purpose. A teleological explanation relates to the purpose of a phenomenon; a functional explanation relates to its function. Carl Hempel (1959) regards *purpose* as a wider concept than *function*, he considers therefore that functional analysis and explanation is contained within teleology. Other philosophers of science consider that Hempel gives too restricted a connotation to the concept of function. We shall restrict ourselves here to suggesting that teleological and functional forms of explanation are closely related to each other. What interests us is the close association between the traditional view of geography as a discipline seeking synthesis and the functional-teleological analyses and forms of explanation. It has been regarded as logically sound to make the synthesis, or 'wholeness', our goal, so that each phenomenon should be analysed with a view to explaining its purpose or function within the whole.

Early in the twentieth century there was a reaction in many disciplines against the simple and deterministic cause–effect arguments and forms of analysis which had characterized the nineteenth century. This welled up into what might be called *functionalist philosophy*, which sought to replace expressions of cause and effect with expressions which emphasized associations. It tried to develop functional analysis and explanatory forms to replace the *mechanical explanations* so characteristic of physics. The term 'mechanic' (from the Greek *mekhane* – arrangement or machine) is used in philosophy to characterize explanatory measures and world views which have used machines as models of both organic and inorganic change. The tendency to prefer functional to mechanical explanations was most marked in biology where attention was directed to complex organisms which must be analysed primarily as 'indivisible wholes'. A flower, for example, can neither be fully understood through an analysis of its stamens, petals, etc. in isolation, nor effectively studied only in its individual 'wholeness' but must also be related to the ecological environment within which it is growing.

There appears to be a range of phenomena which can best be described and analysed with reference to a 'unity' or to a 'system'. It is not because such a 'unity' or 'system' is necessarily governed by an overriding or predetermined purpose, but because individual phenomena must be understood in the light of functional associations and circular causations within the 'wholeness'.

During the first part of the twentieth century, functionalism characterized the outlook not only of biologists but also of many social anthropologists, notably Bronislaw Kaspar Malinowski (1884–1942), and sociologists. Functionalism also affected psychology and economics to some extent, eventually achieving a considerable penetration into those sciences.

Functionalism affected much geographical research in the late nineteenth and early twentieth centuries and philosophy was strongly interwoven with method. Wrigley (1965, p. 15), points out that some French regional geographers, notably Jean Brunhes (1869–1930), were markedly influenced by functional social anthropologists. Just as Malinowski regarded culture as an 'indivisible wholeness' from which an explanation for single occurrences might be derived, the individual region provided a 'unity' for the French regional school of geography. The region was considered to be a functional unit – an 'organism' that was more than the sum of its parts. Hettner and Hartshorne shared this philosophical viewpoint. Alongside his maintenance of the belief that the region is a functional unity that gives a 'wholeness', Hartshorne (1950) emphasized the need for a functional approach to political geography. Here we can seek a link with Ratzel's views (1897) in discussing the *raison d'être* of the state in terms of its 'cohesive geographical forces'.

In political science this was developed by Talcott Parsons in the 1950s and 1960s as the *structural-functionalist* approach connected with structuralism and systems analysis (see p. 138). A function in this connection is defined as an activity performed by a structure which maintains a system of which it is a part (a definition which requires a deeper understanding of system analysis to become intelligible). The essence of structural-functionalism 'is the system-maintaining activity and the functional approach allows widely differing societies to be analysed because it emphasises their basic functional characteristics which in turn, it is argued, are reflected in deep-seated relatively permanent structural characteristics' (Morgan, 1975, p. 291). The important point here is that the Parsons model has an implicit assumption of an equilibrium-seeking social system which contrasts it with the dynamic model of Karl Marx.

The methodological difficulties with both functionalism and systems analysis begin when we want to analyse influences that change the structure of the system. The Norwegian political scientist Rokkan (1970) has, however, developed Parsons's functionalist framework further to cope specially with the dynamics of the nation-building process, and so has demonstrated that functionalism and systems analysis are not necessarily connected with equilibrium rather than change.

At about the same time as the 'quantitative revolution', geographers began to distinguish between their basic philosophical beliefs and their use of methods which corresponded with them. Stoddart (1967, p. 519) pointed out in reference to functionalism, that the theme of organic analogies had once been very well developed in biology and philosophy, but it had long since been discarded there. Harvey also rejected the functionalist philosophy. In maintaining (1969, p. 445) however, that 'to attack functionalism as a philosophy is not, therefore, to attack it as a methodology', he also suggested that essential insight is achieved by establishing hypotheses of functional connections. The methodological strength of functionalism lies in its support of reciprocal relationships, conditions and feedback in complex systems of organizational structures.

Throughout the long history of geography, many basic elements in its thinking have been relatively stable. There has always been a view of geography as a discipline of synthesis. *Holism* has been there the whole time even if it has changed its character rather markedly. Once it signified some indefinable gift of God; now we talk of it in a methodological way as a functional system that can be subjected to systems analysis.

Before we look further at the most recent developments in geographical method, including systems analysis, we must inspect some of the divisions and difficulties of functional analysis. This is because an evaluation of functional analysis forms a necessary basis for the development of systems analysis.

The use of functional analysis

Functional explanatory models are very common in geography. New York can be explained in terms of its functions as a chief port on the eastern US seaboard, the chief financial centre of North America, and so on. Smaller towns can be 'explained' in terms of the function in a central place hierarchy. Such explanations are usually wholly verbal; they represent a form of description but do not produce any more firm evidence to support an argument.

In order to demonstrate how a functional analysis operates, we may take a central place or market that serves the needs of an economy for exchange of goods and services. Is this explanation sufficient? Central places may *seem* to exist for exchange purposes but may *really* satisfy men's needs to meet each other; the trade function is *manifest* but the social function is *latent*. How far, by asking which are the latent functions and which are the manifest functions, can we develop distinctive kinds of explanation?

In so far as goods and services can only be exchanged at central places, and that such exchange is a necessary part of the economy under investigation, the difference between manifest and latent functions is of no particular explanatory interest. Central places can be explained in accordance with their manifest function. Such a simple explanation is not satisfactory, however, where there are such functional alternatives as pedlars and tinkers. Where such alternatives exist, the central place may nevertheless be preferred. In such a case it would be reasonable to suggest the latent form as an explanation.

It often happens that there are several candidates for one function. A functional explanation of the location of a town or a factory, for example, is not usually a sufficient explanation. There are almost always other locations just as satisfactory for the purpose.

In most cases, functional analysis only demonstrates the *necessary* location conditions for a town or factory to flourish. It will seldom indicate which conditions are *sufficient* to make any one location the only possible location. Functional analysis can be useful in enabling us to discern some of the conditions necessary for a phenomenon to function within a given system. We cannot, however, ascertain both the necessary and sufficient conditions for a tenable and unambiguous explanation. There is no reason to overlook the functional elements in our attempts at explanation, but we must appreciate the possibility of logical weaknesses in the method.

Individual theoreticians of science have maintained that functional relations are to a considerable extent tenable only within systems that maintain and regulate themselves. The simplest example of such a system is a water-heating system regulated by a thermostat. The function of the thermostat is to register the variations in temperature and to signal them so that an even temperature may be maintained. If we try to imagine this function in terms of social conditions, we would restrict functional explanations to relative static communities where the functions help to support the inner balance of the system. Now we know that the communities geographers are most interested in studying have undergone major developments. A location that could have been explained by functional needs a decade ago is maintained today only as a result of *geographical inertia*; Pittsburgh and Lanarkshire can only be explained as steel-making centres in relation to the industrial location necessities and economic conditions of the nineteenth century. Harvey (1969 p. 437) maintained that these views on the logic of functional analysis should only be related to the version of functional analysis as defined by Hempel (1959, pp. 5-10). The latter defined functional analysis narrowly: 'the contribution that some item makes toward the maintenance of some given system'. It is also possible to define function as a mathematical expression between variables or as an *indicator* of their use-value.

Even if the concept of function is interpreted narrowly, functional analysis may be a useful point of departure for the formulation of individual theories and, perhaps more significantly, for research into alternative methods for the study of complicated systems and the structures of organizations. It may, for example, be useful to ask how central places function in an economy because this question raises a range of other questions and draws our attention to the complexity of the systems within which we work. Whether or not we are going to derive anything useful from functional analysis depends on the extent to which we can specify a system clearly.

Proposals to use systems analysis and therefore to make use of *general systems theory* in geography were put forward in a number of papers around 1970. Chorley (1973a, p. 162) said that the application of systems analysis 'greeted by some as a conceptual breakthrough and by others as a jargon ridden statement of the obvious, has at least served to highlight and rationalise some of the important and long-continued methodological difficulties which geographers have faced'. Systems analysis has been used as a methodological tool to build a new form of geographical synthesis. The role of men in the natural ecosystem is again presented as a common object of study for physical and human geography and 'geography as human ecology' has returned as a subject for discussion.

Geography as human ecology

While the use of a more formalized systems theory has only been introduced into geography recently, systemic thinking has been of much longer duration. The history of systemic thinking in geography is closely associated with functional analysis and the consideration of regions as complex organisms or unities and with a viewpoint of geography as human ecology.

The most obvious of the antecendents of systemic thinking was the school of thought which, at the beginning of the twentieth century, wished to define geography as *human ecology*. The ecological concepts we find implicit in the works of Vidal de la Blache are, however, rather different from those enunciated by Harlan Barrows in his presidential address to the Association of American Geographers in 1922 (Barrows, 1923), in which he considered that geography should concentrate on the study of man's associations with his natural environment. His main argument was that the subject had diversified too much and that specialized branches like geomorphology, climatology and biogeography should be separated from the subject, and that geography should concentrate on those themes that lead towards synthesis, with an economic regional geography occupying a central place. Apart from this he gave no clear directions about methods of research; for this reason, and because 'natural science' geographers exerted a powerful influence on the discipline at that time, these ideas made little impact on the 1920s. Barrows's paper 'Geography as human ecology' was, however, often cited later.

The concept of human ecology may need further clarification. *Ecology* (from the Greek *oikos* = home place; *logos* = doctrine) was first used by the German biologist and popular philosopher Ernst Haeckel in 1868. Biologists classify ecology as the study of the relationships between animals, plants and their environments. Ecologists should, from this definition, study the natural relationships whereby particular species of plants and animals are dependent on each other and on the non-organic environment (climate, soil, the chemical composition of atmosphere and water, etc.). The aspects of ecology that impinge on humanity's biological nature, and its relationship to the natural environment, should therefore form the subject matter of *human ecology*.

For many years, ecology had a somewhat anonymous existence in biological research. During recent decades, however, interest in ecology has burgeoned in the context of increasing concern about the protection of nature. These marked advances in biological research are largely due to the development of a new direction within ecology called *systems ecology* which studies the construction and function of the *ecosystem*.

An ecosystem (Figure 5.1) consists of the biological community at a specific place and the environmental physical circumstances that influence and are influenced by that biological community. The ecosystem is not only the sum of flora and fauna, water, air and soil, for the most critical element is the circulation within the system: the solar energy which comes in, the transport of water and gases, the change of inorganic material into organic material, growth and movement. An ecosystem may be defined for any and every geographical study region from a small puddle to the globe itself.

A significant result of systems ecology has been the development of

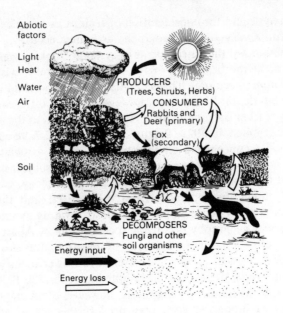

Figure 5.1 A generalized ecosystem (after Bliss *et al.*, 1969)

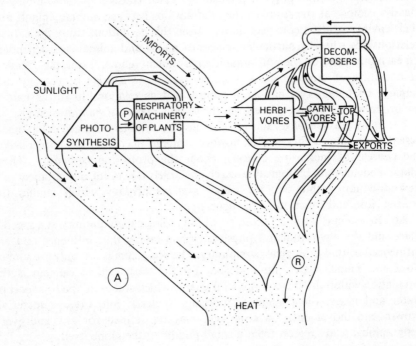

Figure 5.2 Odum's conception of energy flow (after Odum) 1960, from Stoddart, 1967)

perational models of circulations and relations between the parts (Figure .2), including the means of subsistence, within the ecosystem. So much new nowledge has been produced that radical revision of elementary text books as become necessary.

If we develop the slogan 'geography as human ecology' we must be aware of he tools of modern biological systems ecology which offer many pportunities for quantitative analysis. Aase (1970, p. 13) pointed out that, Individual quantitative techniques offer possibilities for registering variables f a physical geographical nature and of analysing them alongside social ariables'. He emphasized the necessity for a grouping of subjects that not nly study one or many factors working upon the environment within a egional framework but also have an overall view of both social aspects and ie way in which environmental processes operate.

Stoddart (1967) shows how the concept of ecosystem has four elements that iterest geographers. Firstly it is monistic: it brings together the worlds of an, animals and plants within a single system wherein the interactions etween the components can be analysed, to a large extent, by quantitative iethods. Ecosystem analysis, by emphasizing the functions and characteristics f whole systems rather than any particular relationship within them, bypasses iscussion of determinism and the conflict between physical and human eography.

Secondly, the ecosystem is structured in a more or less orderly, rational and nderstandable way. A particular advantage is that as fast as the structures of n ecosystem are developed, they can be checked and investigated. Thirdly, :osystems function: they include a permanent through-put of material and iergy. To make a geographical analogy, the system contains not only the erceptible lines of communication but also the goods and people who use iem (cf. landscape geography, pp. 36–40). Fourthly, the ecosystem is a type of :neral system that uses and can make use of general developed theories of 'stems analysis.

Stoddart maintains that ecosystem analysis gives the geographer a tool with hich he can work (1967, p. 534), though emphasizing that the model-building f the biologists cannot be carried over directly into geography. Chorley nsiders, therefore (1973a, p. 157) that 'the ecological model may fail as a pposed key to the general understanding of the relations between modern ciety and nature, and therefore as a basis for contemporary geographical idies, because it casts social man in too subordinate and ineffectual a role.'

When humanity began to clear forests and plough the land, the biosphere as changed from a system working in itself and for itself to a resource for one the species within the system. Humanity became a conscious manipulator of e ecosystem in order to develop the resources in which it was interested to eir maximum use. Chorley (1973a, p. 160) suggests that the ecosystems ologists study are characterized by negative feedbacks which almost always irt to work as soon as something upsets the stability of the system. In the

case of a rapid growth in the numbers of an animal species, nature hits back by
failing to supply nutrition for the increased numbers, and high death rate
intervene until the balance is restored again. The systems in which humanity i
an active participant incorporate stronger positive feedbacks. Human being
counter nature's rectification by conscious action. When the cultivation c
wheat in the drier areas of the North American prairies was about to result in
negative natural feedback, in the form of drought and dustbowl condition
the farmers, instead of giving up agriculture and allowing the ecosystem t
return to its original balance, continued to grow wheat although in stri
cultivation every other year. Humanity very often succeeds in replacing
natural ecosystem by a human-made one. The process of change and c
technical and economic development therefore has much greater significanc
for the analysis of the systems in which human beings participate than in th
systems analysed by biologists.

The ecosystem model has balance, equilibrium, cycling and stability as i
basic elements. Chorley (1973a, p. 161) considers that one of the fundament
difficulties facing the development of geographical research today is tha
geographers may become so involved in such concepts as to overlook tl
positive possibilities for the manipulation of resources and ecosystems. F
refers to Wrigley's characterization of the regional method of Vidal de
Blache (see p. 34) and maintains that the Industrial Revolution has made tl
ecological model inappropriate as a basis for the study of modern industri
communities.

The ecosystem model, Chorley maintains, will be of geographic
significance in so far as humanity can be said to function in the same way
other species. It loses significance to the extent that human beings succeed
manipulating nature. The use of the ecosystem concept in geographic
analysis raises two important questions: are our human systems so much mo
complex than the biological parts of ecosystems as to limit seriously tl
geographical use of the model? If so, to what extent does humanity control tl
system within which it lives?

To the first of these questions a biologist will definitely answer no, huma
made systems are much less complex than natural ecosystems; in
manipulation of nature humanity always simplifies it. In biological terms,
Mid-West wheat field, because of the dominance of one species, is mu
simpler than the natural prairie it succeeded, and an important ecologic
observation is that simple ecosystems are much more liable to negati
feedback than complex natural ecosystems. This is also a problem with t
town, surely the most manipulated of all ecosystems. Here, simplificati
creates a lot of dead ends. Sewage, for example, is channelled into what wou
be called a dead end in a systems analysis, that is, a limited recipient th
cannot transform and recirculate the organic matter, a resource that is th
lost. Most pollution problems are of a similar character, resulting fro
humanity's manipulation and simplification of the natural ecosystem,

creating dead ends and ultimately serious negative feedbacks. In this process valuable resources for humankind are depleted. Humanity may be able to control the system, but if it wants to avoid serious repercussions in the long run, it would be wise to work *with* nature and not against it. The ecosystem approach is of real value in this connection.

This brings us to the current debate about environmental values and the use of resources. Geographers have largely been left out of this debate so far, partly because of the shadow cast by the unproductive conflict between possibilism and determinism during the early twentieth century. I think personally that geographers are so afraid of being branded determinists that there is little risk, as Chorley suggests, that geographers will become indoctrinated with oversimplified ecosystem models and apply them uncritically to social systems. I believe there is a greater danger that the development of the subject will come to a dead end because we do not dare to use what we can of ecosystem analysis and the concepts associated with it. Use of the quantitative models which seemed to be working well in the 1960s may lead us to link ourselves too closely with the models and concepts of economics.

Chisholm (1975, p. 52) points out that the trouble with economics is that many of its theories, though logically consistent, are difficult to verify. The field of economics is littered with elegantly and logically constructed but non-operative theories of economic growth and development. Similar comments might be made about many theories geographers derived from economics in the wake of the quantitative revolution. We may note 'the inadequacies of location theory and the unresolved dispute as to whether urban hierarchies should be based on a $K = 3$, $K = 4$, or $K = 7$ system' (Chisholm, 1975, p. 51). The danger with economics and also with geographical research, which has been modelled on economic theory, is that in order to achieve intellectual rigour we have to assume away many inconvenient complications. Then we suddenly realize these complications may be the main issues. Some of the complications might be analysed better through ecological models, although it is quite clear that these also have their limitations. It is important for us as geographers, that our discipline, with its traditional links with both natural and social sciences, is in a rather good position to exploit the interesting and important themes of conflict between what is ecologically desirable and what is economically advantageous.

Individual geographers have tried to bring theories from ecosystem analysis to bear on problems of the interaction of human beings with nature. Eyre, in his book *The Real Wealth of Nations* (1978), criticizes Adam Smith's (1776) view that the wealth of a nation is solely the amount and quality of the labour it possesses and the efficiency with which it sets it to work. Smith's point of view might have been reasonable in 1776, states Eyre, but today the supply of natural resources will increasingly be the crucial problem. So Eyre proceeds in an ambitious attempt to provide a calculation of the natural resource wealth of the earth and its nations. Simmons provides an understanding of humanity's effects on the biosphere in his textbook *Biogeography* (1979). In another book (1974, 1981) he presents an overview of the ecosystems of the world ranging from those least affected by men to the most urbanized systems. Simmons points out (1974, p. 35) that both economists and ecologists are putting forward theories which are necessary for the understanding of the relationships between humanity and nature. It is the concepts of the economist, however, that dominate our outlook today.

> The perspectives of ecology are different from those of economics, for they stress limits rather than continued growth, stability rather than continuous development, and they operate on a different time scale, for the amortization period of capital is replaced by that of evolution of ecosystems and of organisms. So some reconciliation of the two systems of thought might be held to be desirable in which the findings of one science might be translated with some precision into its impact upon the other, and the values suggested by ecology might become operational *dicta* of economics and vice versa.

Those who describe geography as human ecology have often defined the concept too narrowly and have presented studies of humanity's relationship to its environment as if it only encompasses humanity's relationship to nature and not to its total physical and social environment. For the individual, the environment is much more than just nature. Kirk (1963, p. 364) has described the geographical environment in terms which may possibly provide a useful starting point for a discussion of systems in which both ecological and social science theories and concepts may be relevant.

Figure 5.3 lists the factors we may need to consider in such an analysis, but the diagram gives us no guidance in the development of operational models for ecosystems dominated by humankind, or simply for systems where natural,

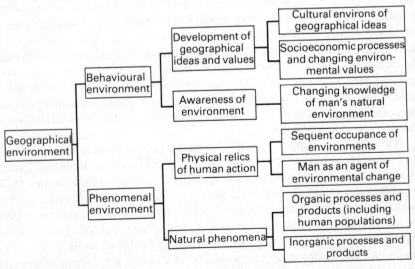

Figure 5.3   Geography and the environment (from Kirk, 1963)

economic and social factors interact. Everyone agrees that all such systems are rather complicated, but in order to obtain a better insight into the behavioural environment of humankind we would need to consider the humanistic and structuralistic approaches discussed in Chapter 4. Kirk's model might profitably be compared with the realist model in Figure 4.3c (p. 113). Figure 5.4 attempts to accommodate Kirk's model and a realist model. The

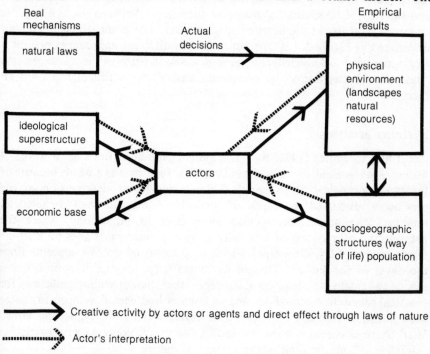

Creative activity by actors or agents and direct effect through laws of nature

Actor's interpretation

Figure 5.4 A developed realist explanatory model

'phenomenal environment', the natural phenomena and physical relics of human actions, are of course, a part of the empirical world. Kirk's 'awareness of environment' is involved in the agent's interpretation of the physical environment. The empirical world or level also comprises a number of socio-geographic patterns of welfare, demographic structure, political divisions, etc., which are important for interpretation and action. If in Kirk's model, we exclude 'human populations' from the factors affecting 'natural phenomena' those laws of nature are singled out which, 'in principle', create those parts of the phenomenal environment that are independent of man. We say 'in principle' because, as we shall show later, many natural processes are modified or frustrated by human action. Figure 5.4 places the human actor (the agent) in a central position. Creative action and the actor's interpretations are clearly stressed. Kirk also stresses the 'cultural environs of geographical ideas' and 'changing geographical values' which correspond to the ideological base, or superstructure, whereas 'socio-economic processes' are related to the economic base. We may here see the contours of a system model, possibly bridging the differences between empiricist, structuralist and humanistic approaches.. The study of results forms the core of empiricist research: interpretations by the individual agent are the main concerns of humanists, and the role of 'mechanisms' acting as chamshafts between the real and the empirical level lies at the heart of structuralism. The point stressed here and underlined in Figure 5.4 is that none of these different approaches present a single true road to knowledge; an accommodation between them is necessary. And so is a better knowledge of systems analysis, of which Figure 5.4 is an example.

Systems analysis

According to James (1972, p. 11), a *system* may be defined as 'a whole (a person, a state, a culture, a business firm) that functions as a whole because of the interdependence of its parts'. This sounds like a new version of the previously discussed concepts of organism and *Ganzheit* (wholeness, totality). The connection is also quite clear in philosophy, where the presentation of a system of internally cross-connected parts goes back to the Greek philosophers. Geographers have used forms of systems concepts since the dawn of the subject. Despite its venerability, a systemic approach has tended to remain a philosophical concept rather than providing guidelines for practical research. No methods and techniques had been developed to enable the analysis of complex systems in an accurate way before the Second World War. Systems concepts were invoked in descriptive concepts with particular reference to consideration of the balance of nature.

The first *general systems theory* was put forward by Ludwig von Bertalanffy, who began his professional career as a biologist during the 1920s. In biology he discovered that colleagues tried to increase their knowledge of the nature of organisms by dissecting them into smaller and smaller parts. It struck him that, until we study the individual organism as a system of multifarious associated parts we would not really understand the laws that govern the life of that organism. After a while, he realized that this idea could be extended to non-biological systems and that these systems had many common characteristics over a range of sciences. It was possible to develop a general systems theory that gave the same analytical framework and procedure for all sciences. A general system is a higher-order generalization of a multiplicity of systems individual sciences have recognized. Von Bertalanffy saw general systems theory as a way of uniting the sciences, but when he presented this idea at a philosophical seminar in Chicago in 1937, the academic world was not ready for such a theory.

At that time the tendency was to concentrate on detailed investigation of separate phenomena and scholars were sceptical of general theories. Physics was almost the only science concerned with general theory. The majority of research workers at that time were looking for cause–effect explanations. Since the Second World War, however, the growing quantity of multidisciplinary research attempts to investigate more complex phenomena, and the development of statistical methods and computer technology, have prepared science for general systems theory.

The development of *cybernetics* (from the Greek *kybernete* = helmsman) is particularly relevant here. This new branch of science was founded in 1949 by a group of American scholars led by the mathematician and physicist Norbert Wiener, and may be defined as the study of regulating and self-regulating mechanisms in nature and technology. A *regulatory mechanism* follows a programme, a prescribed course of action that produces a predetermined operation. A water tap is a simple regulatory mechanism, and a thermostat is a *self-regulating mechanism* normally used to maintain a predetermined level of operation constant. In nature, there are a very large number of self-regulating mechanisms, such as the automatic regulation of body temperature. Wiener believed that these self-regulating mechanisms follow certain common laws and that they can be described mathematically in the same way. Whilst the regulation is very precise in nature, in human societies it is defective. Wiener considered that cybernetics could also be used in economic and political fields and that only by using cybernetics could humanity achieve good government.

Cybernetics is primarily concerned with the control mechanisms in systems and with communication processes which determine their successful working. It places emphasis on the interaction between components rather than making sharp distinctions between cause and effect. Between two components, causal mechanism may work both ways. An impulse that starts in one part of the system will work its way back to its origin after being transformed through a range of partial processes in other parts of the system. Part of the mathematical basis for cybernetics is found in information theory. Cybernetics is now regarded as a useful discipline for approaching the more philosophical aspects of general systems theory von Bertalanffy began to explore in papers and books during the 1950s and 1960s, leading to his most-quoted book *General Systems Theory: Foundations, Development, Applications* in 1968. To understand something of his theory we must have a more precise understanding of systems concepts.

The kinds of system we can analyse are abstractions. Every real system (such as a landscape) is indivisibly complex. A real system is composed of an endless number of variables that different research workers, with different aims, may, with good reason, analyse in different ways. We may form several different abstract systems from one real system. As a method, systems analysis concerns abstraction rather than truth. The system must therefore be seen as a useful abstraction or model that enables a particular form of analysis to be made.

The abstract character of a system is emphasized when we realize that a

system, if it is to be analysed, must be 'closed'. An 'open' system interconnect
with its surroundings. All real systems (such as landscapes) are open systems
When we analyse a system we can only consider a finite number of element
within the system and the reciprocal relations between them. The elements an
connections we are not able to consider in such an analysis must be disregarde
completely. We have to assume they do not affect the system. In the analysi
of a region, we can of course take into account individual influences and singl
elements not geographically located within the predetermined area or regior
The abstract system remains closed all the same because we enclose thos
elements and relationships in our conceptual model. The system is nc
synonymous with the geographically bounded landscape, but is congruent wit
the model we have made of it, represented by the elements and connections w
have chosen to enclose or consider.

In other words, we can only study a system after we have determined it
boundaries. This presents no mathematical problem since the boundaries dra
themselves in so far as some elements are defined as belonging to the systei
and some as lying outside it, although it is not all that easy to choose thos
elements in practical geographical research. The demarcation may see
obvious in some cases, as when the system is discrete and has well-define
connections with the surrounding environment. These connections can then b
built into the model or we may exclude them. As an example of such a systen
Harvey (1969, p. 457) describes a firm which functions within an economy o
the basis of a particular set of economic circumstances. When we analyse th
internal relations and elements *within* the firm as a closed system, we mu
regard these circumstances as unchangeable. To extend the boundaries c
the system so as to include the changing social and political relationships in th
society of which the firm is a part may well alter the result of the analysis. Sc
even in this simple case the drawing of the boundaries creates problems.

The necessity of abstraction and closing also applies to cause and effe
analysis and to more theoretical temporal analyses. When we say that A caus
B, we have determined that A and B shall be fixed elements that stand in
predetermined relationship to each other and that no other elements will affe
the connection. This means that we have determined a closed system around
and B. We can therefore regard a cause–effect analysis as a form of systen
analysis where the assumption of a one-way operation severely simplifies th
system and its reciprocating activities.

By identifying the set of *elements* we believe best describes the real syste
we can construct an abstract system in order to model a real situation. Fc
example, in a large industrial company engaged in several branches of activit
the head office and each of the branch offices form its constituent element
Mathematically expressed, the system consists of a set of elements $A = (a_1, a_2$
$\ldots a_n)$. To this expression should be added an element a_0 that represents tl
environment of the system. In this case, a_0 can be the economic system with
which the firm operates. We can then infer a new set of elements $B = (a_0, a$

$a_2 \ldots a_n$), which includes all the elements in the system plus an extra element that represents the environment. We can then investigate the *connections* between these elements. Analysing the company, we can see whether there are any connections between the branches, and, if so, between which branches, or whether there is only direct contact between the head office and the individual branches. We can observe whether the contacts go both ways and what the contact model implies. Let r_{ij} represent the connection between an element a_j and another a_i. If $r_{ij} = 0$, there is no direct connection between element a_i and element a_j. In our example this would imply that a particular branch has no contact with another branch. All these connections can be expressed as a new set $R = (r_{0n}, r_{02} \ldots r_{0n}, r_{12}, r_{13} \ldots r_{(n-1)n})$. A system (Figure 5.5) can therefore be defined in the following terms: every set $S = (A, R)$ is a system. In general, therefore, a system consists of:

(1) a set of fixed elements with variable characteristics;
(2) a set of connections between the elements in the system;
(3) a set of connections ($r_{01} \ldots r_{0n}$) between the elements in the system and its environment.

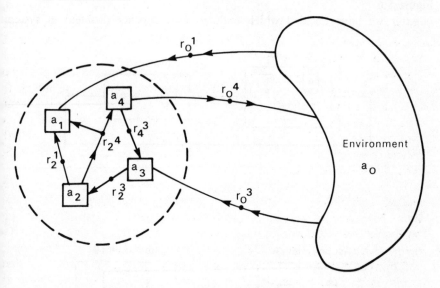

Figure 5.5 A system and its environment. The diagram shows links between the elements within the system (broken circle) and between the elements and their environment

We can study three basic aspects of every system: structure; function; development. The structure is the sum of the elements and the connections between them. Function concerns the flows (exchange relationships) that occupy the connections. Development represents the changes in both structure and function that may take place over time.

Elements are the basic units in the *structure* of a system. From a mathematical point of view an element, like a point in geometry, has no definition. A mathematical analysis of a system can therefore proceed without further consideration of the nature of elements, but we need to conceptualize the phenomena in such a way that they can be handled like elements in mathematical analysis. There are two fundamental problems here. The first is a scale problem; an economic system, for instance, may be said to consist of firms and organizations. Organizations such as trade unions are also themselves systems that include branches and groups of workers on the shop floor. The latter group is also a system of individuals, each of whom may be visualized as a biological system, and so on. Whatever we choose to regard as an element at a particular level of analysis, may also be a system at a lower level of analysis. This brings a host of problems with it. We can, for example, regard an element as an indivisible unit (like a branch in a firm resolving or acting on a resolution). A branch can also be seen as a loose association of lower-order elements (individuals in the branch who have contacts with other individuals in other branches). These two points of view are developed in Figure 5.6.

After we have decided which scale to use, another problem in system

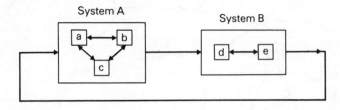

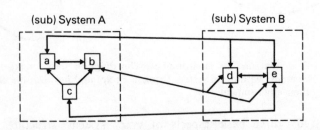

Figure 5.6   Systems and sub-systems. The upper diagram shows system A and system B interacting as units, with smaller system interactions going on within each system. The lower diagram shows systems A and B interacting at lower levels (from Blalock and Blalock, 1959)

uilding is how to identify the elements. Identification is particularly difficult *hen we are dealing with phenomena that have continuous distributions, as, >r example, when precipitation forms an element in a system. Identification is asiest with clearly separated elements, such as farms. In mathematical ystems theory, single elements are variables. In order to use the apparatus of 1athematical analysis we must often formulate an element as a unit whose 1dividuality we study rather than define it as an individual itself.

Further components in the structure of systems are the relationships or links etween the elements. We may consider three different basic forms of :lationship: a *series relation* (Figure 5.7) concerns single causal relationships

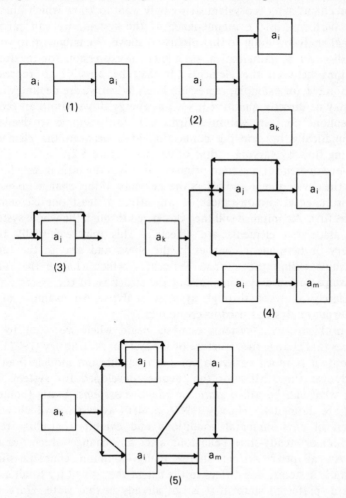

igure 5.7 Relations between elements in systems: (1) Series relation; (2) parallel relation; (3) feedback relation; (4) simple compound relation; (5) complex compound relation (adapted from Harvey, 1969)

that may be linked in causal orders. A *parallel relation* (Figure 5.7) occurs
when two or more elements affect a third or, inversely, when one element
affects two or more others. Such relationships are found in the more
complicated cause-effect systems (p. 123). A *negative feedback relationship*
describes a situation where an element eventually influences itself. These three
basic forms of relationship can be linked in a variety of ways in order to
construct complicated systems (Figure 5.7).

The *function* of a system is concerned with the flows, influences and
reactions within the network provided by its structure. Analyses of function
are concerned with the internal flow in the system, such as the energy flow
and food chains in an ecosystem. If we only want to know which function the
element performs in the maintenance of the system, we can carry out a
functional analysis similar to that discussed above. We may wish to go further
and to discover a mathematical or numerical expression for the functional
associations between the elements. It may be possible to represent the
association by, for example, regression lines. When we are dealing with flows
which may be directly quantified, such as energy flows within an ecosystem
and telephone contacts within a firm, it is fairly simple to display them
diagrammatically by drawing connecting lines between the elements and
illustrating flow by varying widths of arrows (Figure 5.2).

The *development* of a system primarily involves the influences which come
in from the environment and affect the elements. If any change takes place in
the environmental circumstances, it will affect at least one element in the
system at first. An impulse will then be carried through the whole system until
all the associated elements are affected. This may eventually result in
temporary or permanent changes in the flows and also in the functional
relationships within the system. Influences which change the functional
relationships within a system, but not the structure of the system, are more
appropriately analysed through systems analysis. An example of this is
input–output analysis as used in economics.

Our problems with systems analysis begin when we want to analyse
influences that change the structure of the system. As Chorley (1973a, p. 16)
points out, it is much easier to construct equilibrium models than models
changed over time. Most of the theories developed for systems analysis
concern what can be called *static* or *adaptive systems*. Static (homeostatic)
systems are defined by Harvey (1969, p. 460) as systems which resist any
alteration in environmental conditions and exhibit a gradual return to
equilibrium or steady-state behaviour after any change which has affected
them. An adaptive system shares many common characteristics with
homeostatic systems, but differs to the extent that it will try to alter its state
towards a 'preferred state' if it is not already in that state. Harvey (1969,
p. 461) suggests that these developments are most characteristic of systems
which have normally been regarded as goal-seeking. As a concrete example he
suggests that a preferred situation for a journey-to-work system is when the

emand for workers by a factory can be met from the working population of the neighbouring housing estates. 'If a rehousing project takes residences further away from an employment opportunity then the system adapts by altering the parameter of the distance function.' The system adapts itself to the new situation but without undergoing any real change in its structure. The theory of what Harvey calls dynamic and controlled systems is less well developed. In *dynamic systems* a feedback mechanism results in the system changing itself through a series of unrepeated states. Feedback can, for example, lead to a situation where new, preferred circumstances are identified. economic growth models can be seen as such dynamic systems. The problem with such models is, however, that they *only* exhibit the dynamic aspect. horley (1973a, p. 164) maintains that real systems are neither in equilibrium nor dynamic, but that they lurch from one non-equilibrium state to another. He suggests this is especially true of those systems geographers are most interested in studying, namely the ecosystems of the earth, which humanity constantly affects and changes. The ecosystems modelled by biologists are, however, to be classified as static (or to some extent adaptive) systems.

Geographers are primarily interested in studying systems whose most important functional variables are spatial circumstances such as location, distance, extent, density per areal unit, and so on. A system where one or more of the functionally important variables are spatial may be described as a *geographical system*. Although the majority of ecosystem models do not contain spatial variables, it is relatively simple to build such variables into this type of model. This signifies that geographical systems must easily allow themselves to be constructed as static or adaptive systems. It is difficult to make a geographical system dynamic for then we must combine time and space in the same model. Space may be expressed in two dimensions by cartographical abstraction, but when we introduce time we need a three-dimensional presentation. We may be able to present a satisfactory explanation for such a system but it is very difficult to handle and analyse. These problems have been thoroughly analysed in the presentation of *time-space models* which have recently been developed in Lund (see Carlstein *al.*, 1978).

Some problems may be solved by developing geographical models which may be classified as *controlled systems*, which are defined by Harvey (1969, p. 2) as systems in which the operator has some control over the inputs. *systems control theory*, which has developed within cybernetics, is based on such systems. Controlled systems are particularly useful in planning situations when the objective is known and the input in the economic geographic system has been defined. In most cases we can control certain of the inputs, but others are either impossible or too expensive to manipulate. If we wish, for example, to maximize agricultural production, we may be in a position to control the input of artificial fertilizers, but we cannot control the climate. Partially controlled systems are therefore of great interest. In future applied geography

might well focus on the development of models for controlled systems ar
attempt to show how spatial systems can be organized or developed by tl
manipulation of a few key factors.

Chorley (1973a, p. 166) maintains that 'the kind of geographic
methodology which . . . is increasingly necessary is analogous to that used
analysing a man-machine system. In the geographical context the "machine"
made up of those systems structures of the physical and biologic
environment which man is increasingly able to manipulate [either advertent
or inadvertently].'

Our increased knowledge of environmental conditions, as described in tl
biologist's ecosystem, leads us to appreciate the extent of the need for tl
development of planning and control systems. Many of the scientists engag
in research into possible future conditions fear that the positive feedba
mechanisms in the form of technological development and control which ha
led to an exponential increase in population, industrial production, etc., wi
in the long run, result in a dramatic crisis of pollution, hunger and shortage
resources. One of the causes of such a crisis would be the long-ter
suppression of natural negative feedback mechanisms (Meadows et al. 197.

Chorley suggests, however (1973a, p. 167), that this is unlikely to give rise
a situation where humanity loses its control over nature. It is important th
this challenge be met with new positive feedback in the form of better planni
and control – a task for geographers. Let us consider the Sahel catastropl
which is analysed in a systems model (Figure 5.8) by the Danish geograph
Reenberg (1982). She uses the model to illustrate the great number of possil
causes for the increasing desertification process in the Sahel belt of Afric
One possible explanation is climatic change (on the left side of the figur
Climatic changes may be due to such strictly natural factors as have operat
many times before in the history of the earth and may even have such speci
causes as increased vulcanism. Climatic change may also be induced by hum
activity through increased industrialization and pollution. The assumpti
that the increased desertification is due to climatic change can be test
empirically by a series of meteorological observations taken over time.

Geographers, having studied the Sahel problem, prefer the theor
presented on the right side of the model. Here it is not possible to postulat
simple chain of causes and effects since many of the elements intermingle a
work on each other in a complex way. Some elements are associated w
traditional ways of life in the region. Many tribes calculate their wealth
terms of head of cattle and so tend to overgraze. Other traditions may inclu
slash-and-burn methods of improving pasture and agricultural land, t
collection of fuelwood and the production of charcoal. As long as exter
influences were small, some sort of natural balance was struck, regulated
mortality in drought periods. External influences (called 'imperialism'
Figure 5.8) have encouraged the use of the more fertile parts of the region
the production of cash crops for sale in the more industrialized countries.

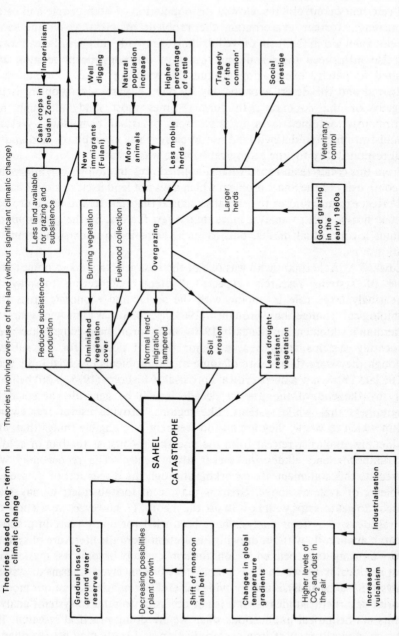

Figure 5.8 A practical example of systems analysis. Reasons for the Sahel catastrophe (after Reenberg, 1982)

the areas of subsistence agriculture have been reduced and pressures on these areas increased. Well-meaning western initiatives such as medical provision and veterinary control have allowed the population of both people and cattle to increase, further exacerbating the problem of pressure on the land. Development aid in the form of well-drilling to provide supplies of clean water has also influenced the wandering routes of the nomadic population and resulted in patchy overgrazing around the watering places. Vegetation is destroyed and the desert expands day by day. A particular problem is the 'tragedy of the common'. In former times most land, although not continuously occupied, was in some sort of tribal ownership. Western administration often defined land not in current use as common land and so local responsibility for the ecological balance was lost.

From this concrete and somewhat simplified presentation we can appreciate the complexity of the Sahel problem which does not lend itself to simple cause-and-effect explanations or to general structural theories. In a research project, we may not be able to analyse more than a few factors. So the *system model* remains a conceptual model, but, as such, helps us to understand complex relationships.

Edward A. Ackerman, who was one of the first geographers to point to the value of systems research, expected 'systems engineering to play an increasingly large role in coping with the social and economic crisis that technological change has brought' (1963, p. 436). Within ten years of Ackerman's statement, in the early 1970s, many prominent geographers were advocating systems analysis as a major field of activity for the subject although they were fully aware of some of the problems involved in its use.

The late 1970s saw a more critical appraisal. Chisholm (1975, p.36) believed that 'by the end of the present decade it will be generally accepted by geographers that while systems, like regions, provide useful framework within which to work, they are all too frequently intangible things that with maddening regularity retreat from the researcher – just as the bag of gold at the rainbow's end eludes the seeker after riches.' The reader may well appreciate this statement after working through the discussion of theoretical problems of systems above. Systems may seem too abstract; it may seem difficult to get to grips with how to use the theory. If, however, we see how the central ideas of systems analysis have been used for many years in practical research apparently without drawing inspiration from the literature of system theory or using its associated jargon, the concept may become less mysterious. Most practical work we do in geography may be conceived in terms of system analysis. Systems analysis may provide a useful systematization of our models, theories or structured ideas, but it is not necessary to refer to systems analysis and its mathematical implications when we are doing practical research. For instance, a world map of iron ore production and trade may be described in systemic terms: the elements are the producing and the consuming centres, the relations or links are the trading lines, the amount of iron transported along the different lines depict the function, and maps showing these situations at specific time intervals would describe the development of the system.

Gregory (1978, pp. 42-7) criticizes both systems analysis and general systems theory on the ground that they are intrinsically associated with positivism. The concept of one systems theory which is relevant for all the sciences may be seen as a fruit of the positivist concept of one science, one method. He is further afraid that the prominence given to control systems may lead to *instrumentalism* (see p. 105): 'In case this is misunderstood,' he states (1978, p. 45),

the sincerity or otherwise of the advocates of systems analysis is not at issue; rather, the positive conception of science to which they subscribe *in itself* entails a particular conception of practical life, irrespective of what their own intentions might be, and the connection with the two are determined by what Habermas describes as a deep-seated *cognitive interest* in technical control.

This is clearly a problem because it might be difficult to take care of the individual within the great system. In general we calculate and model average situations and build our control models on this basis, whereas the needs and opportunities of individuals and groups may deviate far from this average.

As to the political bias of systems analysis, as indicated by Gregory, we may refer to Harvey (1974, p. 270), who states that 'systems-theoretic formulations are sophisticated enough (in principle) to do everything Marx sought to do except to transform concepts and categories dialectically and thereby transform the nature of the system from within',

New advances within the field of systems analysis have been made and demonstrated by Bennett and Chorley (1978) and by Wilson (1981). Systems analysis is still a relatively young discipline and needs further development in order to handle complex geographical phenomena. In the words of Simmons and Cox (1985, p. 50), 'the ability of systems analysis to handle holistic ideas in geography is not yet proven, nor as yet disproven: as with other quantitative approaches it is premature to deliver final verdicts'. Simmons and Cox identify systems analysis as a 'quantitative approach' not because it necessarily depends on numeracy or quantitative data, but because a systems model (Figure 5.5, p. 141) is built upon mathematical principles. Mabogunje (1976) has shown that systems analysis is well adapted to give a conceptual understanding of rural–urban migration in developing countries. Quantitative data on migration patterns are virtually non-existent but this deficiency can partially be overcome by a systems model that presents the elements and relationships at work.

Description, analysis, prognosis

Asbjörn Nordgård (1972, p. 29) says that in the development of a science we can distinguish three broad stages: descriptive, analytical and predictive. Description is the first step and the simplest; it is concerned with the description and mapping of phenomena. The analytical stage moves a step further by looking for explanations and seeking the laws behind what has been observed. By the predictive stage, the laws have been studied so thoroughly that we can use models to predict occurrences.

During the 1970s, geographers suggested that the discipline was moving into the predictive stage. While trying to develop models for controlled systems which may be used to guide development in the future, Aase (1970) considered that geographers must involve themselves in the formation of planning syntheses. Chorley (1973a) argued that geographers should be concerned with the formation of controlled systems. Berry (1973a) recommended 'process metageography' and the analysis of complex systems as guides to decision making on environmental location conditions. Hägerstrand (1973) said that we must try to use our experience of translating the world into geometrical terms in order to develop a time–space geometry with particular emphasis on entering projects with a limited space budget and hoped that this might develop a pattern of future-oriented deductive thinking in geography not previously possible. Garrison (1973, p. 247) declared, 'While our current concern with systems and relations represents a high level of understanding, it is not nearly high enough. It must extend to the alternative scenarios that these and new relations might follow, and to the problem of choice among these alternative futures.'

Nordgaard maintains that, for geographers, the predictive stage is still far ahead. The nature of the discipline suggests a strong emphasis on reasoned description. Little by little, he hopes our explanations may become more precise and quantitative – so that the predictive stage draws closer (Nordgaard 1972, p. 29).

Bartels (1973) presents a schema (Figure 5.9) which, in a rather instructive way, shows the main stages in the development of geographical research from the descriptive through the analytical towards the predictive stage. Figure 5. may usefully be compared with Figure 3.3, p. 58). There is no need to add to what has already been said on the development of the subject apart from pointing out that the quantitative 'revolution' turned geography into predominantly analytical discipline and that this was the most significant aspect of the shift in interest within the subject which took place during the 1950s and 1960s. The predictive stage has hardly arrived yet.

Haggett (1983, p. 598) points out that the adoption of 'future geography' is something new amongst geographers. If we look at papers in journals, books and maps published by geographers in 1982 he says we find the majority relate to the world as it was in the early 1980s, the spatial models, ecological relationships and the regional systems which could be analysed at that time. Some of the research workers were involved in describing and interpreting the geography of earlier decades and centuries. Only a few research projects were about the geography of the future. Haggett illustrates this with a simple diagram (Figure 5.10). He explains the lack of treatment of comtemporar

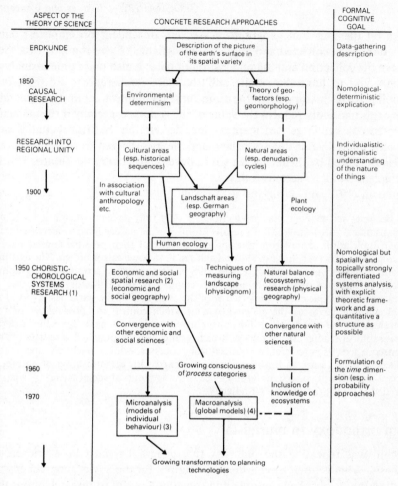

Figure 5.9 The development of research in geography (from Bartels, 1973)

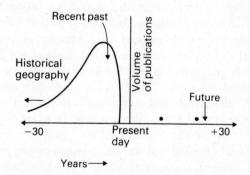

igure 5.10 The time distribution of geographical research. Most published geographical research deals with the recent past-very little is concerned with the future (from Haggett, 1983)

affairs by the fact that geographers are very dependent on empirical data which have been collected and published by officials. There is a long time gap between the collection and the publication of data; it also takes time to analyse the data and to have the results published. Research reports are therefore beginning to be historical by the time they are published. In our dynamic society this markedly reduces the value of the results, especially if the material presented consists largely of mapping and description. Statistical studies can have only limited value unless the laws and theories derived from them and the models suggested by them can be used to develop or govern the future. This is the challenge which faces us today.

Anuchin (1973, pp. 61–2) put it this way:

> It becomes self-evident that production can only fully develop when it is based on geographical forecasting. Man's means of influencing nature have so increased that their application cannot continue without a study of their possible consequences. Geography, however, has not shown itself ready to solve this problem. The existing main branches (geomorphology, hydrology, demography, economic geography etc.), in spite of their usefulness, are completely unsatisfactory when one i concerned with questions connected with the evolution of the variables involved in regional complexes of the geoenvironment which control the possibilities of the development of production. For this purpose one must have synthetic genera geographical studies, the results of which would provide practical forecasts of the consequences of interference with natural processes, which inevitably are taking place. It is necessary to have a science concerned with the utilisation of nature, a science which will connect natural science with the group of social sciences – what is needed is a geography without adjectives.

From orthodoxy to pluralism

Anuchin was repeating the old view that geography must be a science of synthesis. What is interesting is the justification, for the Soviet geographer was asserting that geography can only add something useful to research about the future if it can establish a geographical synthesis between humanity and nature. We should note, however, that when Anuchin (1960) put forward these ideas it led to the so-called Anuchin controversy within Soviet geography Other Russian geographers maintained that Marxist dogma precluded a synthesis of natural and social sciences and that the separate development of human and physical geography in the Soviet Union was derived from the classification of sciences made by Engels in the nineteenth century, based on the principles of dialectical and historical materialism. The Anuchin controversy, however, tailed off as the practical tasks of Soviet geography appeared to be more urgent than ideological discussion. Critics soon realized that the 'acceptance of physical and economic geography as two independent sciences does not prevent their overlapping and ability to merge in one complex' (Poksisevskij *et al.*, 1964, p. 154). The East German geographer Kohl (1968) suggested that the low public esteem in which geography was held was due to its subdivision into human and physical branches and suggested that there should be a dialectical understanding of the unity of man and nature. Gerasimov (1969, p. 51), a leading Soviet geographer, deplored the fact that geography attracted little attention in the UNESCO international research project 'Man and the Biosphere' despite the fact that geography sees the relationship between humanity and its environment as its main research theme. During the 1970s, research into humanity–environment questions became a focal point for Soviet and east European geography (Weichhart, 1980, p. 129). It is the main field of work for many departments of geography, and geographers also take part in many interdisciplinary research projects.

Whereas geographers in the communist countries have adopted a practical and pragmatic standpoint in relation to the problems of geographical synthesis, the adherents of the developing school of *Marxist structuralism* in the West are generally more dogmatic. The aim of Marxist geographers is to 'understand society within the knowledge framework of the only holistic scientific theory of human praxis: historical materialism' (Hurst, 1985, p. 60). The insights into nature provided by an empirically oriented physical geography have no value in this context. A human ecology approach can only retard scientific progress (Asheim, 1987).

Biilman (1981) suggests that from a dogmatic Marxist standpoint there is no place for geography as an independent science. Hurst (1985) is quite clear that historical materialism has no need of geography or any other fragment of social science as presently constituted. They must be rejected or reconstituted into one united Marxist social science. 'For geographers to become Marxists, they have as a professional or academic group to commit suicide' (Hurst, 1985, p. 77). Hurst criticizes Marxist geographers like Peet (1981) and Soja (1980) for trying to save geography through the advocacy of *spatial dialectics* or *socio-spatial dialetics* as new approaches. He maintains that these are mere fetishisms and are unscientific. Hurst also deplores the recent revival of the *anarchist* tradition deriving from Réclus and Kropotkin, into a modern *populist geography* or 'applied people's geography' as advocated by Harvey (1984). Harvey's proposal to activate theory and practice at the 'grassroot level' and advance the interests of the people in a truly democratic way is rejected by Hurst as idealist.

Hurst presents an extreme Marxist viewpoint on the merger of geography and other social sciences into a unified historical materialist science. Most Marxist geographers still find some virtue in a separate geographical science, but the majority of those in the West consider geography to be exclusively a social science. Gregory (1978, pp. 170–1) regards the idea of geography as a bridge between the natural and social sciences as more of a pious hope or useful excuse than as a serious proposition. One reason why geography has not developed this synthesis very far is that the natural and social sciences keep pulling it in different directions. Hannerberg (1961, 1968), though not a declared radical geographer, argued that the systematic branches of geography are separate sciences in their own right: it only creates logical difficulties to regard them as integrated parts of a synthetic discipline of geography. He states that the idea of geography as a discipline of synthesis is so general as to have no meaning in concrete scientific work. Even Johnston (1983b, 1986a) finds it to be philosophically indefensible to merge human and physical geography and regards them as more or less separate disciplines.

Simmons and Cox (1985), however, point to the findings of the physicist David Bohm (1980) that the explicit and manifest order of consciousness is not ultimately distinct from that of matter, implying that there is really no distinct dualism between physical and human science. Weichhart (1975) also argues that there is no reason to assume a fundamental conflict or indissoluble dichotomy between physical and human geography: there is no need to reject the unity of geography on philosophical grounds.

A geographical synthesis remains as difficult to achieve now as at any earlier period in the history of the subject. Granö (1987) believes that the difficulties we have had in establishing a clear-cut *disciplinary matrix* may be due to the way in which the discipline was institutionalized in the universities during the late nineteenth century by political decision. It was only then that geography was given a cognitive content by the first professors. They defended the infant discipline by trying in every way to emphasize the distinctions between geography and other subjects. With this in mind, the history of geography was extended backwards in time with particular reference to its *cosmographic* character. This was in line with the political expectations of governments and leading members of the geographical societies who had supported the establishment of geography at universities. At the same time the professors sought to prove their *scientific* abilities in relation to other scientists through advanced and specialist studies into such fields as glacial morphology and rural settlement patterns. The monistic unity of geography, observes Granö, was absolutely indispensable in order to justify its existence alongside other disciplines but it did not suit the thematic, discipline-oriented structure of the universities. Geography itself gradually formed a group made up of different disciplines with no single theoretical framework, although aiming at geographical synthesis in order to justify its separate existence. One of the most difficult problems of geography has been to create a model scientific treatment of humanity–environment relations.

For a long period, the discipline-oriented structure of the universities functioned well. The institutions were small and they trained *specialists* to become university teachers and for certain professions (law, medicine, etc.) and also supplied qualified schoolteachers for disciplines corresponding to those at university. It was only in countries where geography became an important school subject that it achieved academic status and respect by the general public.

Since the Second World War, traditional university research, constricted within the framework of its separate disciplines, has been increasingly supplemented by problem-oriented or applied research. Applied research is often grouped into sectors which reflect the organization of government funding bodies rather than the traditional university subjects. A new and interdisciplinary job market has been created at the same time as the number of traditional, discipline-oriented posts is declining in both universities and schools. In planning, for example, posts are advertised at national and local levels that do not specify training in any one specific discipline at the same time as the number of staff is being reduced in many university departments. Consequently, the discipline-oriented structure of the universities has come under severe stress. The essentially democratic decision-making processes of the European universities have retarded these developments but the hierarchical structure of American universities (soon to be imposed in Britain) has led to the closure of many single subject departments there and has facilitated the establishment of sector-oriented centres such as regional and environmental studies. To an increasing extent, the European universities, challenged by sectorally oriented education in other higher education centres (polytechnics in Britain; district high schools in Scandinavia), are lowering the barriers between disciplines and establishing new, integrated patterns of study.

Granö (1987) argues that these developments should suit geography very well since it has less easily adapted to discipline-oriented research than to the problem-oriented research fields the learned geographical societies have always supported. To the extent that geography has maintained its cosmographic structure within university institutions, it may be able to play an effective role in modern problem-oriented contract research, provided that geographers are outward-looking, active and ready to co-operate with colleagues who can offer different specialisms to their own.

The tendency of physical geography to become more involved in applied research is particularly promising in this context. Orme (1985, p. 264) points out that physical geography, while lacking any distinct status in so far as its raw materials are shared by other natural sciences, can yet play an important role by emphasizing synthesis. The task is to create a working synthesis of data based on geomorphological, climatological and biogeographical studies into a comprehensive expression of the physical environment. It is not sufficient to rest there. 'The physical geographer must also be practical and keen to apply findings to such areas as resource management, regional development and urban planning.' (Orme, 1985, p. 265). Exclusive specialist research on, for example, deglaciation processes in Scottish glens becomes less attractive to such a programme. Narrowly focused academic research is of declining relevance in the present job market for doctoral candidates. It seems, however, clear that departments of geography are well suited to work in a broad field of applied research and could profit from a working geographical synthesis.

A new synthesis?

Haggett (1983) has attempted to answer this question. He has tried to develop a new form of synthesis which diverges from the traditional division of the subject (Figure 5.11). He emphasizes that the historical divisions are important if only because universities use them as a basis for their courses. It is more valuable, he thinks, to divide the subject up in relation to the way in which it analyses its problems. The three new main groups are defined as follows.

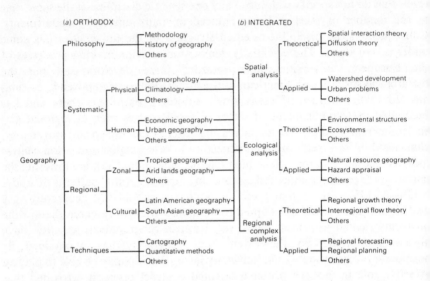

Figure 5.11   The internal structure of geography (from Haggett, 1983)

(1) *Spatial analysis* concerns itself with the variations in the localization and distribution of a significant phenomenon or group of phenomena; for instance, the analysis of variations in population density or poverty in rural areas. Which factors control the distribution pattern? How can these patterns be modified so that the distribution becomes more effective or just?

(2) *Ecological analysis* concerns itself with the study of connections between human and environmental variables. In this type of analysis we are studying the relations within particular bounded geographical spaces rather than the spatial variations between regions.

(3) *Regional complex analysis* combines the results of spatial and ecological analysis. Appropriate regional units are identified by areal differentiations. Connecting lines and flows between the individual regions may then be observed.

In the development of his textbook, Haggett (1972, 1983) has tried to arrange his themes under these headings. His work shows clearly, however, that satisfactory models for complex regional systems, let alone complex ecosystems, have not yet been developed. It is necessary to present models developed through spatial analysis within the traditional systematic branches of the subject.

Weichhart (1975) has made another attempt at a better organizational plan for the discipline in order to promote geographical synthesis. He refutes the notion that 'geography as human ecology' can form a leading concept for the whole of geography. Humanity–environment questions will only be part of the research field but need to become a more important part. Returning to Uhlig's (1971) organizational plan (Figure 1.3, p. 9), Weichhart (1975) classifies the *geofactors* which are the important elements of the *geosphere* into three groups: abiotic, biotic and human-induced. *Abiotic* factors are geology, soil, climatic features, ocean currents, etc.; *biotic* factors include vegetation, animal life and humanity as a biological creature; *man-induced* factors are settlement, transportation, industry, social structures etc. Weichhart (1975, p. 98) maintains that it is possible on this basis to recognise four problem categories (Figure 5.12), under which most possible geographical research questions could be grouped. In systematic geography, at the lower stages of integration, we describe and explain, possibly through spatial theories or laws, the spatial variation of the *single* geofactors, be they abiotic, biotic or man-induced. In this connection the other geofactors are taken into consideration only to the degree to which they influence the spatial variation of the geofactor under consideration. This contrasts with other categories of geographical problem where several geofactors are taken into account at the same time. We are looking for complex system relations that exist between several geofactors. Taking the current division of labour within the discipline into consideration, Weichhart (1975, p. 99) envisages three groups.

First it is possible to study the system relations between all or a number of the abiotic or biotic geofactors – geography as a physical geographical synthesis. The leading threads might include a nomothetic oriented typology of natural landscapes or a process-oriented description of the evolution of the landscapes in a certain region.

On the human side, we may study the systems relations between all or a number of man-induced factors, and may in this connection, seek inspiration from the *realist* model (Figure 4.3 p. 113). The catalogue of relevant problems would, however, be incomplete without consideration of the interrelations between abiotic, biotic and man-induced factors which constitute the man-environment system. Weichhart (1975 p. 98) makes the point that this does not imply that the totality of geofactors are brought into consideration. Geographical research has shown that the abiotic and biotic parameters needed to describe and explain the patterns of nature may not be identical to those needed to explain and describe the complex of relations between humanity and nature. Relief structures recede into the background; soil, vegetation and hydrological features become more important. Among human-induced factors, those which may be important to an understanding of social geographical structures may have little significance for the relations between

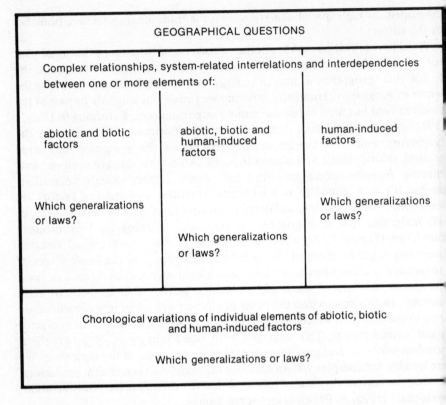

```
┌─────────────────────────────────────────────────────────────────┐
│                      GEOGRAPHICAL QUESTIONS                        │
├─────────────────────────────────────────────────────────────────┤
│  Complex relationships, system-related interrelations and inter-  │
│  dependencies between one or more elements of:                     │
│                                                                    │
│  abiotic and biotic      abiotic, biotic and     human-induced     │
│  factors                 human-induced            factors          │
│                          factors                                   │
│                                                                    │
│  Which generalizations                            Which generaliza-│
│  or laws?                                          tions or laws?   │
│                          Which generalizations                     │
│                          or laws?                                  │
├─────────────────────────────────────────────────────────────────┤
│  Chorological variations of individual elements of abiotic, biotic │
│              and human-induced factors                             │
│                                                                    │
│              Which generalizations or laws?                        │
└─────────────────────────────────────────────────────────────────┘
```

Figure 5.12   Problem categories within geography (after Weichhart, 1975)

humanity and nature. The study of humanity–environment relations i
therefore not the same as a total synthesis of all the geofactors (Figure 5.12
  The original German organizational plan for geography shown in Figu
1.3, p. 9), distinguishes between general or systematic *(allgemein*
geography, with its nomothetic aspects, and *special* or regional geography
with its idiographic aspects. Landscape geography is seen as a transitio
between the systematic and the regional. In real life, however, as Weichha
(1975, p. 100) observes, the general and the special are indissolubly joine
When we try to distinguish between them, we either fall into what Johnstc
(1985, p. 335) calls the *singularity trap* or into the *generalization tra*
Avoidance of either of these traps involves treating every place and region n
as singular but as *unique* products of individual responses to general processe
  For this reason, Weichhart (1975, p. 104), in his new organizational plan f
geography (Figure 5.13) makes no distinctions between general and spec
geography but contrasts *allgemeine Geographie*, focusing on the study of
single geofactor in a regional or global context, with *complex geograph*
which studies system relations between several geofactors in a regional

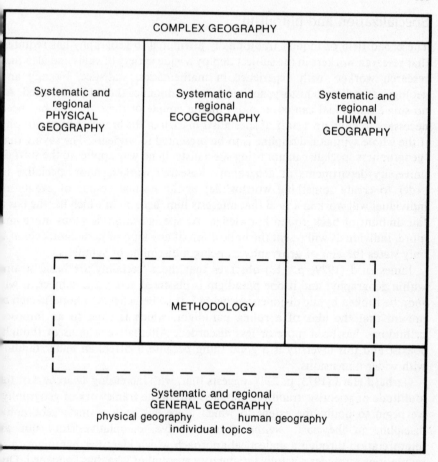

Figure 5.13 A modified organizational plan of geography (after Weichhart, 1975)

world context. Complex geography is divided into three parts corresponding to the grouping of problems in Figure 5.12 and does not therefore represent a total synthesis of all possible geofactors but only of those of importance for the chosen problem field. The field of *ecogeography*, which Weichhart believes is becoming increasingly important, studies the system relations between those geofactors of particular importance for humanity-environment problems.

While this organizational plan may not be the ultimate answer to the problem of geographical synthesis, it provides a useful framework for the sort of applied research projects of growing importance in geography. Many German departments use the threefold division of complex geography to provide a framework for those degree courses in geography which train planners for public and private service.

Specialization and pluralism

The broad field of inquiry traditionally attributed to geography has required that research workers in the subject deploy a wide variety of skills and also that research workers with experience in mathematics, statistics, biology and geology, as well as in history, sociology and economics should be recruited. As no single individual can cover more than a couple of these fields it has been necessary to build up a staff of specialists in each of the branches of geography if the whole synthetic discipline is to be presented to students. The saying that 'geographers specialize in not being specialists' in no way applies to the staff of university departments of geography. Research workers must specialize in order to create something worthwhile; in the normal course of events an individual will work in a field that interests him/her and in which he/she has a fair amount of background knowledge. As specialization develops more and more, individuals will resent the imposition of any kind of paradigm, even if it only states the aim of geography as being a discipline of synthesis.

James Bird (1979, p. 118) observes that there 'certainly are basic strains within geography, and if one paradigm is plastered across the subject, it will soon be broken by the disjunctions below'. It is, he believes, a hopeful sign at present that the idea of a ruling paradigm, which is close to an imposed orthodoxy, has been more or less discarded. Alternative schools of thought coexist and this diversity is a good thing because it offers an understanding with wider dimensions.

Gerhard Hard (1973, p. 237) suggests that, with increasing awareness of the multitude of scientific traditions pursued within the framework of geography we begin to doubt the extent to which there has been a single geographic discipline in the past. Neither a consecutive, cumulative story nor an interpretation through a dialectical approach which identifies paradigms and revolutions, provides a wholly satisfactory account of what has happened. Our perspective on the history of a discipline is always more or less influenced by the norms and outlook of the present generation. We see history from the standpoint of the present day. Whether we emphasize the continuity and gradual growth of a science or dwell on its discontinuities and revolutions, we tacitly assume a single line of progress to the present situation. Perhaps we should stress the heterogeneity of geography with its many-faceted and rich traditions.

Hard takes a fresh look at Fenneman's circles (Figure 1.1, p. 4); are the real geographers only those who integrate all the branches of the discipline in their research? If so, there are very few real geographers. Hard uses Venn diagrams to develop his argument (Figure 5.14). The first example, though simple, is not totally unrealistic, where the term 'real geographer' may only be applied to those who are committed to (a) geomorphology, or (b) cultural landscape morphology, or both (shaded on Figure 5.14 I). If, however, synthesis is the sole aim of geography, a 'real geographer' must study both the physical and

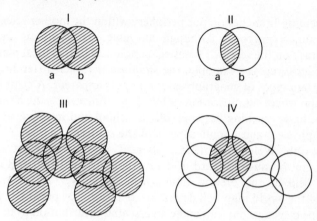

Figure 5.14 Different definitions of a 'geographer' (shaded). The circles symbolize closely connected research themes: a, geomorphologists; b, landscape morphologists I-IV are explained in the text (adapted from Hard, 1973, p. 235)

the cultural morphology of the landscape in order to qualify (Figure 5.14 II). If we consider the research themes actually being pursued by self-styled geographers, the figure expands (Figure 5.14 III) to include climatologists, geomorphologists, biogeographers, ecogeographers, landscape geographers of different brands, economic geographers, locational theorists, behavioural geographers, and so on. It is too restrictive (Figure 5.14 IV) to include only ecogeographers attempting a synthesis of natural and human factors among the 'real geographers'. Capelle (1979, p. 64) suggests that Fenneman's geography was an inward-looking discipline, whereas 'geography today has become outward-looking, although not aggressively so, towards compatible sister sciences on its periphery'. Hartshorne (1939, pp. 243–5) described geography as an 'integrative' discipline, but that is not the same as regarding it as an 'integrated' discipline. There is an integrative task of transmitting impulses from branch to branch within the structure, but there is no need to withdraw from the periphery.

We may still postulate a core or a nerve centre, but to regard regional geography as this core is no longer helpful. The core may rather be defined in Ackerman's (1963, p. 433) term as 'thinking geographically':

> To structure his mind in terms of spatial distributions and their correlations is a most important tool for anyone following our discipline. The more the better. If there is any really meaningful distinction among scientists, it is this mental structuring. It is one reason why we should approach analogues from other fields, as from physics, with the utmost care. The mental substrates for inspiration differ from field to field.

This mental structuring is our trademark and an integrative effort to keep all the fast-emerging branches on our periphery within the mother science should be our common purpose. Although an integrated synthesis may be an impossible task on the research frontier, in practical life, in local planning and in school education, for example, the situation is rather different. Here the need for certain types of geographical synthesis is apparent. A synthesis is also a realistic aim where simplification rather than refinement is the objective. For this reason, basic teaching in geography at school and in universities should cover both physical and human aspects of the subject.

I have, with Weichhart (1975), stressed *ecogeography* as integrative geography, not because I regard it as geography proper, but because it is an important field at the present time when humanity's use of the natural resources of the world may well determine its future. My personal view is that the discipline of geography can make an essential contribution to the planning of a future for humankind, and that in this context geography should base its analysis of humanity's activity more on ecological than on economic analogies. The reader may prefer another choice: there are a number offered. There are still, for example, many quantitative–positivist geographers who believe we should plan our future societies with the help of models derived from economics. A growing number of geographers, on the other hand, are discarding what they term 'neo-classical economics' and seeking a strategy for a new society through the development of a radical geography based on historical–dialectical methods and Marxist philosophy. Other critics of the 'quantitative revolution' have tried to establish what has been termed humanistic geography (Ley and Samuels, 1978). They have been criticized by Marxists who allege that the humanists are only trying to understand man and the world of his experience through hermeneutic methods, but that they are not committed to changes that are both possible and necessary.

On the other wing of the discipline, physical geographers try to explain the complex of relationships which form the physical landscape. As physical geographers gradually move into the realm of applied science, they may well have important contributions to make.

Perhaps none of these schools of thought will emerge as 'the geography of the future' but we should try to retain them all within the structure of the discipline. As to the future, we may add, following Bird (1979, p. 124), that 'the geographer will never be the master of his fate: his very reason always progresses by leading him into the unknown and unforeseen where he learns new things'.

References

Aase, A. (1970) Geografi og samfunn. Noen tendenser og problemer i dagens samfunnsgeografi, *Norsk Geogr. Tidsskr.*, Vol. 24, pp. 1–21.

Abler, P., Adams, J. S. and Gould, P. (1972) *Spatial Organization: The Geographer's View of the World*, Prentice-Hall, London.

Ackerman, E. A. (1945) Geographic training, wartime research and immediate professional objectives, *Ann. Assoc. Am. Geogrs.*, Vol. 35, pp. 121–43.

Ackerman, E. A. (1958) *Geography as a Fundamental Research Discipline*, University of Chicago, Dept. of Geography Research Paper No. 53.

Ackerman, E. A. (1963) Where is a research frontier?, *Ann. Assoc. Geogrs*, Vol. 53, pp. 429–40.

Adams, J. D. (1968) *A Review of Behaviour and Location*, LSE Graduate School Discussion Paper No. 20, London.

Anderle, O. F. (1960) A plea for theoretical history, *History and Theory*, Vol. 1, pp. 27–56.

Andrews, H. F. (1986) The early life of Paul Vidal de Blache and the makings of modern geography, *Trans. Inst. Br. Geogr. N. S.*, Vol. 11, pp. 174–82.

Anuchin, V. A. (1960) *Teoreticheskiye proplemy geografii*, Moscow.

Anuchin V.A. (1973) Theory of geography, in R. J. Chorley (ed.) *Directions in Geography*, Methuen, London, pp. 43–63.

Appleton, J. (1975) *The Experience of Landscape*, Wiley, Chichester.

Aquist, A. C. (1981) *Kuhns paradigmteori. Ett forsök till tillämpning på kulturgeografi*, Rapporter og notiser 61, Inst. f. Kulturgeografi, Lund.

Asheim, B. T. (1987) A critical evaluation of postwar developments in human geography in Scandinavia, *Progress in Human Geography*, Vol. 11, no. 3, pp. 333–353.

Bagrow, L. (1945) The origin of Ptolemy's 'Geographia', *Geografiska annaler*, 1945, pp. 318–87.

Banse, E. (1924) *Die Seele der Geographie Geschichte einer Entwicklung*, Braunschweig und Hamburg.

Barrows, H. H. (1923) Geography as human ecology, *Ann. Assoc. Am. Geogrs*, Vol. 13, pp. 1–14.

Bartels, D. (1968) *Zur wissenschaftstheoretischen Grundlegung einer Geographie des Menschen*, Beihefte zur geographische Zeitschrift, 19 F, Steiner, Wiesbaden.

Bartels, D. (1973) Between theory and metatheory, in R. J. Chorley (ed.) *Directions in Geography*, Methuen, London, pp. 23–42.

Beck, H. (1982) *Grosse Geographen. Pioniere–Aussenseiter–Gelehrte*, Dietrich Reimer Verlag, Berlin.

Bennett, R. J. (1985) Quantification and relevance, in R. J. Johnston (ed.) *The future of geography*, Methuen, London, pp. 211–224.

Bennett, R. J. and Chorley, R. J. (eds.) (1978) *Environmental Systems: Philosophy Analysis and Control*, Methuen, London.

Bennett, R. J. and Wrigley, N. (eds.) (1981) *Quantitative Geography: A British View* Routledge & Kegan Paul, London.

Beresford, M. (1951) The lost villages of medieval England, *Geogr. J.*, Vol. 117, pp 129–47.

Bernal, J. D. (1969) *Science in History:* Vol. 4, *The Social Sciences: Conclusion*, C. A Watts, London.

Berry, B. J. L. (1973a) A paradigm for modern geography, in R. J. Chorley (ed. *Directions in Geography*, Methuen, London, pp. 3–21.

Berry, B. J. L. (1973b) *The Human Consequences of Urbanization*, Macmillan London.

Berry, B. J. L. (1974) Review of D. Harvey *Social Justice and the City*, *Antipode*, Vol 6, pp. 142–5, 148.

Biilman, O. (1981) *Geografi, tradisjoner og perspektiver*, Geografforlaget, Brenderup

Bird, J. (1975) Methodological implications for geography from the philosophy of K R. Popper, *Scottish Geogr. Mag.*, Vol. 91, pp. 153–63.

Bird, J. (1977) Methodology and philosophy, *Progress in Human Geogr.*, Vol. 1, pp 104–10.

Bird, J. (1979) Methodology and philosophy, progress report, *Progress in Human Geography*, Vol. 3, pp. 117–20.

Blalock, H. M. and Blalock, A. (1959) Toward a clarification of systems analysis in th social sciences, *Philosophy Sci.*, Vol. 26, pp. 84–96.

Bliss, L. W. *et al*, (1969) *Laboratory Manual for General Botany*, 4th edn, Ho Rinehart & Winston, New York.

Bobek, H. and Schmithüsen, J. (1949) Die Landschaft im logischen System d Geographie, *Erdkunde*, Vol. 3, pp.112–20.

Bohm, D. (1980) *Wholeness and implicate order*, Routledge & Kegan Paul, London

Braithwaite, R. B. (1953) *Scientific Explanation*, Cambridge University Press.

Breitbart, M. M. (1981) Peter Kropotkin, the anarchist geographer, in D. R. Stoddar *Geography, Ideology and Social Concern*, Blackwell, Oxford, pp. 134–53.

Broek, J. O. M. (1965) *Geography, its Scope and Spirit*, Merrill, Colombus, Ohio.

Broek, J. O. M. and Webb, J. W. (1973) *A Geography of Mankind*, McGraw-Hi New York.

Brown, E. H., (ed.) (1980) *Geography, Yesterday and Tomorrow*, Oxford Universi Press.

Brunhes, J. (1912) *La geographie humaine, essai de classification positive, principes exemples*, Paris.

Bunge, W. (1962) *Theoretical Geography* (2nd edn 1966) Lund Studies in Geograph Ser. C1 (Lund, Sweden: Gleerup).

Bunge, W. (1973) Ethics and logic in geography, in R. J. Chorley (ed.) *Directions Geography*, London, Methuen, pp. 371–81.

Burton, I. (1963) The quantitative revolution and theoretical geography, *Canadi Geogr.*, Vol. 7, pp. 151–62.

Buttimer, A. (1978) Charisma and context: the challenge of la Géographie Humaine, D. Ley and M. S. Samuels (eds.) *Humanistic Geography, Prospects and Problen* Maaroufa Press, Chicago, pp. 58–76.

Buttimer, A. (1981) On people, paradigms and 'progress' in geography, in D. R. Stoddart (ed.) *Geography, Ideology and Social Concern,* Blackwell, Oxford, pp. 81–98.

Buttimer, A. (1983) *The Practice of Geography,* Longmans, London and New York.

Buttimer, A. and Seamon, D. (eds.) (1980) *The Human Experience of Space and Place,* Croom Helm, Beckenham.

Capel, H. (1981) Institutionalization of geography and strategies of change, in D. R. Stoddart (ed.) *Geography, Ideology and Social Concern,* Blackwell, Oxford, pp. 37–69.

Capelle, R. B. jr (1979) On the periphery of geography, *J. Geog.,* Vol. 78, pp. 64–8.

Carlstein, T. *et al.* (1978) *Timing Space and Spacing Time* (3 Vols.), Arnold, London.

Chabot, G. (1950) Les conceptions françaises de la science géographique, *Norsk Geogr. Tidsskr.,* Vol. 12, pp. 309–21.

Chisholm, M. (1975) *Human Geography: Evolution or Revolution?* Pelican, Harmondsworth.

Chorley, R. J. (1973a) Geography as human ecology, in R. J. Chorley (ed.) *Directions in Geography,* Methuen, London, pp. 155–69.

Chorley, R. J. (ed.) (1973b) *Directions in Geography,* Methuen, London.

Chorley, R. J. and Haggett, P. (eds.) (1965) *Frontiers in Geographical Teaching,* Methuen, London.

Chorley, R. J. and Haggett, P. (eds.) (1967) *Models in Geography,* Methuen, London.

Christaller, W. (1933) Die zentralen Orte in Süddeutschland, Jena, English trans. C. W. Baskin (1966) *Central Places in Southern Germany,* Prentice-Hall, Englewood Cliffs, N. J.

Christaller, W. (1968) Wie ich zur der Theorie derzentralen Orte gekommen bin, *Geog. Z.,* Vol. 56, pp. 88–101.

Claval, P. (1980) Epistemology and the history of geographical thought, *Prog. Human Geog.,* Vol. 4, pp. 371–84.

Coates, B. E. and Rawstron, E. M. (1971) *Regional Variations in Britain,* Batsford, London.

Coates, B. E., Johnston, R. J. and Knox, P. L. (1977) *Geography and Inequality,* Oxford University Press.

Collingwood, R. (1946) *The Idea of History,* Oxford Unviversity Press.

Cornu, A. (1955) *Marx et Engels,* Presses Universitaires de France, Paris.

Darwin, C. (1859) *The Origin of Species,* London.

Davies, W. K. (1972) *The Conceptual Revolution in Geography,* University of London Press.

Demangeon, A. (1905) *La Picardie et les régions voisines, Artois, Cambresis, Beauvaises,* Armand Colin, Paris.

Dickinson, R. E. (1939) Landscape and society, *Scot. Geog. Mag.,* Vol. 55, pp. 1–14.

Dickinson, R. E. (1969) *The Makers of Modern Geography,* Routledge & Kegan Paul, London.

Dickinson, R. E. (1970) *Regional Ecology, the Study of Man's Environment,* Wiley, New York.

Dray, W. H. (1966) *Laws and Explanation in History,* Oxford University Press.

Dunbar, G. S. (1981) Elisée Réclus, an anarchist geographer, in D. R. Stoddart, (ed.) *Geography, Ideology and Social Concern,* Blackwell, Oxford, pp. 154–64.

Duncan, J. S. (1985) Individual action and political power: a structuration perspective, in R. J. Johnston (ed.) *The Future of Geography,* Methuen, London, pp. 174–89.

Entrikin, N. J. (1976) Contemporary humanism in geography, *Ann. Assoc. Am. Geogrs.,* Vol. 66, pp. 615–32.

Eyre, S. R. (1978) *The Real Wealth of Nations,* Arnold, London.

Fawcett, C. B. (1919) *The Provinces of England* (rev. edn 1960), Hutchinson, London.

Febvre, L. (1922) *La terre et l'evolution humaine,* in the series *L'Evolution de l'Humanité, Paris,* English trans. 1925, *A Geographical Introduction to History,* Knopf, London.

Fenneman, N. M. (1919) The circumference of geography, *Ann. Assoc. Am. Geogrs.,* Vol. 9, pp. 3–11. Reprinted in F. E. Dohrs, L. M. Sommers and D. R. Petterson (eds.) (1958) *Outside Readings in Geography,* Crowell, New York, pp. 2–10.

Fischer, E., Campbell, R. D. and Miller, E. S. (1969) *A Question of Place: The Development of Geographic Thought,* Beatty, Arlington, Virginia.

Fochler-Hauke, G. (ed.) (1959) *Geographie,* Das Fischer Lexikon, Frankfurt.

Forer, P. (1978) A place for plastic space, *Progr. Human Geog.,* Vol. 2, pp. 230–67.

Freeman, T. W. (1961) *A Hundred Years of Geography,* Duckworth, London.

Freeman, T. W. (1980) The Royal Geographical Society and the development of geography, in E. H. Brown (ed.) *Geography, Yesterday and Tomorrow,* Oxford University Press, pp. 1–99.

Freeman, T. W. and Pinchemel, P. (eds.) (1978) *Geographers, Bibliographical Studies,* Vol. 2, Mansell, London.

Freeman, T. W. and Pinchemel, P. (eds.) (1980) *Geographers, Bibliographical Studies,* Vol. 4, Mansell, London.

Garrison, W. L. (1959–60) Spatial structure of the economy, *Ann. Assoc. Am. Geogrs* Vol. 49, pp. 232–9, 471–82; Vol. 50, pp. 357–73.

Garrison, W. L. (1973) Future geographies, in R. J. Chorley (ed.) *Directions in Geography,* Methuen, London, pp. 237–49.

Gerasimov, I. P. (1969) Die Wissenschaft von der Biosphäre und ihrer Umgestaltung *Petermanns Mitteilungen,* Vol. 113, pp. 49–51.

Gerland, G. (1887) Die wissenschaftliche Aufgabe der Geographie, ihre Methode und ihre Stellung im praktischen Leben, *Beiträge zur Geophysik,* Vol. 1, pp. 4–54.

Giddens, A. (1979) *Central Problems in Social Theory,* Macmillan, London.

Giddens, A. (1984) *The Construction of Society,* Polity Press, Oxford.

Giese, E. (1981) The development and present state of research into 'quantitative geography' in the German-speaking countries, in G. Bahrenberg and V. Streit (eds. *German Quantitative Geography,* Münstersche Geographische Arbeiten 11, pp 9–25.

Gould, P. and White, R. (1974) *Mental Maps,* Penguin, Harmondsworth.

Gradmann, R. (1931) *Süd-Deutschland,* 2, vols. J. Engelhorn, Stuttgart.

Granö, J. G. (1929) Reine Geographie, *Acta Geographica,* Vol. 2, No. 2, pp. 1–202

Granö, O. (1981) External influence and internal change in the development of geography, in D. R. Stoddart (ed.) *Geography, Ideology and Social Change* Blackwell, Oxford, pp. 17–36.

Granö, O. (1986) Finnish geography 1880–1980, *Highlight of the Decades,* University of Turku, duplicated.

Granö, O. (1987) Vetenskapens institutionella struktur och geografins utveklin *Nordisk Samhällsgeografisk Tidsskrift,* Vol. 5, pp. 3–8.

Gray, F. (1975) Non-explanation in urban geography, *Area,* Vol. 7, pp. 228–35.

Greene, T. M. (ed.) (1957) *Kant Selections,* Scribner, New York.

Gregory, D. (1978) *Ideology, Science and Human Geography,* Hutchinson, London

Guelke, L. (1974) An idealist alternative in human geography, *Ann. Assoc. Am. Geogrs.,* Vol. 64, pp. 193–202.

Guelke, L. (1977a) The role of laws in human geography, *Prog. Human Geog.,* Vol. No. 3, pp. 376–86.

Guelke, L. (1977b) Regional geography, *Professional Geogr.,* Vol. 29, pp. 1–7.

Guelke, L. (1978) Geography and logical positivism, in D. T. Herbert and R. Johnston (eds.) *Geography and the Human Environment, Progress in research a applications,* Vol. 1, John Wiley, Chichester, pp. 35–61.

Guelke, L. (1981) Idealism, in M. E. Harvey and B. P. Holly (eds.) *Themes in Geographic Thought*, Croom Helm, Beckenham, pp. 133–47.

Guelke, L (1982) *Historical Understanding in Geography: An Idealistic Approach*, Cambridge University Press.

Guess, R. (1981) *The Idea of a Critical Theory: Habermas and the Frankfurt School*, Cambridge University Press.

Hägerstrand, T. (1953) Innovationsförloppet ur korologisk synpunkt, *Medd. Från Lunds Universitets Geografiska Institution. Avhandling* nr. 25, trans. A. Pred (1967) *Innovation Diffusion as a Spatial Process*, University of Chicago Press.

Hägerstrand, T. (1973) The domain of human geography, in R. J. Chorley (ed.) *Directions in Geography*, Methuen, London, pp. 67–87.

Haggett, P. (1965) *Locational Analysis in Human Geography*, Arnold, London.

Haggett, P. (1972) *Geography: A Modern Synthesis* (3rd edn 1983), Harper & Row, New York.

Haggett, P., Cliff, A. D. and Frey, A. (1977) *Locational Analysis in Human Geography*, Arnold, London.

Hannerberg, D. (1961, 1968) *Att Studera Kulturgeografi*, Scandinavian University Books, Stockholm.

Hard, G. (1973) *Die Geographie, eine wissenschaftstheoretische Einfürung*, DeGruyter, Berlin.

Harris, C. D. and Ullman, E. L. (1945) The nature of cities, *Ann. Am. Acad. Pol. Soc. Sci.*, Vol. 242, pp. 7–17.

Hartshorne, R. (1939) The nature of geography, a critical survey of current thought in the light of the past, *Ann. Assoc. Am. Geogrs.*, Vol. 29, pp. 173–658.

Hartshorne, R. (1950) The functional approach in political geography, *Ann. Assoc. Am. Geogrs.*, Vol. 40, pp. 95–130.

Hartshorne, R. (1955) 'Exceptionalism in Geography' re-examined, *Ann. Am. Geogrs.*, Vol. 45, pp. 205–44.

Hartshorne, R. (1959) *Perspective on the Nature of Geography*, Rand McNally, Chicago.

Harvey, D. (1969) *Explanation in Geography*, Arnold, London.

Harvey, D. (1973) *Social Justice and the City*, Arnold, London.

Harvey, D. (1974) Population, resources and the ideology of science, *Econ. Geog.*, Vol. 50, pp. 256–77.

Harvey, D. (1984) On the history and present condition of geography: an historical materialist manifesto, *Pro. Geogr.*, Vol. 36, pp.1–11.

Harvey, D. (1985a) *The Urbanization of Capital*, Blackwell, Oxford.

Harvey, D. (1985b) *Consciousness and the Urban Experience*, Blackwell, Oxford.

Harvey, M. E. and Holly, B. P. (eds.) (1981) *Themes in Geographic Thought*, Croom Helm, Beckenham.

Hassinger, H. (1919) Über einige Aufgaben geographischer Forschung und Lehre, *Kartographische und schulgeographische Zeitschrift*, Vol. 8, pp. 65–76.

Hegel, G. W. F. (1975) *Lectures on the Philosophy of World History*, Cambridge University Press.

Hempel, C. G. (1959) The logic of functional analysis, in L. Gross (ed.) *Symposium on Sociological Theory*, Harper & Row, Evanston.

Henriksen, G. (1973) *Grunnlagsproblemer og interaksjon–en metageografisk analyse*, Hovedfagsoppgave i geografi, Geografisk Institutt, Universitetet i Bergen.

Hettner, A. (1927) *Die Geographie, ihre Geschichte, ihr Wesen und ihre Methoden*, Ferdinand Hirt, Breslau.

Hettner, A. (1929) Methodische Zeit–und Streitfragen. Neue Folge, *Geographische Zeitschrift*, Vol. 35, pp. 264–86, 332–44.

Hettner, A. (1930) Zur 'Stellungnahme von Seiten der Schulgeographie',

Geographische Anzeiger, Vol. 31, pp. 353–6.

Howard, E. (1902) *Garden Cities of Tomorrow,* London.

Huntington, E. (1915) *Civilization and Climate,* Yale University Press, New Haven, CT.

Hurst, M. E. E. (1985) Geography has neither existence nor future, in R. J. Johnston (ed.) *The Future of Geography,* Methuen, London, pp. 59–91.

Huxley, T. H. (1977) *Physiography,* Macmillan, London.

James, P. E. (1972) *All Possible Worlds: A History of Geographical Ideas,* Odyssey Press, Indianapolis.

Johannessen, K. S. (1985) *Tradisjoner og skoler i moderne vitenskapsfilosofi,* Sigma, Bergen.

Johansson, I. (1973) Anglosaxisk vetenskapsfilosofi, *Positivism, Marxism, kritisk teori,* Pan/Nordsteds, Stockholm, pp. 7–67.

Johnston, R. J. (1968) Choice in classification, the subjectivity of objective method, *Ann. Assoc. Am. Geogrs.,* Vol. 58, pp. 575–89.

Johnston, R. J. (1978) Paradigms and revolutions or evolution, *Prog. Human Geog,* Vol. 2, pp. 189–206.

Johnston, R. J. (1979) *Geography and Geographers: Anglo-American Human Geography since 1945,* Arnold, London.

Johnston, R. J. (1980) On the nature of explanation in human geography, *Transactions, IBG,* Vol. 5, pp. 402–12.

Johnston, R. J. (1983b) *Philosophy and Human Geography,* Arnold, London.

Johnston, R. J. (1985) *The Future of Geography,* Methuen, London.

Johnston, R. J. (1986a) *Philosophy and Human Geography,* 2nd edn, Arnold, London.

Johnston, R. J. (1986b) *On Human Geography,* Blackwell, Oxford.

Johnston, R. J. (1987) *Geography and Geographers: Anglo-American Human Geography since 1945* (3rd edn), Arnold, London.

Kant, E. (1946) Den indre omflyttingen i Estland i samband med de estniska städerns omland, *Svensk Geografisk Årsbok,* Vol. 22, pp. 83–124.

Kant, E. (1951) Omlandsforskning och sektoranalys, in G. Enequist (ed.) *Tätorter och Omland,* Lundequistska Bokhandelen, Uppsala, pp. 19–49.

Keltie, J. S. (1886) Geographical education: report to the Council of the Royal Geographical Society, *Suppl. Papers Royal Geog. Soc.,* No. 1, pp. 439–594.

King, L. J. and Golledge, R. G. (1978) *Cities, Space and Behaviour,* Prentice-Hall, Englewood Cliffs, NJ.

Kirk, W. (1963) Problems of Geography, *Geography,* Vol. 48, pp. 357–71.

Knox, P. L. (1975) *Social Well-Being: A Spatial Perspective,* Oxford University Press.

Kohl, H. (1968) Bedeutung und Entwicklungsfragen der Geographie, in den Deutsche Demokratischen Republik *Petermanns Mitteilungen,* Vol. 112, pp. 3–8.

Kropotkin, P. (1885) What Geography ought to be, *Nineteenth Century,* Vol. 18, pp. 940–56.

Kropotkin, P. (1924) *Ethics: Origin and Development,* New York.

Kuhn, T. S. (1962, 1970a) *The Structure of Scientific Revolutions,* University Chicago Press.

Kuhn, T. S. (1970b) Reflections on my critics, in I. Lakatos and A. Musgrave (eds) *Criticism and the Growth of Knowledge,* Cambridge University Press, pp. 231–7.

Lange, G. (1961) Varenius über die Grundfrage der Geographie, *Petermanns Geographische Mitteilungen,* Vol. 105, pp. 274–83.

Leser, H. (1980) *Geographie,* Das Geographische Seminar, Westermann, Braunschweig.

Ley, D. and Samuels, M. (1978) *Humanistic Geography, Prospects and Problems,* Maaroufa Press, Chicago.

Lukermann, F. (1958) Towards a more geographic economic geography, *Professional Geogr.*, Vol. 10, No. 1, pp. 1–10.

Mabogunje, A. (1976) Systems approach to a theory of rural-urban migration, in J. Beishon and C. Peters (eds.) *Systems Behaviour* (2nd edn), Harper & Row/Open University Press, London, pp. 304–13.

Mair, A. (1986) Thomas Kuhn an understanding geography, *Prog. Human Geogr.*, Vol. 10, pp. 345–69.

Malmberg, T. (1980) *Human Territoriality,* The Hague, Mouton.

Marsh, G. P. (1864) *Man and Nature, or Physical Geography as Modified by Human Action,* Schribners, New York.

Martin, G. J. (1985) Paradigm change: a history of geography in the United States 1892–1925, *National Geographic Research,* spring 1985, pp. 217–35.

Massey, D. (1984) *Spatial Division of Labour: Social Structures and the Geography of Production,* Macmillan, London.

Masterman, M. (1970) The nature of a paradigm, in I. Lakatos and A. Musgrave (eds.), *Criticism and the Growth of Knowledge,* Cambridge University Press, pp. 59–90.

Mead, W. (1954) Ridge and furrow in Buckinghamshire, *Geogr. J.,* Vol. 120, pp. 34–42.

Meadows, D. H., Meadows, D. L., Randers, J. and Behrens, W. W. (1972) *The Limits to Growth,* Earth Island, London.

Meijer, H. (1981) *Zuyder Zee–Lake Ijssel,* Haag: IDG, Utrecht.

Minshull, R. (1970) *The Changing Nature of Geography,* Hutchinson, London.

Montefiore, A. C. and Williams, W. W. (1955) Determinism and possibilism, *Geographical Studies,* Vol. 2, pp. 1–11.

Morgan, M. A. (1975) Values and political geography, in R. Peel *et al.* (ed.) *Processes in Physical and Human Geography, Bristol Essays,* Heinemann, London, pp. 287–304.

Morrill, R. L. (1965) *Migration and the growth of urban settlement,* Lund Studies in Geography, Ser. B, 24, Gleerup, Lund, Sweden.

Morrill, R. L. (1974) Review of D. Harvey, *Social Justice and the City, Ann. Assoc. Am. Geogrs.,* Vol. 64, pp. 475–7.

Morrill, R. L. (1984) Recollection of the 'Quantitative Revolution's' early years: the University of Washington 1955–65, in M. Billinge, D. Gregory and R. Martin (eds.) *Recollection of a Revolution,* Macmillan, London, pp. 57–72.

Morrill, R. L. and Wohlenberg, E. H. (1971) *The Geography of Poverty in the United States,* McGraw-Hill, New York.

Muehrceke, P. (1981) Maps in geography, in L. Guelke (ed.) *Maps in Modern Geography, Cartographica Monographs 27* University of Toronto Press, Toronto, pp. 1–14.

Myrdal, G. (1953) The relation between social theory and social policy, *Br. J. Sociol.,* Vol. 23, pp. 210–42.

Neef, E. (1982) Geographie–einmal anders gesehen, *Geographische Zeitschrift,* Vol. 70, pp. 241–60.

Newcomb, R. M. (1979) Planning the past, *Studies in Historical Geography,* Dawson/Archon, London.

Nordgård, A. (1972) *Korologiske metoder,* Geografisk Institutt, Oslo.

Odum, H. T. (1960) Ecological potential and analogue circuits for the ecosystem, *Am. Scientist,* Vol. 48, pp. 1–8.

Olsson, G. (1974) Servitude and inequality in spatial planning: ideology and methodology in conflict, *Antipode,* Vol. 6, No. 1, pp. 16–21. Reprinted in R. Peet (ed.) (1977) *Radical Geography,* Methuen, London.

Olsson, G. (1975) *Birds in Egg,* Michigan Geog. Publ. No. 15, Ann Arbor.

Olsson, G. (1978) Of ambiguity or far cries from a memorialising mamafesta, in D. Ley and M. Samuels (eds.) *Humanistic Geography: Prospect and Problems,* Croom Helm, Beckenham, pp. 109-22.

Orme, A. (1985) Understanding and predicting the physical world, in R. J. Johnston (ed.) *The Future of Geography,* Methuen, London, pp. 258-75.

Paffen, K. H. (1955) Die natürlichen Landschaften und Ihre raümliche Gliederung, *Forshgn. Z dt. Landeskunde 68.*

Peet, R. (ed.) (1977) *Radical Geography,* Methuen, London.

Peet, R. (1981) Spatial dialectics and Marxist geography, *Prog. Human Geogr.,* Vol. 5, pp. 105-10.

Peet, R. (1985) The social origins of environmental determinism, *Ann. Assoc. Am. Geogrs.,* Vol. 75, pp. 309-33.

Penck, A. (1894) *Morphologie der Erdoberflache,* Stuttgart.

Penck, A. (1901-9) *Die Alpen in Eisalter,* Vols. 1-3, Stuttgart.

Penck, A. (1928) Neuere Geographie, *Zeitschrift d. Gesellsch. f. Erdkunde zu Berlin,* Berlin, pp. 31-56.

Peschel, O. (1870) *Neue Probleme der vergleichenden Erdkunde als Versuch einer Morphologie der Erdoberfläche,* Duncker und Humblot, Leipzig.

Pickles, J. (1985) *Phenomenology, Science and Geography,* Cambridge University Press.

Poksisevskij, V. V. *et al.* (1964) The regional concept in Soviet geography, in F. I Hamilton (ed.) *Abstracts of Papers,* IGU, London.

Popper, K. (1970) Normal science and its dangers, in F. Lakatos and A. Musgrave (eds.) *Criticism and the Growth of Knowledge,* Cambridge University Press, pp 51-8.

Pred, A. (1967) *Behaviour and Location:* Part I, *Foundations for a Geographic and Dynamic Location Theory,* Gleerup, Lund.

Pred, A. (1969) *Behaviour and Location:* Part II, *Foundations for a Geographic and Dynamic Location Theory,* Gleerup, Lund.

Putnam, H. (1981) The 'corroboration' of theories, in I. Hacking (ed.) *Scientific Revolutions,* Oxford Unversity Press, pp. 60-79.

Quaini, M. (1982) *Geography and Marxism,* Blackwell, Oxford.

Ratzel, F. (1882) *Anthropogeographie:* I, *Oder Grundzüge der Anwendung de Erdkunde auf die Geschichte,* Engelhorn, Stuttgart.

Ratzel, F. (1891) *Antropogeographie:* II, *Die geographische Verbrietung de Menschen,* Engelhorn, Stuttgart.

Ratzel, F. (1897) *Politische Geographie,* Oldenburg, Munich.

Réclus, E. (1866-7) *La terre,* Hachette, Paris.

Réclus, E. (1875-94) *Nouvelle géographie universelle,* Hachette, Paris.

Réclus, E. (1905-8) *L'homme et la terre,* 6 vols., Paris.

Reenberg, A. (1982) *Det katastroferamte Sahel,* Geografforlaget, Brenderup.

Ritter, C. (1822-59) *Die Erdkunde, im Verhältnis zur Natur und zur Geschichte de Menschen, oder allgemeine vergleichende Geographie als sichere Grundlage de Studiums und Unterrichts in Physikalischen und historischen Wissenschaften,* 1 vols., Reimer, Berlin.

Rokkan, S. (1970) *Citizens, Elections, Parties,* Universitetsforlaget, Oslo.

Rostow, W. W. (1960) *The Stages of Economic Growth,* Cambridge University Pres

Sack, R. D. (1972) Geography, geometry and explanation, *Ann. Am. Assoc. Geogrs* Vol. 62, pp. 61-78.

Sack, R. D. (1974) Chorology and spatial analysis, *Ann. Assoc. Am. Geogrs.,* Vol. 6 pp. 439-52.

Sack, R. D. (1980) *Conceptions of Space in Social Thought,* Macmillan, London.

Sack, R. D. (1986) *Human Territoriality, Its Theory and History,* Cambridg University Press.

Sauer, C. O. (1925) *The Morphology of Landscape,* University of California *Publs. in Geog.,* Vol. 2, pp. 19–35.

Sauer, C. O. (1963) *Land and Life,* ed. J. B. Leighley, University of California Press, Berkeley.

Sayer, A. (1985) Realism and geography, in R. J. Johnston (ed.) *The Future of Geography,* Methuen, London, pp. 159–73.

Schaefer, F. (1953) Exceptionalism in geography, *Ann. Assoc. Am. Geogrs.,* Vol. 43, pp. 226–49.

Schilpp, P. A. (ed.) (1963) *The Philosophy of Rudolph Carnap,* Open Court, La Salle, Ill.

Schlüter, O. (1906) *Die Ziele der Geographie des Menschen,* München, Berlin.

Schlüter, O. (1920) Die Erdkunde im Verhältnis zu der Natur–und Geisteswissenschaften, *Geographische Anzeiger,* Vol. 21. pp. 145–52, 212–21.

Schmieder, O. (1964) Alexander von Humboldt: Persönlichkeit, wissenschaftliches Werk und Auswirkung auf die moderne Länderkunde, *Geog. Z.,* Vol. 52, pp. 81–95.

Schmithüsen, J. (1976) *Allgemeine Geosynergetik,* De Gruyter, Berlin.

Scholten, A. (1980) Al-Muqaddasi *c.* 945–*c.* 988, in T. W. Freeman and P. Pinchemel (eds.) *Geographers, Bibliographical Studies,* Vol. 4, Mansell, London, pp. 1–6.

Schultz, H. D. (1980) *Die deutschsprachige Geographie von 1800 bis 1970,* Abhandlung des geographischen Instituts–Antropogeographie, Band 29, Selbstverlag des geographischen Instituts der Freien Universität Berlin.

Schumacher, E. F. (1974) *Small Is Beautiful: A Study of Economics as if People Mattered,* Abacus, London.

Semple, E. C. (1911) *Influences of Geographical Environment,* Henry Holt, New York.

Simmons, I. G. (1974, 1981) *The Ecology of Natural Resources,* Arnold, London.

Simmons. I. G. (1979) *Biogeography: Natural and Cultural,* Arnold, London.

Simmons, I. G. and Cox, N. J. (1985) Holistic and reductionistic perspectives in geography, in R. J. Johnston (ed.) *The Future of Geography,* Methuen, London, pp. 43–58.

Simpson, G. G. (1963) Historical science, in C. C. Albritton (ed.) *The Fabric of Geology,* Addison Wesley, Reading, Mass.

Skjervheim, H. (1974) Objectivism and the study of man, *Inquiry,* Vol. 17, pp. 213–39, 265–302.

Smith, A. (1776) *An Inquiry into the Nature and Causes of the Wealth of Nations,* London.

Smith, D. M. (1979) *Where the Grass in Greener: Living in an Unequal World,* Penguin, London.

Soja, E. (1980) The socio-spatial dialectic, *Ann. Assoc. Am. Geogr.,* Vol. 70, pp. 207–25.

Somerville, M. (1848) *Physical Geography,* London.

Sømme, A. (ed.) (1965) *Fjellbygd og feriefjell,* Cappelen, Oslo.

Stamp, D. (1966) Ten Years on, *Trans. Inst. Br. Geogrs.,* Vol. 40, pp. 11–20.

Steers, J. A. (1946) *The Coastline of England and Wales,* Cambridge University Press.

Steiner, D. (1965) Die Faktorenanalyse: eine modernes statistisches Hilfsmittel des Geographen für die objektive Raumgliederung und Typenbildung, *Geographica Helvetica,* Vol. 20, pp. 20–34.

Stevenson, W. I. (1978) Patrick Geddes 1854-1932, in T. W. Freeman and P. Pinchemel (eds.) *Geographers, Bibliographical Studies,* Vol. 2, Mansell, London, pp. 53–65.

Stewart, J. Q. (1947) Empirical mathematical rules concerning the distribution and equilibrium population, *Geog. Rev.,* Vol. 37, pp. 461–85.

Stoddart, D. R. (1966) Darwin's impact on geography, *Ann. Assoc. Am. Geogrs.,* Vol. 56, pp. 683–98.

Stoddart, D. R. (1967) Organism and ecosystem as geographical models, in R. J. Chorley and P. Haggett (eds.) *Models in Geography*, Methuen, London, pp. 511–48.
Stoddart, D. R. (1975) 'That Victorian Science'–Huxley's 'Physiography' and its impact on geography, *Trans. Inst. Br. Geogrs.*, Vol. 66, pp. 17–40.
Stoddart, D. R. (1986) *On Geography*, Blackwell, Oxford.
Taaffe, E. J. (ed.) (1970) *Geography*, Prentice-Hall, Englewood Cliffs, NJ.
Tatham, G. (1951) Geography in the nineteenth century, in G. Taylor (ed.) *Geography in the Twentieth Century*, Methuen, London, pp. 28–69.
Taylor, G. (ed.) (1951) *Geography in the Twentieth Century*, Methuen, London.
Taylor, P. J. (1976) An interpretation of the quantification debate in British Geography, *Trans. Inst. Br. Geogrs.*, Vol. 1, new series, pp. 129–42.
Taylor, P. J. (1985) The value of a geographical perspective, in R. J. Johnston (ed.) *The Future of Geography*, Methuen, London, pp. 92–110.
Thrift, N. J. (1986) The geography of international economic disorder, in R. J. Johnston and P. J. Taylor (eds.) *A World In Crisis. Geographical perspectives*, Blackwell, Oxford, pp. 12–67.
Thrower, N. (1972) *Maps and Man*, Prentice-Hall, Englewood Cliffs, NJ.
Troll, C. (1947) Die geographische Wissenschaft in Deutschland in dem Jahren 1933 bis 1945, *Erdkunde*, Vol. 1, pp. 3–48.
Tuan Yi-Fu (1971) Geography, phenomenology, and the study of human nature, *Canadian Geogr.*, Vol. 15, pp. 181–92.
Tuan Yi-Fu (1974) Space and Place: Humanistic Perspectives, *Progr. Geog.*, Vol. 6, pp. 211–52.
Tuan Yi-Fu (1976) Humanistic Geography, *Ann. Assoc. Am. Geogrs.*, Vol. 66, pp. 266–76.
Tuan Yi-Fu (1977) *Space and Place: The Perspectives of Experience*, University of Minnesota Press; Arnold, London.
Tuan Yi-Fu (1978) Literature and geography: implications for geographical research, in D. Ley and M. S. Samuels (eds.) *Humanistic Geography: Prospects and Problems*, Maaroufa, Chicago, pp. 194–206.
Tuan Yi-Fu (1980) *Landscapes of Fear*, Pantheon, New York; Blackwell, Oxford.
Uhlig, H. (1967) Methodische Begriffe der Geographie, besonders der Landschaftkunde. Separat-Vorabdruck aus *Westermanns Lexikon* der Geographie, Westermann, Braunschweig.
Uhlig, H. (1971) Organization and system of geography, *Geoforum*, Vol. 7, pp. 7–38.
Uhlig, H. (1973) Landschaftökologie. *Das Wesen der Landschaft*, Wissenschaftliche Buchgesellschaft, Darmstadt, pp. 268–85.
Ullmann, E. (1941) A theory of location for cities, *Am. J. Sociol.*, Vol. 46, pp. 835–64.
van Valkenburg, S. (1952) The German school of geography, in G. Taylor (ed.) *Geography in the Twentieth Century*, Methuen, London, pp. 91–117.
Varenius, B. (1650) *Geographia Generalis*, Amsterdam.
Vidal de la Blache, P. (1903) *Tableau de la géographie de la France*, Hachette, Paris.
Vidal de la Blache, P. (1917) *La France de l'est*, Armand Colin, Paris.
Vidal de la Blache, P. (1921) *Principes de la geographie humaine*, trans. 1926 as *Principles of Human Geography*, Constable, London.
von Bertalanffy, L. (1968) *General Systems Theory: Foundations, Development, Applications*, George Brazilier, New York.
von Humboldt, A. (1845–62) *Kosmos: Entwurf einer physische Weltbeschreibung*, 5 Vols., Cotta, Stuttgart. English trans. E. C. Otté 1849–58, H. G. Bohn, London.
von Thünen, J. H. (1826) *Der Isolierte Staat in Beziehung auf Landwirtschaft und Nationalökonomie*, Hamburg, English trans. C. M. Wartenburg (1966) *Von Thünen's Isolated State*, ed. P. Hall, Pergamon, Oxford.

Waibel, L. (1933) Was verstehen wir unter Landschaftskunde? *Geogr. Anzeiger,* Vol. 34, pp. 197–207.

Wärneryd, O. (1977) Kulturgeografi–Samhaltsgeografi *Samhällsventenskapliga studiernas historik,* Lund, pp. 20–31.

Warntz, W. (1959) *Towards a Geography of Price: A Study in Geo-Econometrics,* University of Pennsylvania Press, Philadelphia.

Warntz, W. (1964) A new map of the surface of population potentials for the United States, 1960, *Geogr. Rev.,* Vol. 54, pp. 170–84.

Weber, A. (1909) *Über der Standort der Industrien,* Tübingen, trans. C. Friederich (1929) *Alfred Weber's Theory of the Location of Industries,* Chicago University Press.

Weber, M. (1949) *The Methodology of Social Sciences.* English trans. of three articles published in German in 1904, 1905, 1917 ed. E. A. Shils and H. A. Finch, Free Press, Glencoe, IL.

Weichhart, P. (1975) Gesucht: Eine human-ökologisch orientierte Teildisziplin der komplexen Geographie, *Ber. z. dt. Landeskunde,* Vol, 54, pp. 125–32.

Weichhart, P. (1980) *Geographie im Umbruch, Franz Deuticke, Wien.*

Weight, E. (1957) *Die Geographie,* Westermann.

White, G. (1973) Natural hazards research, in R. J. Chorley (ed.) *Directions in Geography,* Methuen, London, pp. 193–216.

White, G. (1974) Edward Ackerman 1911–73, *Ann. Assoc. Am. Geogrs.,* Vol. 64, pp. 197–309.

White, R. and Gould, P. (1974) *Mental Maps,* Penguin, Harmondsworth.

Whittlesey, D. (1929) Sequent occupance, *Ann. Assoc. Am. Geogrs.,* Vol. 19, pp. 162–5.

Widberg, J. (1978) *Geografi, från naturvetenskap til samhällsvetenskap: En idéhistorisk översikt.* 3-betygsuppsats, Inst. för Kultur. och Economisk Geog., Lund.

Wilson, A. G. (1981) *Geography and the Environment, Systems Analytical Methods,* Wiley, Chichester.

Wolpert, J. (1964) The decision process in spatial context, *Ann. Assoc. Am. Geogrs.,* Vol. 54, pp. 337–58.

Wrigley, E. A. (1965) Changes in the philosophy of geography, in R. K. Chorley and P. Haggett (eds.) *Frontiers in Geographical Teaching,* Methuen, London, pp. 3–20.

Yeates, M. (1968) *An Introduction to Quantitative Analysis in Economic Geography,* McGraw-Hill, New York.

Author and Personality Index

Subject Index